EXPEDIENT IDENTITY

THE ESCALATING ASSERTION OF ARAB INDIVIDUALITY IN ISRAEL

RAPHAEL ISRAELI

Strategic Book Publishing and Rights Co.

Strategic Book Publishing and Rights Co., LLC
USA | Singapore
www.sbpra.net

For information about special discounts for bulk purchases, please contact Strategic Book Publishing and Rights Co., LLC Special Sales, at bookorder@sbpra.net.

ISBN: 978-1-952269-54-7

Contents

Apologia and Acknowledgments

The 2019-2020 three successive (and abortive) national election campaigns, which failed to break the deadlock between Right and Left in the Israeli Knesset, were marked by the impressive increase in the Arab representation in the Israeli Parliament, from 10 to 12 and then 15 mandates (out of the total 120 membership in the House), engendering much fear in much of the Israeli public about the incremental takeover of Israeli politics by the mostly unfriendly, and often subversive Arab vote, and emboldening the previously much passive Israeli Arab public to claim an increasingly active part in Israel's political process and a determining share in its decision making, as citizens of "equal rights" in Israel's democratic system.

Had the Israeli Arabs been truly committed to their Israeli identity and resigned to accept their lot as a minority in the Jewish State, the rise of their power in the Israeli Knesset would not have been noticed so adversely; had they, like the Muslims of Britain and the Jews of America played within the political rules of their country and with the predominant political actors among their compatriots: British Muslims within the Labor and the Tory parties (which have allowed Mayor Khan to be elected in London) and Muslims and Jews in the US within the Democratic and Republican parties (which enabled Muslim and Jewish Senators and Congressmen to be elected to the Senate and the House), then all would have been normal and predictable. But Israeli Arabs, who even resent that appellation, preferring to identify as "Palestinians citizens of Israel", as if their British or American counter-examples would insist on the "Pakistani- British national" or the "Israeli-Jewish American citizen" appellations. Moreover, what makes the situation of Israeli Arabs even more irritating and problematic is that they plainly, entirely and openly make of the Palestinian cause theirs, and since their country has been at odds, and often in a hostile confrontation, with their people, they automatically find themselves in an impossible conflict of identities that cannot be overbridged.

Hence the inevitable impulse of Israelis and others to try to comprehend what makes the Israeli Arabs tick, what governs the ever-changing tenor of their stated identity; to explain the built-in contradictions in their conduct and their zigzagging political behavior; and to try to crack the code of their often enigmatic actions that seem to undermine their status and socio-political stance in Israel instead of enhancing it. Indeed, it often appears that while accommodation, moderation and reconciliation with the Israeli Jewish majority would serve best their interests in the long run, if they only could act with patience, low profile and forbearance, their rush to engage in confrontational debates and rifts, and in one-upmanship with the Israeli establishment, sounds threatening to the Israeli fear- and complex stricken population that is still steeped in and pursued by the post-traumatic *sho'a* disturbances which haunt it.

The immediate trigger for this volume was an interview with me which renowned journalist Nadav Shragai of Jerusalem published in the Israeli daily *Israel Ha-yom* on March 23, 2020, on the occasion of the inauguration of the 23rd Knesset in Israel where the high visibility and impact of the Joint Arab Party was much in evidence. This interview has engendered several responses, for the most part positive, but some critical too, which reflected the deep division in the Israeli constituency between the minority of human rights champions who would prioritize the application of "democratic" principles of equality at any price, and the majority of experience-hardened commoners who have learned to take seriously threats to their national existence.

As always, I am extremely indebted to the Harry Truman Research Institute for the Advancement of Peace at Hebrew University, Jerusalem, my home base for the past half century, for the office space and logistical assistance it has afforded me that long; and to my many friends and colleagues who have showered on me their plentiful remarks and constructive insights, as well as some scathing criticism which I attempted to heed. All blame remains exclusively mine, nonetheless, for all the errors of fact and judgment that I may have unwittingly made in the process.

Jerusalem, during the memorable weeks of isolation in my home while the coronavirus crisis lockdown forced all of us indoors in March and April, 2020.

Introduction

To be a Palestinian Arab in Israel

Since its inception (1948) Israel has been haunted by the question of its large Arab-Palestinian minority in view of the fact that the country has remained in an unsettled conflict situation with its Palestinian people which remains destitute and stateless partly within Israel, partly across the border in Jordan, and partly on its doorstep in the West Bank and Gaza, which have been almost continuously under Israeli rule or close watch since the 1967 Six-day War. At times the Arab minority in Israel, which amounted to ca 15% in 1949 (150,000 out of 700,000) ascended to 21% in 2020 (close to 2 million out of 9 million). That Arab population which shuns its appellation as "Israeli Arabs" and has opted for the self-identifying designation of "Palestinian citizens of Israel", states its Israeli technical and instrumental "civil identity"; at other times its ethno-national identity takes over, and the clash between country where it dwells and the nation to which it belongs becomes inevitable. All the more so, since the realization is always there that the Israeli Arabs cannot reconcile to the fact that while prior of 1948 they used to constitute the majority in their land of West Palestine, under Ottoman and then British rule, in the order of two thirds (over one million out of slightly over one million and a half)), they have shrunk to a 21% minority in 2020, despite their twelve-fold growth in absolute numbers during the intervening 7 decades of the existence of the state of Israel.

In spite of today's Arab Joint List Party's list in the Israeli Knesset, which has grown to become the third largest political party in Israeli politics, its clamoring for integration into Israeli society of which it claims to be part and parcel, and its determination to take an active part in Israeli decision making, still the Jewish majority of the state is reluctant to confide in Israeli Arabs and share with them the most intimate avenues of power, in view of the hostile political positions often taken by their elected leadership, which apparently represents the vast majority of their constituency, despite some claims to the contrary. That support can be gauged by the elections results, but there is no way to evaluate the precise political inclinations among the Arabs who vote for the List, because no one can penetrate the thinking and beliefs of all Arab individuals. What can be verified and tested is only what their leaders write, say and do, and the steady growth of the Arab population's support for its Unified Arab List, from about half the Arab constituency until a decade ago, while the rest voted for the vast spectrum of the general (namely Zionist) parties, from the extreme Right to the extreme Left, to 80% these days, with the shrinking rest opting for the establishment parties of Israel. In other words, that process of gradual alienation heralds a widening gap towards separation and secession which undercut and undermine all the attempts, by Jews and Arabs alike, to claim integration and participation of the Arabs in the country's political makeup. Rather, it signals a new determination to struggle from a position of force and equality in the competition for power. That is what the Israeli Jewish majority most deeply dreads, which impelled it to legislate the Nation-State Law that the Arabs most abhor as the major obstacle on their way to attain an equal share of power with a view of stripping Israel of its Jewish and Zionist nature and turning it into a "state of its citizens ", a code word for a bi-national state.

The Land Day of 1976 and then "al-Aqsa Intifada" of 2000,

when the Arabs of Israel rose in rebellion against the Israeli establishment and against the Jewish nature of the state, were one successive chain of events which constituted this watershed in Israeli life and signaled the shift of the relatively docile and resigned conduct of the Arab population in the country. That change was arguably triggered as a result of the 1967 War, as Israel brought the West Bank and Gaza under its rule, and its Arabs discovered that they were an organic part of their Palestinian kin in those territories, thus reviving the old feeling of belonging to a retrieved majority in the united space of Palestine. In January, 2008, despite the relative calm that had reigned among the Arabs of Israel after they had acted in unison with their brethren in the West Bank and Gaza to signal heir common identity during the 2000 unrest, it was still possible to go beyond the events reported by the Israeli media and detect a direct link between the unsettled issues of the awakened joint Palestinian awareness on both sides of the Israeli Green Line and the current events of the day. The Israeli Prime Minister's Office in fact released a communique which stated:

> Approximately 20 Israeli Arabs from Jisr A-Zarka and the Wadi Ara region were recently arrested in a joint ISA (Israeli Security Agency)-Israeli Police operation on suspicion of involvement in illegally trafficking in weapons and munitions. Six of those arrested were indicted on 27 January, 2008. The principal accused was Hamza Masri, 24, from Kafr Kara, who was accused of trafficking in weapons and munitions with Shahar Hanina, 41, the head of *Tanzim*, a PLO subsidiary in Qalqiliya. It was claimed that in 2005, Masri had acquired a pistol for Hanina, as well as a 15 kg bag of potassium for use in preparing explosives, while Masri was fully aware of its intended use. Masri was arrested in 2005 and warned about his ties with Hanina, whom he knew headed the

PLO affiliated *Aqsa Martyrs Brigades* in Qalqiliya. Upon his release later that year, Masri continued his links with Hanina. Masri purchased tens of thousands of dollars worth of weapons and munitions for Hanina, including an M-16, a hunting rifle and a laser sight for an M-16.

Over the past year, many cases were uncovered regarding ties involving arms between criminal elements in Israel and terrorist operatives in Judea and Samaria and in the Gaza Strip. Security forces are constantly engaged in a constant war on the trade and smuggling of arms, including from IDF bases, and their sale to terrorist operatives in the territories. These ties between terrorists and criminals holding Israeli identity cards facilitate the acquisition of arms and ammunition which ultimately are used in attacks against Israel. The danger inherent in these ties is seen in the case of Hamas operatives and arms dealers from Jabel Mukabber in East Jerusalem, who were ultimately arrested. They were found to have had ties with two Hamas operatives who carried out the shooting attack at Sheikh Sa'ed Checkpoint, in the separation fence around Jerusalem, in May 2007. One of the persons arrested provided the terrorists with a weapon a few hours before the attack, in which two Israeli security forces were injured, one of them seriously. The terrorists, who hold Israeli identity cards and live in Jabel Mukabber, were killed in an exchange of fire during the incident. Under questioning, the detainees admitted that they were involved in extensive trade in arms with criminal elements, Arab Israelis from the North, and also Hamas operatives from Hebron and Bido, a village in the Ramallah District. The questioning also revealed that one of the terrorists acquired the pistol used in the attack a few hours before the attack, and that he had received it from Anan Muhammad Halaila, 21 an arms dealer and also resident of Jabel Mukabber. He came up with those of other detainees as persons who had been involved in attempts to steal weapons from IDF soldiers with the intent of selling them[1].

This was just one example of the criminal, often backed up by ideological partnership among Palestinian Arabs on both sides of the divide. Another example occurred in March 2008 when Israeli security forces uncovered a network of arms dealers from the Nazareth area, who sold munitions that had been stolen from the IDF to Palestinians in the West Bank. Among those arrested was Arkan Bashir, a volunteer Muslim IDF soldier who admitted under questioning that he stole munitions from the IDF and sold them to arms dealers, who then sold them to Ahmad Boz, a Fatah operative from Nablus, who was arrested. That ISA Report of 2007 also made clear the continued problem of Israeli Arab violence:

> A prominent phenomenon that has appeared over the years, and was renewed in 2007, is the throwing of stones and Molotov cocktails at Israeli vehicles. In 2007 there were dozens of cases of stone-throwing inside Israel, with the major focal points being Route 443 and on roads in northern Israel [where the Arab population is relatively dense] and in the southern part of the country [the Beesheba area where the Bedouin population is thriving]. Toward the end of the year Molotov cocktails were also hurled at cars traveling Route 443 [from the Coastal Plain to Jerusalem]. In 2007 Security forces carried out a number of actions in which they arrested and questioned dozens of Arabs who threw stones and Molotov

---

[1] IMRA, January 27, 2008, extracted from an ISA Report.

cocktails at Israeli vehicles, civilians and IDF troops, on a daily basis, endangering the lives of the passengers in the vehicles[2].

These samples of the Israeli Arab-partnership with their Palestinian kin demonstrated that Israeli Arabs no longer looked at Israel with resignation as to their minority status, where they would have every interest to live in peace and obey the laws that inter alia also protect them, but they were shifting their focus gradually to a confrontational attitude born out of their growing identification with other Palestinians which contributed to their surging Palestinian identity at the expense of their Israeli make up. This, while up to the 1967 War the Arabs of Israel were gradually evolving an Israeli character, which had impelled them to volunteer in time of emergency as a replacement to the Jewish work force which was mobilized for war, in the 2000s the newly expanded loyalty to other Palestinians, distanced them from Israel. Their leadership and politicians accordingly greatly shifted their public interest from the tedious internal affairs of their Arab compatriots, to the more glamorous and popular engagement with Palestinian issues which attracted international attention.

It seemed that just like following the Balfour Declaration of 1917, which had confirmed the worst fears of the Arabs regarding the hidden agenda of the Zionists, who step by step were realizing their blueprint of establishing their separate entity in what the Arabs considered as their Palestine, so was the victorious Zionist state of the post-1967 era determined to expand its presence in the West Bank and Gaza. Hence the jointly adopted new mantra of "ending the Israeli occupation" which became the war cry of all Palestinians on both sides of the divide. From now on, their joint struggle would

---

[2] Ibid. The report may be found in full at http//www.mfa.gov.il/NR/rdonlyres/75FC2B98=A581-4C89-88AC-7C3C1DiBC097/0/Terrorism2007report.pdf

not be confined to diplomatic pressures and occasional outbursts of hostility against the Jews to scare them off from implementing their Zionist plans, but would be devoted to building up into a systematic political and armed struggle, the PLO leading it from the Palestinian entity, and the Israeli Arabs siding with it and hammering in onto the Israeli public opinion from within the Israeli Knesset and playing on the conscience of the Israeli Left and the Israeli intelligentsia that leans to the Left.

One will have noticed that while at the outset of the conflict in Palestine, the clashes were ethnicity and religion-based, capitalizing on the traditional hatred and contempt towards the Jews in the Arab and Islamic worlds to help recruit Muslims against them, they later settled into a more political and national pattern under the British Mandate, where international relations, interests and sensitivities of other Arab countries and the predominant powers of the day dictated the world agenda. Hence, the increasing Islamic and Arab quality of the conflict, which led to an impasse. As the involvement of other Arab countries accorded to the conflict an all-Arab national character, its specifically Palestinian quality was dimmed and it became known as the Arab-Israeli conflict where the clash between two nationalities, the Arab and the Zionist, engaged in an inconclusive orgy of fighting and then in an equally open-ended series of armistices, truces and cease-fires which perpetuated the temporary nature of that never-ending conflict. Only after the 1967 War and the taking over of the Palestinian territories by Israel, did the conflict revert to its Palestinian roots which left it stuck there, while with Egypt and Jordan Israel concluded peace treaties, shaky and uncertain as they may be. The foolishness that Israel mindlessly committed by signing the Oslo Accords and bringing in its Palestinian nemesis, far from alleviating the situation, on the contrary sunk it deeper into the quagmire of this unresolved and insoluble dispute.

All through, one wondered why, against all odds, the smaller and better organized *Yishuv* and then Israel could in the final analysis beat its more numerous and richer Arab competitors. Yuval Harari put it in a concise and brilliant insight, that is shared by many historians:

> History provides ample evidence for the crucial importance of large scale cooperation. Victory almost invariably went to those who cooperated better… in conflicts between different human groups. Thus Rome conquered Greece not because the Romans had larger brains or better tool-making techniques, but because they were able to cooperate more effectively. Throughout history, disciplined armies routed disorganized hordes, and unified elites dominated the disorderly masses. In 1914, for example, 3 million Russian noblemen, officials and business people, lorded it over 180 million farmers and workers. The Russian elite knew how to cooperate in defense of its common interests, whereas the 180 million commoners were incapable of effective mobilization. Indeed, much of the elites' efforts focused on ensuring that the 180 million people at the bottom would never learn to cooperate.[3]

The tiny Jewish *Yishuv* in Palestine also observed with horror that while their brethren were harshly persecuted in Germany towards their incarceration and extermination throughout Europe, it was the Palestinian leadership, headed by Haj Amin al-Husseini, which collaborated with Nazi Germany to achieve that genocidal goal. They could not therefore be expected at any stage of their struggle with the Palestinians to show much sympathy for their rivals. On the contrary, on many instances when their military clashes with

---

[3] Yuval Noah Harari, *Homo Deus: A Brief History of Tomorrow*, Vintage Books, London, 2016, pp. 154-5.

the Palestinians ended up in massive removals of Arabs when they lost battles, many Jewish combatants who had only recently emerged as survivors of the Holocaust who found shelter in the nascent Jewish state, reflected on their condition as victors compared to their wholesale victimhood at the hand of the Nazis, wishing that European Jews had been "just " disinherited and uprooted by their persecutors instead of burned in the crematoria of Auschwitz. That comparison has become a sub-conscious element in their deeply ingrained suspicion of the ultimate lethal goals of the Arabs towards the Jewish state.

The Arabs could not care less about Jewish extermination in Europe, in fact their chief Palestinian mufti, Haj Amin, started collaborating with the Nazis, leading the two parties to share the idea of the final solution.

Evidence from Arab sources lends credibility to that suspicion and has led to the toughening of Israeli positions in the negotiations that have taken place between the parties along the years, including during the Oslo process (1993-2015) which failed dismally despite the valiant efforts of President Obama and Secretary Kerry to breath oxygen into it. In fact, even the restrictive British White Paper that had been issued by Neville Chamberlain, the co-author of the Munich Agreement, a few months before the outbreak of the war in 1939, and stipulated that seventy-five thousand immigration certificates only would be authorized by the mandatory power to incoming Jewish refugees, in their time of desperate distress, was cruelly scuttled by the Palestinian leadership. This act that could never be forgotten by the surviving Jews whose thinking and sentiments were conditioned by it ever after. For according to Walid Khalidi, one of the senior Palestinian scholars of Middle Eastern affairs, the White Paper also stipulated that when that quota was exhausted, further Jewish immigration would be contingent upon

Arab agreement, "which clearly would not be forthcoming,"[4], because, since the beginning of the Zionist settlement in Palestine, the Arabs had been dead set against Jewish immigration and settlement in the land. It was supposedly the memorandum written by Musa Alami and George Antonius, two of the prominent Palestinian leaders, in the absence of Haj Amin who had been exiled by the British, and signed by all Arab senior officials and submitted to the British High Commissioner in Palestine in 1936, which complained about British unjust policies in Palestine, that started to tilt that policy toward the issuance of the White Paper. Musa Alami joined the Palestinian delegation in 1939 to the London Round Table, which directly triggered the publication of the White Paper.

These heavy residues of fear, suspicion, lived experiences, in addition to the many wars, disruption, uprooting, disinheritance, destruction and a prolonged refugee status on both sides of the divide have turned the coexistence of the Jewish majority and the Arab minority in Israel into a near impossibility. Developing into two separate societies, which are referred to, by both sides as "social groups", or "social sectors" or to the Arabs and Jews as two divergent entities, and never as one society in spite of sharing the country for many decades after Israel was founded does not spell out integration and unity, and has turned Israel into a brewing cauldron of uneasy agitation, uncertain future and doubts about the possibility of attaining any permanent satisfactory solutions. Two different societies have emerged, whose culture, religion, national sentiment and ethnic aspirations are so far apart from each other, and so hostile to each other, that mixing them together has grown like trying to mix water and oil, and whatever one attempts, at the end of the day the oil will always float on the surface and the water will sink at the bottom. For the Jewish-Palestinian dispute has failed to come

---

[4] Walid Khalidi, *Journal of Palestinian Studies*, Vol. XXXV, No 1, Autumn 2005, pp. 60-79.

to its end, and is on the contrary constantly escalating, by the all-Arab and Islamic input that has contributed to its amplification. Worse, no leadership has emerged in sight and no new thinking has been in evidence to signal, except marginally, the willingness of the Jewish majority to abdicate the Jewish rule, sovereignty, nationalism and prevalence it has regained after two millennia of expectation and yearning; nor the readiness of the Arab erstwhile majority turned minority, to abandon its traditional contempt of Jewish rule, or to reinstall its domination over the Palestine it had lost in 1948. Quite the contrary, they seek to regain their hegemony by first attaining equality and parity in a bi-national state with the Jews, and then seeking to prevail demographically by allowing the "right of return" of the Palestinians to be implemented.

Sometimes ill-informed Israelis wonder why Arabs in Israel, rather than welcoming and blessing their good fortune of living under Israeli rule, which has clearly advanced their social and economic status, allowed their agriculture a quantum jump of centuries, initiated them into democracy and freedom, prolonged their life expectancy, afforded them high education and access into the professions, unprecedented progress and liberation for their women and the undreamed opportunity to taste Israeli high-tech, would elect to live in denial of all that. In fact, while the older generation among them would show signs or recognition and gratitude to Israel for all the bounty it showered on them, the younger generation, with some exceptions, would impute that immense progress in their society to their own endeavor, talent and initiative which were attained inspite of the "discrimination, oppression and persecution" that they have been suffering in Israel, and therefore they feel no obligation to be thankful. Quite the contrary, without those obstructions put on their way by Israel, they claim, they would have run forward much faster in the path of progress. They do not explain how their Palestinian and Arab compatriots who were free from those Israeli obstructions have remained far behind and are looking with longing and envy to the immense advance the Israeli Arabs have made. Israeli Arabs themselves watch their Palestinian kin in the Arab world and other Arabs in the Middle East, and evince no desire to be in their place. In fact, any time there was mention of a peace settlement between Israel and its neighbors, affording an opportunity to Israeli Arabs to move "to the freedom, prosperity and bliss of Palestinian or another Arab rule", they recoiled in horror from that prospect and elected to continue to "suffer" under Israeli oppression.

CHAPTER ONE

Being Palestinian Amidst a Plurality of Identities

The birth of Israel in 1948, which had been preceded by half a century of a Zionist trickling immigration of Jews into Palestine, has established a new major element of Jewish national presence in the Middle East in the midst of a turbulent Arab world. This addition has been rejected by the Arab majority in this hostile space, not only due to its contending claim to the land of Palestine, but also due to the Zionist immigration ambition to settle the fledgling Jewish state, while denigration of the Jews was part of the ingrained anti-Jewish attitudes of Islam that had been consecrated by 14 centuries of the sacred sources of the Qur'an and the Hadith, and the horrifying practice of *dhimmitude* throughout the Islamic realm, that will be discussed below.[5] Nonetheless, the stunning success of the Zionist enterprise which endeavored to pave the road for the Jewish return to their ancient land against all odds, has succeeded to found the State of Israel in 1948. Though barely half a million Jews had populated the land in those momentous moments of Jewish history, hardly sufficient to ensure its viability then, it has grown

---

[5] For details, see Andy Bostom, *The Legacy of Islamic Anti-Semitism*, Prometheus Books, NY, 2008; and Bat Ye'or, *Islam and Dhimmitude: Where Civilizations Collide*, Fairleigh Dickinson University Press, Lancaster, 2002. For a specific illustration, see R. Israeli, *Paranoia, Inferiority Complex and Fanaticism: Muslim Attitudes Towards Jews,* Strategic Books, TX, 2018.

70 years later (in 2020) into a Jewish state of 8 million souls, which encompasses more than half the world's Jewry. But Arab and Muslim rejectionism ignores this reality and has consistently refused to recognize and accept the notion of a Jewish state, insisting on the definition of Judaism as a faith, which therefore can continue to survive while scattered among other nations (like Islam, Buddhism and Christianity), and not a nation parallel to the Arabs, French or Germans who require a national and territorial definition as part of their identity.

After the birth of Israel and as its remaining Arab inhabitants turned into a minority, the traditional notions of population definitions were reversed: the Jews were now the sovereign majority, dominating the erstwhile Arab majority turned minority. That minority, constituting over 20% of the Israeli population today, was divided by definition between their country of Israel where they dwelt, and their Palestinian people, in surrounding Arab countries and refugee camps, which remained in a condition of war with Israel. But in practice, for all intents and purposes, they continued to constitute part and parcel of the Palestinian people, boosted by their Arab and Islamic common heritage which enriched and intensified (and complicated) their quest for identity.

1. The Israeli Arabs as Israelis

The Israeli aspect of the Arab identity in Israel has turned for most Muslims among them, over the years, into a technical and utilitarian necessity that can be drawn upon to get a passport, to claim rights and perks, and to enjoy free life, a long life expectancy and social services in a high-tech and advanced society, the like of which does not exist in any Arab country. But Israel has also become in their eyes the punch-bag that they can beat when they complain about discrimination and oppression, lay down their grievances and recriminations, whose eternal victims they claim to be. Paradoxically, opposed as they are to the very notion of the Jewish state, which they seek to alter even to their own detriment, they would by no means renounce its citizenship which they find beneficial to them without admitting it openly. Their main perennial claim of discrimination in every aspect of Israeli life, based on the fact that their achievements compared to those of the Jewish majority are inferior, must be gauged against some yardstick in order to gain credence. Discrimination is not only a subjective feeling, allowing every group to claim being victim to discrimination and oppression, but also an objective state of affairs which can be tested, verified and measured. For example, the Arabs lodge the claim that they are discriminated against in general, compared to the Jews. Had all Jews been well-off, well-educated and employed in high positions, and all Arabs poor, uneducated and unemployed, then one could understand this claim of discrimination and feeling of oppression. However, there are many Arabs better off, better educated and better employed than Jews, something that indicates in their midst a differential in capacity, diligence, education, ambition, entrepreneurship etc, as among any other group. Many Arab villages are poorer than Jewish villages, but some of them are better off too. Among Jewish populations we also find the poor and the wealthy, employed and unemployed, educated and uneducated; if so, who discriminates against the disadvantaged Jews in this case? Take the villages of Umm al-Fahm in the Triangle and Abu-Ghosh near Jerusalem. The former is poorer, it also dips in violence, occasionally attacks Israeli traffic on the main highway and engages in crime, arms smuggling and hostile demonstrations against Israel; so much so that some Israelis still prefer to keep away from it after the October 2000 uprising of the Arabs in that area. The latter is a rich village, that has always lived peacefully and traded constructively with Jews, so we find it thriving and flooded by Israeli visitors and shoppers. Both villages are Arab and both populations are Arab. Then, where is the discrimination, except in Arab conduct?

One can measure discrimination also from the angle of what one receives from the state versus what one gives to it. And here we find, to our amazement, that Arabs are positively discriminated: they do not serve their military service which almost every Jewish kid is obligated to do, and do not otherwise lift their finger to defend what they call their country only when it comes to getting benefits from it. They side with their country's enemies, contribute little to their own productivity and advancement; but on the other hand, they take the lion's share in social benefits which are paid for by the taxes of the Jewish majority. They do not pay their share of taxes, but they contribute double their proportion in crime in the country, which has to be policed and tackled with the tax money of the Jewish majority. In short, the Arabs are a burden on the state more than they take their fair share of duty or contribute to its welfare. There is discrimination, but in favor of the Arabs, not against them. Their clamors notwithstanding, what the Arabs wish to establish is not an equality of rights between all the citizens of the country, but a new nobility with all the privileges but without any duties to fulfill toward the state. They regard themselves are deserving of all the social services, payments and allowances, but exempt of any duty of any sort, because they are Arabs. Such a privileged citizenry does not exist in any democratic and modern country. Arab alienation from the country's mainstream, which stems from their tribal, emotional and instinctive identification with any Palestinian or Arab act or position against Israel, and is not mitigated by any reasoned ideological or rational concept, indeed dubs Israel's most important day in the country's secular calendar – Independence Day- the *Nakbah*, namely the Disaster. This means that if the day of celebration of the state is shared as a day of mourning by its Arab citizens, then how can they demand to be treated as friends enjoying equal rights in a country whose demise some of them are seeking, and which others among them view as an enemy, whose powers have to be eroded, whose gains and glory must be debunked or reduced, and whose misfortunes have to be celebrated.

This alienation causes the Arab minority to isolate itself to the extent possible, to cultivate a sub-culture of their own, and to turn inwards in education, language, religion, and even politics and economics, in order to decrease their dependence on the Israeli establishment, while at the same time developing their sense of victimhood and punching the Israeli bag whenever their expectations are not met. For the Israelis would, in their eyes, always be the aggressors, the murderers, the oppressors and the occupiers, even when they defend themselves against Arab terrorism, while the Palestinians would always be by definition right and victims of their country's oppression. Hence the "understanding" and leniency among the Arabs in Israel towards crime in their midst, which is two-fold their proportion in the population in the country, especially when it concerns "ideological" crime which brings no benefit to its perpetrators contrary to the case of economic crimes. On the other hand this criminal behavior is sure to cause security, reputation, and other damages to the country they dislike, like murdering Israeli soldiers, spying or joining terrorist organizations, launching arsons of fields and forests, counterfeiting of official documents, throwing rocks on passing traffic, or resisting the implementation of the law, often under the cover of the immunity that their Knesset members enjoy, and the like. In general, Arabs can hardly be caught "red handed" celebrating Israel's joys or successes, or mourning its failures and misfortunes.

On top of everything, they throw responsibility for their own crimes onto Israel, which "fails" to control their rising criminality. But when crime among themselves becomes unbearable, they demand protection from Israeli authorities as of right, being "loyal Israeli citizens". They forget that the social contract between a state and its citizens requires not only that it protect them, but that they be equally committed to its defense when attacked or threatened. The Arabs of Israel only conveniently embrace the first part of that principle that serves them, but totally deny and reject its second part which obliges them. Moreover, whenever Arab volunteers (Some Christians, Bedouins and more rarely Muslims) join the military, they are accused of treason, discouraged, their families harassed, and when they fall in combat, their funerals are refused in Muslim cemeteries for the unforgivable sin of defending their country. All these anomalies in social conduct within a democratic and open society, stem principally from the fact that the state of Israel, far from nipping in the bud this counter-normative behavior of the rebellious Arab minority, has permitted, even consecrated, the growth in its midst of those two separate and vastly differentiated sets of values for the Jews and the Arabs. Arab children do not share the same school curricula, generating a reality where the Arabs, who study in their own language their own history and culture, grow to respect their own heritage, not that of their state. They become accustomed to the idea that their country's independence is their own "catastrophe", and they naturally side with their country's enemies rather than with it. They also get used, as a matter of course, that not only are they absolved from duties in defending their land, but they occasionally even gang up against it to its detriment on the way to its ultimate demise.

The alienation of the Arabs in Israel, which has originally stemmed from their separate habitat in their towns and villages, and from the prevalence of Jewish rule following the 1948 War that they lost against their hopes and expectations, has expanded from the domain of education into to the political arena. Initially, except for the Communist Party that was led by Jews but was made up by Arab voters, Christians and Muslims, most Arab politicians had founded their factions as affiliates of existing major Israeli mainstream parties. But in the long run, realizing that involvement in politics in a democratic system, that they learned to work admirably, was the best avenue to defend their rights and privileges, they formed their own independent parties, hailing various shades of Arab nationalism and of anti-Israeli hostility. Not content with the large variety of Israeli political parties, from the extreme left to the extreme right, where every shade of opinion could find its expression, the Arabs of Israel found it necessary to establish their own political groupings, one of them (National Democratic Alliance-*Balad*) referring to a "national" base that is Arab, not Israeli. This is not an expression of a desire for integration into the country's political process as they claim. Those Arab parties, which usually co-opt a token anti-Zionist Israeli Jew of the extreme Left, to advertise their all-Israeli character, are not concerned in their platforms with general mainstream Israeli issues, like security, Jewish immigration, protection of and concern for the Jewish Diaspora worldwide, settlement of the land and reinforcing Israel's economy, unless they are intent to criticize, condemn and vilify the Jewish state of Israel, by falsely and libelously accusing it of "racism, apartheid and oppression", while they are bathing in the freest, most liberal, prosperous and advanced country in the entire Middle Eastern space.

Another indication of the Arabs' intent to denigrate the state of Israel and undermine it and not to integrate into it, has been to rally under the umbrella of the Joint Arab List 80% of all Arab voters, while until merely a decade ago half the Arab population in Israel voted for the mainstream Israeli parties. That is called alienation, not integration. The Arab separate political parties which shun the Jewish-dominated Israeli parties that are customarily founded on various shades of the Zionist endeavor, are only concerned with the sectorial needs of the Arabs, as if they lived alone in their own land. One of them, the *Hadash* Party, for example, a vestige of the Communist Party which withered after the dismantling of the Soviet Union, had demanded in its platform that was submitted to the Labor Party of Ehud Barak that the Druze minority which participates in Israel's defense by enlisting in the IDF, should desist from its zealous loyalty to their country and from their national service in its armed forces. It is as if during World War Two the German minority living in the US should incite their countrymen to refrain from participating in the war effort of their country against Nazi Germany, or the Japanese minority living in California, should solicit the same for the Pacific War with Imperial Japan. It is noteworthy that those rare Israeli Arabs who joined the Israeli parties are also the only ones who made it to the upper echelons of the political system, not by virtue of being Arabs, but because they distinguished themselves within their Israeli parties. Exactly like Muslims, Jews or Sikhs in Europe and the US who made it to the top of the political system of their countries by adhering to the existing mainstream parties, not by creating separate groupings loyal to their faith or national backgrounds.

The other Arab political groupings too, while shunning their country and calumniating its system, are enjoying its bounty, without lifting a finger to abide by their duties towards it, keep clamoring for a quota regime that should apportion to them, solely on their "merit" of being Arab, many government posts, state budgets and autonomous educational and cultural assets proportional to their numbers. Yielding to their demands would turn the country effectively into a bi-national state and bring about its demise like the Lebanese state which consists of a flimsy "balance" between communal groups, and has consequently descended into chaos. Would France or Britain tolerate that their Muslims should establish their own Islamic, Arab- National or Pakistani-National, political bodies and run for Parliament under those appellations, rather than join the existing Socialists or RPR in France or Labor or Tories in England, in order to participate in the political game? So "national" and alienated Arab politics in Israel have become, that most of their political leaders have started clamoring for the "right of return" of Palestinian refugees to Israel, which would mean the end of the Jewish state that they did not help build but whose demise they herald.

Alienation from the Jewish state is also expressed on the symbolic level. Not only have Israeli Arabs been on record as demanding changes in the Israeli anthem and flag (equivalent to Muslims in Scandinavia, Greece or Switzerland demanding that the national flags of their adoptive countries be cleared of the Cross that adorns them). On another level, the Muslim radicals among them are boycotting Israeli elections, lest the elected be constrained to swear fealty to the laws of the country while at the same time they, and other Arabs have violently and virulently attacked the Israeli law of Nation-state which simply establishes the state of Israel as the Jewish state, as an evidence similar to proclaiming Germany the state of the Germans and France for the French. The catch here is that the Arabs in particular and Muslims in general, refuse to recognize the existence of Jewry as a people and nation, deserving of self determination and statehood, the argument that should delegitimize the very existence of Israel in general, as Palestinians and the BDS movement worldwide would have it. Conversely, they strongly argue that Judaism is only a faith, which like other religions (Christianity, Islam, Buddhism etc) can exist within many nationalities.

Others have also developed notions of a gradual secession from the Jewish entity. At first, that tendency has been expressed by a national leadership elected among the Arab heads of local councils, which purports to speak, together with the Arab Knesset members, for the entire Arab population of Israel. But there are also spreading talks of autonomy, of one sort or another, and an insistent demand that the country cease to be Jewish and become in fact bi-national. To mollify the shock to the Jewish majority, which has been horrified by such statements, that idea is sold under the euphemistic slogan of "the state of its citizens", which ultimately amounts to the same, since the Arabs would have to be recognized, not as individuals as is the case today, but as a corporative body on an equal footing with the Jews. Moreover, that bi-national entity, after it absorbs the returning Palestinian refugees that Israeli Arabs advocate, would became another Palestinian-majority state (the fourth, after Jordan, the PLO-led West Bank and Hamas-governed Gaza), while Jews are denied any statehood in that concept. That is why Israel insists on being recognized and accepted as a Jewish state, and that is why Israeli Jews are most terrified of and deterred from being denied their Jewish identity. This is also why Israeli Arabs are gaining their place as potentially inimical to Jewish sovereignty in the country, as demonstrated by their virulent opposition to the Israeli Nation State Law that has raised so much turbulence among all non-Jewish minorities in the country.

These trends have gained momentum since the Israeli government has tried to find a permanent solution to the other Bedouins who roam the Negev in southern Israel and parts of the Galilee in its north. Those two hundred thousand Arabs, who had been accustomed to live in open spaces that recognize no international borders, and had considered all those empty spaces where they wandered as theirs, have had tremendous difficulties to internalize the changes which occurred since 1948 in modern Israel. The new requirements put an end to nomadic life and demanded that for the sake of rendering social services, like schools and clinics, the state needed them to concentrate in townships built with government aid. The Bedouins complied in part, but they continue also to lay claim to the state lands where they were used to graze their herds as their own, and have been demanding, sometimes violently, that those lands be recognized and registered as their own property. They are also alarmed by the pace of Israeli settlement and development of the Negev and the Galilee, which the Bedouins regard as encroaching upon their "rights". Most threatening for the scattered Israelis who live in the south and in isolated settlements ("observatories") in the north, has been the mushrooming around them of dozens of tent and shack clusters, dubbed the "illegal" or "unrecognized" villages, which have been inhabited for decades by Bedouins without any basic services of health, education or infrastructure, like electricity or running water. It is quite odd to observe those flimsy habitations, where the dirt driveways are occupied by automobiles, topped with a forest of TV antennas, but devoid of toilets or other sanitary installations. While for the Bedouins, supported by the rest of the Israeli Arabs and some leftist Israelis, this may be their only way to fulfill their claim on the land, for the neighboring Israelis that means chaos in urban planning, deteriorating living conditions for thousands of Bedouins and a sense of siege, like the urban centers of south America which are surrounded by the *favela* shacks of poverty and crime. The Bedouin menace is easy to imagine in such an environment, especially as the Bedouins, aided and incited by other Arab nationalists and by the Israeli Leftist radicals, have been consistently rejecting any compromise settlement by the Israeli authorities.

2. Israeli Arabs as Palestinians

The Palestinian identity of Israeli Arabs has become so dominant, that most of them, including those who serve in the Israeli Knesset, dub themselves Palestinians, who under duress would also admit that they are "of Israeli citizenship". Thank you. The more salient the Palestinian identity becomes, the more the Israeli aspect of the Arab-Israeli self perception recedes and is relegated to a secondary plan. The dilemma remains insoluble for Israel as long as the conflict between Israel and the rest of the Arabs is not settled: since the Arabs in Israel are not inclined to side in that dispute with their country, in which they struggle to be equal citizens, but rather with its enemies, they are bound to feel Palestinian rather than Israeli along this divide. One could say that at least in this regard they have made their choice and they are no longer "torn between their country and their people". But beyond the conflict which compels some individuals to make clear choices, Arabs in Israel have also been promoting their Palestinian identity in some creative and self-perpetuating ways: Palestinian history (genuine or manufactured), literature, art, folklore and culture are appropriated as theirs, Palestinian politics across the border provoke debates among them and prod them to support one party or another, like Fatah, Hamas or Islamic Jihad. And although most of them would refuse to leave the comfort and freedom of Israel for the poverty and oppression of a Palestinian entity, they also express a yearning for Palestinian independence, even, or perhaps especially, if that should be at the expense of their present country and to its detriment.

In their demonstrations against the Israeli authorities, the Arabs often raise enemy banners, voice hostile slogans and do not other-wise shrink from any form of violence that spells out their disgust for their country and their support for other Palestinians. They are not impressed when they are faced with past parallel situations in other places, where German or Japanese minorities in the US and England, for example, were arrested and incarcerated for fear of collaboration with their countries of origin in times of war, while in Israel they are not collectively punished in spite of the ongoing hostilities between Israel and other Arabs, and albeit their own unfriendly attitude towards the country where they live rather com-fortably. They are not impressed because they claim that they were the original inhabitants of the land, while the Israelis are the invad-ers, therefore it is Israel that has to adapt to them, not the other way around. They see no wrong when they shout during their demon-strations: "with our souls and blood we shall liberate you oh Pales-tine/Galilee"; liberate from whom or for whom, this is not stated, but one can easily conjecture. The Jewish majority is supposed to be "understanding", to absorb and swallow and to be tolerant of the Arab whims to the point of masochism. And if anyone should speak up or reproach to the Arabs their discourse, he would be accused of racism, discrimination, apartheid, Islamophobia and what not.

For that reason, law enforcement against Arabs has grown nearly impossible in Israel, as it has been becoming in other countries where a Muslim minority exists[6]. For if the police moves in to disperse illegal gatherings, to dismantle illegal construction or simply to enforce the law, both the Arab leadership and the press that pertains to the liberal left, are poised to condemn the police for its "excess of force", and instead of strengthening the hands of the security forces in their ungrateful job, the latter feel abandoned and singled-out as "brutal", something that crystallizes their determination to interfere less forcefully in the future. This attitude was dramatically illustrated once and again during the Land Day that is commemorated each March 30 (since 1976) where the Arabs go wild in their villages, hoist Hizbullah and Hamas banners and brandish anti-Israel slogans, with the Israeli police remaining outside the perimeters of the villages as if they were extra-territorial enclaves, and then reporting that the Land Day "was quiet and uneventful". (the exact same scenario unfolds daily in the Muslim neighborhoods of Paris, Malmo, Sydney and London with Muslim rebellious and unruly immigrants). This is, of course, the recipe for the escalation of violence and hostility the next year around, when everyone knows that those acts of Muslim enmity towards their country remain unpunished. Similarly, Israeli Arabs demonstrate for their Palestinian brethren, support their *Intifadah*, send medical and logistical aid to them and visit the bereaved families who lost their dear ones in their clashes against Israeli police or during acts of terrorism against Israel (never were such condolences presented to the bereaved Israeli families of Palestinian terrorism victims).

3. Israeli Arabs as Arabs

The Arabs of Israel are also part of the large Arab nation which comprises over 350 million people and 22 countries around the Middle East and North Africa. Not only do they sense culturally,

---

[6] See e. g. R. Israeli, *Muslim Minorities in Modern States: The Challenge of Assimilation,* Transaction, N.J, 2009.

historically, demographically, ethnically, linguistically and religiously part of that mass of people and countries, but by being a component of that larger entity, they feel engrossed in their sense of constituting the majority in the Middle East in spite of their being a minority in Israel. For them, it is Israel that is besieged by the Arab majority, not they by their majority host culture of Jews. And once again, as long as the Arab-Israeli conflict persists, and the Palestinian issue is only part of it (and not necessarily the most important thereof), the Arabs of Israel would consistently and perennially find themselves aligned with their brethren- the sworn enemies of their country. For them the Arab world is the great ocean where they can always seek shelter and solace, away from the suffocating Israeli aquarium in which they are trying to survive for the moment. Indeed, through the Arab countries that have signed a peace accord with Israel (Egypt and Jordan), and later through Syria and Lebanon too before they sank into civil war and chaos since 2011, Israeli Arabs were finding ways to relate to the Arab world. However, peace accords notwith-standing, the dilemmas of the Israeli Arabs are not resolved, inasmuch as the populace of those countries which signed peace with Israel remain as hostile as they were in the pre-peace period, if one judges by their sustained anti-Semitic campaigns, the media onslaughts on Israel, the cold-peace maintained by the Arab authorities and the strong and vocal oppositions to Israel in both the establishment and popular circles, especially in the midst of the radical Muslims among them. That means that though the official "peace" ought to facilitate the relations of Israeli Arabs to the wide Arab world, the persistence of the anti-Jewish and anti-Israeli stereotypes there does not make the interaction with them any easier. Moreover, Israeli Arabs, far from condemning those calumniations of their country in the Arab media, tend to cite them as "proofs" of their own recriminations against their country.

The great hopes that the Israeli Arabs attach to their links with the greater Arab world are related to the legendary idea of Arab unity, or Pan-Arabism, which alone can represent the collective strength of all Arabs and make them confident in their capacity to bend the world to their whim. They are aware that previous attempts at unity, which were exemplified by bilateral, trilateral or quadripartite unions between various Arab countries, did not hold for long, and that even in the midst of the 22-member Arab League, disunity has for long stultified any concerted action by that body. Especially bad did the situation become after the Iraq War (2003-5), in which all Arabs evinced their impotence to avert the war, and then were scrambling, again in disunity, to respond to the American initiatives for reforms and liberalization. Israeli Arabs, who are probably the closest in their view and upbringing in Israel to those ideas of freedom and democracy, are bewildered by Arab hesitation when facing change, but they would nevertheless rather cling to their Arab patrimony and defend the positions of their kin across the border than join the US and Israel who advocated change and reform. They have been perennially clinging to one Pan-Arab champion or another (Nasser in the 50's through the 1970's, and Saddam in the 1980's and 1990s) as the modern version of Saladin who would deliver them from their problems, while in the process hoping for their country (Israel), like the Crusader state of yesteryear, to succumb under the victory of their champion.

4. Israeli Arabs as Muslims

The Muslim world, which encompasses 1.5 billion Believers, distributed in 57 Muslim-majority states and tens of millions more as minorities in non-Muslim states, provides an even vaster background for the Arab Muslims of Israel to melt into. Moreover, due to the rise in recent years of militant Muslim radicalism, which has often consecrated violence as a legitimate means of struggle, radical Islamic movements have become the most potentially explosive element in many societies, Muslim and non-Muslim, regardless of whether they are set against their Muslim leaders and societies which they seek to metastasize, or against host non-Muslim societies which they want to transform or subdue. Among the Arab minority in Israel the Muslim radicals have become a force to be reckoned with, both as a substitute for the Communist Party which for years had channeled their anti-Israel resentments into Arab national activism, and due to their systematic, long-term and patient work of propaganda (*da'wa*) which penetrates all aspects of life of Muslims. Once the Believers are hooked on the religion as the "alternative" and the "solution" for all life dilemmas, they are no longer open to relative reasoning, and everything becomes absolute and certain, as captured in the dichotomies: Believer/Unbeliever, good/evil, they/us, justice/injustice, liberty/oppression, Divine/Satanic.

The Islamic Movement in Israel, just like its counterparts in the claimed Palestinian territories and in the adjoining Arab countries, thrives on deprivation and tension, since its success hinges on the instant "solutions" it offers to all existential problems of the individual and society. Its leaders, unlike the corrupt and illegitimate dictators who rule Arab societies all around, are attentive to the pains of their populace and enjoy a tremendous popularity among them. Paradoxically, it is their blood-and-sweat messages which sound more credible to the ears of the crowds than the soothing and empty rhetoric of the leaders which leads nowhere. Until the advent of the radical Muslims in the past three decades, it was the Communists under various appellations, at the outset under the leadership of Christian Arabs, who led their communities both in the local councils and in national politics (at the Knesset). But in the recent past, following the collapse of the Soviet Union, the leadership passed to Muslims (though not the pious among them), who are still engaged in their last rear-guard battle for "socialism" of the *Hadash* brand[7]. The Muslim Movement has taken over some mayoralties in the Arab villages and townships, their greatest achievements being the 1988 landslide conquest of Umm al-Fahm, the largest Muslim town in Israel, by Sheikh Ra'id, one of their foremost leaders; and their majority win in the Nazareth City Council in the 1998 elections, something that indicated that all the coming mayors of the largest Arab town in Israel will also become Muslim (after many decades of Christian-Communist rule).

These advances more than indicate not only the exhaustion and irrelevance of the Communists in the new era, but also that the Muslim radicals have both the ideological vocabulary that captivates the minds of people and the organizational clout to turn religion into a powerful mobilizing factor. The Muslim Movement in Israel has split into the Northern Branch, led by charismatic Ra'id, who pushes his followers towards alienation from the state of Israel; and the towns ruled by the movement have become virtual enclaves of Islam, where by-rules enacted by the city-council substitute for national laws to the extent possible. They keep aloof from national politics and do not vote for the Knesset, lest their elected candidates would have to swear allegiance to the laws of the state (Allah Forbid!!). They embraced a radical and aggressive program of rehabilitating old Arab sites that had been destroyed during the 1948 War, and they particularly map and reclaim old religious sites, such as mosques and cemeteries, claiming "holiness" for them. The *Al-Aqsa* organization that was set up by Ra'id, promotes programs for the refurbishing and the expansion of al-Aqsa Mosque in Jerusalem, and assembles tens of thousands of their membership every year in "Muslim Festivals" that are dedicated to boosting Muslim causes and raising Muslim consciousness in the country, at the expense of

---

[7] *Hadash (literally New)*is the acronym for the Front for Democracy and Change, which preserves the tradition of all Communist countries to dub their regimes "Democratic", precisely because they were not. No Western democracy has adopted that custom.

any Israeli orientation or fealty.

The more tame Southern Branch, which does not differ from the radicals ideologically or strategically, but advocates piecemeal advance rather than a one-stroke leap, is aware that political power can be a conduit for achievements within Israeli society, therefore admonishes its supporters to vote for the Knesset, and in fact sends two delegates to the Israeli Parliament who are elected as part of a larger Arab party of four. In that way, while it participates in the political process that is anathema to other Muslim radicals, it can also claim that it does not partake of Israeli politics as an Islamic party as such, but as part of a larger Arab party that seeks its share of the Israeli national cake. In other words, it is present there not in order to determine Israeli policies, in which it has no interest, but in order to make sure that Arabs and Muslims are not outcasts that can be ignored and discriminated against. While the murderers, the arsonists, the saboteurs, the terrorists and the violent demonstrators among Israeli Arabs are more likely to be drawn from the Northern radical branch, which also excels in producing video- and audio cassettes extolling *Islamikaze*[8] bombers, the Southern Branch provides the rank and file for its mass demonstrations and votes for the Muslim delegates who occupy their Knesset seats but do not hide their hostility towards the Jewish state and their desire to put an end to it.

The Muslim Movement acknowledges its being part of the Muslim Brotherhood, including the Hamas, which in their radical and violent manifestations are akin to other Muslim groupings who do not shun murder and terror to attain their goals. That is the reason that while the Southern Muslim Movement in Israel has been raising

---

[8] *Islamikaze,* a coumpound of Islam and Kamikaze was coined by this author to designate Muslim radicals who are prepared to sacrifice themselves (not to commit suicide) in the process of killing their enemies in terrorist attacks. See R. Israeli, *Islamikaze: Manifestations of Islamic Martyrology,* Frank Kass, London, 2008.

funds and generally acting with caution on the outer limits of legality, the Northern Branch has also been maintaining contacts with other Islamic radicals throughout the Arab and Islamic world, and collecting "charities" which are ultimately deflected to terrorist causes. The hyper-activity of Sheikh Ra'id in the international Islamic arena, and his very diversified links with various Muslim movements, especially in Egypt and Turkey, have raised suspicions against him in the security apparatus in Israel. He was arrested by the Israeli security authorities in mid 2003, and was indicted and tried, but convicted in an agreed plea bargain as the legal process tended to linger beyond measure. He was condemned for his illicit links with the Hamas, and his indictment and conviction were backed by tons of documents of his contacts with international Islamic movements and "charities", money transfers from front "charity" organizations into funds that financed questionable endeavors, and many more encroachments on the legal system of the country that might throw some light (some say obscurity) on the international Islamic terrorist networks. But his premature release from prison as a result of his plea bargain, at the end only boosted his popularity among his followers, and hardened his recalcitrance against the Israeli system that he continued to battle[9]. Unrepentant in his defiance of the Israeli system, his movement was outlawed by the Israel cabinet in 2015.

This large variety of criss-crossing identities obliges every Arab in Israel to find his way, as an individual or part of a collective, and to lend his emphasis to one aspect or another of his loyalties, according to time, place and circumstance. There are Arabs in Israel who distance themselves from politics and focus their attention exclusively on their families, communities and livelihood. These would usually move in their Arab and Israeli circles, in the former in terms

---

[9] See Israeli, Raphael, *Islamic Radicalism and Political Violence: the Templars of Islam and Sheikh Ra'id Salah,* Vallentine Mitchell, London, 2008.

of culture and identity, in the latter in the domain of work and making a living. Others who are active in politics, certainly feel more Arab and Palestinian in their endeavor, but also sense the necessity to relate to the Israeli institutions and society in which they operate and on which they depend. "Born-again" Muslims, who have rediscovered the certitudes that the faith can grant to the Believers, find themselves spending their lives in their neighborhood mosques and in the Muslim enclaves that are provided by their villages. Living as an Arab in that environment means mainly to be a Muslim who relates, through his community, to the international *Umma,* or world congregation of Believers. This is no easy situation for anybody to be in, especially in an era of conflict where the individual is called upon to update his identity and shift his loyalty constantly.

Muslims are usually required to live under Muslim rule, but for those who do not it is imperative to make sure that either they live freely enough to bring to bear their beliefs and religious practices, or to seek other lands of asylum. In the case of Israel, the Arabs consider it theirs (albeit under its Palestine appellation), and they are called upon to cling to it, by cultivating the notion of *sabr* (patience, resilience), until ultimately the land reverts to becoming theirs again. Besides, together with their complaints about their discriminatory treatment by the Jewish majority, they are aware that they enjoy the freest, most prosperous, most advanced social services and longest life expectancy that they can expect anywhere in the Muslim world. So their "suffering" is not so bad after all, and they would rather preserve their Israeli citizenship under which they are allowed to ritually complain about being "oppressed", than take any Arab or Muslim citizenship, say the Syrian, Palestinian or Afghani or Pakistani, where they observe daily the displacements and misery that the "Arab Spring" has brought. While they pay lip-service to the Palestinization of their community, and voice in public the "Right of Return", which would flood Israel with returning

Palestinian refugees, they know deep in their hearts that in such a case Israel would turn into another Palestinian state, bereft of its democracy, freedom, prosperity and technology. When they see the state of backwardness and poverty in Gaza and Ramallah that the Palestinians have founded, Israeli Arabs are not particularly eager to make their towns and villages like them, so they elect to advance within Israeli society and try to get positions of professional specialization in preparation for the day when they are called upon to take over the country.

There is a large part played by the Israeli authorities in all this, if one wishes to explain away the dismal failures in instituting a coherent and persistent policy towards the Arab population of Israel. First of all, there are the political parties in Israel who seek the Arab voters on the eve of elections, only to forget their promises the day after. This has understandably driven the Arabs into political cynicism and also encouraged them to establish their own political subsystems. They have come of age and learned something about participatory democracy, about the full-rights slogans that they have heard so often, while in practice they have encountered many restrictions. They got used to the state's custom of appointing token Arab officials or judges, just to prove that the Arabs are not discriminated against, but in fact that evinces exactly the reverse: for if Arabs could accede to high positions without being positively discriminated for by affirmative action, that would have shown that they truly became integrated citizens. Arabs also got accustomed to the demand of loyalty by the state, but at the same time authorities are lenient towards those who overtly operate against it. For example, Ahmed Tibi, a leader of the Israeli-Arab community, later MK, served for years with impunity, as the adviser of Yasser Arafat, an avowed enemy of Israel, while his compatriot, Azmi Bishara, traveled repeatedly, against the law, to enemy territory in Syria, without the government indicting him. Calumniation of the state and incitement against it by Arab MK's and other notables, have become a matter of course, and no one was seriously indicted for trespassing the limits of law. This has brought Bishara, the Head of the *Balad* Party, to transmit information about Israel to his allies in the Hizbullah and to run away from his post in the Knesset to hide in Arab countries before he could be indicted for treason.

It has become routine that Arab leaders in Israel, far from accepting the rulings of courts of law, which usually protect their rights, especially when they convict other Arabs of "ideological" crimes against the state, on the contrary attack the system and blame all manner of machinations against them by the police and the courts. They consistently follow the line that they cannot be wrong because they are themselves wronged, therefore any accusation of encroachment on the law on their part is a mere conspiracy against them in order to frame them and discriminate against them. Since they are vociferous about demanding their rights, but are not asked to fulfill their duties, they regard any call upon them to respect the law as a nuisance or persecution, and reject it with disgust. Therefore, the leniency by the Israeli authorities towards them, far from easing the tensions, on the contrary triggers the contempt and confusion on the part of the Arabs. Indeed, Arabs often realize that their violence pays off, that no one would take them to task and demand that they abide by the law, and that if they should persist in their lawlessness, they are sure to win at the end. That is the mechanism that allowed Bishara to spy against his country, the Bedouins to set up illegal villages and then claim that they are dispossessed when they are evacuated by the authorities, the Arab Members of the Knesset to sit in the Israeli Legislative House and act against its laws, Arab intellectuals to issue papers undermining Israeli existence and sovereignty, and Arab political and religious leaders to side with the enemies of their country and deny the latter's right of self defense. Other Israeli citizens, who see and hear, and are very alert to what is happening in their neighborhood, are increasingly skeptical not only about achieving an acceptable settlement with the Palestinians outwardly, but in view of the total identification of Israeli Arabs with their brethren, that skepticism has been extending to the possibility of livability with their immediate Arab neighbors in Israel proper inwardly. These fears are haunting the Israelis, especially after the trauma of October 2000, more emphatically than ever before. The great surge of the Joint Arab Party, which rose from 10 to 15 Knesset members during the three successive national elections in 2019-2020, did little to ally those fears and suspicions.

The state of Israel has to understand that the issue is not economic, as it is sometimes claimed, and no amount of budget or financial aid would resolve it. This is a growingly acute ideological question translating into issues of identity, future and destiny. The first cry of dissent from Israel by its Arab citizens was voiced during the first Land Day in 1976, when they announced loud and clear that they were Palestinian Arabs; but Israel, instead of waking up to the looming danger, elected to sink the problem in a cataract of apologies, promises, declarations and endless words. Since the two Palestinian *Intifadah*'s that shook the Israeli public (1987 and again 2000), Israel has repeatedly been caught by "surprise", by the violence of the spill of that rebellion over its border, into the Arab-Israeli areas. Most Israelis were stunned by these eruptions within Israel Proper, as if its official soothing declarations of equality should have created love, fraternity and harmony between the two conflicting communities. Israel has learned the hard way that this was never the case, for Israeli policies and responses to the growing crisis have always come too little and too late. The state never realized that these issues ought to be settled by legislation and education, in order to nip in the bud the growth of these wild weeds that are destroying what is left of the fragile co-existence between the two communities. The law should be enforced, enjoyment of rights should hinge on the fulfillment of duties, and the choices should be clearly stated to the Arabs, for themselves to choose.

And yet, Israelis are constantly asking themselves whether the

Arabs of the country are friends of foes? For, due to their increasing vociferousness and the international stature that they claim for themselves, which is fed by the rising national demands of the Palestinians, they came to be seen by the Israeli public as the tip of the iceberg, representing the wider Palestinian, Arab and Islamic circles which have not made much progress towards reconciling with the Israeli presence in their midst. These days are not merely characterized by Arab strife, terror, war, hatred and incitement against Israel, even as terror and killings occasioned by the Arab unrest domestically have overshadowed the peace talks between Israel and the Palestinians; and worldwide legitimacy is given to the Palestinian demands, and to their Arab and Islamic allies' endeavors, especially in Europe, with some lateral support by intellectual and leftist circles in the West. Thus, much doubt is being cast there on the very right to existence of the Jewish state, as manifested by the spread of the BDS propaganda in the world, at a time when Israel, more than ever before, is in dire need of its supporters in order to continue to defend itself. For, the thugs who rule countries like Syria, Libya and Iran, and the terrorist movements like al-Qa'ida, Hamas and Hizbullah, and for a time ISIS, which have shown their mettle in the world scene, are no longer hiding their intentions against the Jews, Israel and anyone who dares to support anything Jewish in the West. Their incitement and hatred are propagated by the Arab and Muslim media almost without regard to the facts, to history or to the truth[10]. Even "respectable" Arabic newspapers that appear in the West, often take upon themselves to diffuse disgusting and libelous anti-Semitic propaganda of the worst kind that is often topped by cartoons or straight anti-Semitic statements of the Western press itself.

---

[10] See R. Israeli, *Hatred, Lies and Violence,* Transaction, NJ, 2014.

Chapter Two

The Jewish and Zionist State— A Sore in the Eye

The rising Zionist movement, which started out as a political theory but soon deployed in Ottoman and then Mandatory British Palestine the necessary tools for its gradual implementation, was the unbearable shift in the status of the Jews, in the eyes of Muslims, from an eternally oppressed and humiliated minority given to the mercy of Muslim rulers, to a proud, independent and successful nation capable of standing up to their former oppressors and even of beating them, in spite of being vastly outnumbered. This act of reversed humiliation of the entire Islamic *Umma*, which has become a constant theme in its hostility towards Israel, the Jews and Zionism, though it happened within three generations of Jewish Zionism's spectacular achievements, has indeed stood out in comparison with the backwardness, helplessness, bitterness and fanaticism which have only increased the sense of frustration among the Muslims, the Arabs and particularly the Palestinians who were directly victimized by this struggle.

Hatred and contempt towards the Jews in the Arab and Muslim worlds, which to this day is exemplified by the recurrent mosque sermons in the citation from the Qur'an that Jews are as the "descendants of apes and pigs", have been rationalized over the centuries by the assumption that if the Jews are irrefutably comparable to animals by the Word of Allah itself, they are thereby dehumanized, as the Nazis would do to them,consider them and act against them centuries later, thereby making them "permissible" for extermination. When Osama Bin Laden admitted in September 2001 that his al-Qa'ida organization had planned and perpetrated the Twin Tower horror, he justified the act as being geared to harm "American and Jewish arrogance", the two actors which blocked Islamic radicals from triumphing in the international arena, the one on the world scale, the other, with all proportions guarded, in the regional area of the Middle East. For Europe, which has nowadays practically capitulated to Islam, those two actors remained the only obstacles resisting Islamic aggression, expansion and terrorism and determined to battle against it.

The reversal of the Jewish condition in the world was triggered and cultivated by Zionism which effected a number of revolutions that upgraded the Jewish nation from a persecuted, oppressed, murdered, underprivileged and trampled upon minority that could be tossed around the globe and prevented from developing its genius, into one of the most successful new nations in the post-World War II process of decolonization and independence of colonized nations. That reversal had begun since the 19th century in the large Jewish communities around the world, especially in Eastern Europe, when the emancipation of Jews on the one hand, and the manifestation of anti-Semitism on the other, as during the epoch-making Dreyfus Affair in France, on the other; aided by the national awakening of other nations who also sought independence from the yoke of their oppressors, as in the case of the Balkan states who sought liberation from the Ottoman occupation[11], all converged to trigger the birth of political Zionism. Political, because the idea of the Jews returning to Zion had endured for centuries before, but as an ideal of redemption that could someday be realized under apocalyptic or eschato-

---

[11] See e.g. Nobel Prize Laureate, Ivo Andric's *The Bridge on the Drina*, Dereta, Belgrade, 2011.

logical circumstances. The socio-political condition of the Jewish Diasporas across the globe was not such as to support the hope or trigger a realistic design to do something about it, due to the dispersion of Jews around the world and their usual state of submission which barely permitted their survival, while there was almost never a real and concrete chance for change. That was the great breakthrough that Theodor Herzl brought about when, taking advantage of the convergence of all those conditions, decided to launch a political movement and a plan of action that he predicted would mature within 50 years into a Jewish state, as indeed it was to be.

The difficulties were enormous due to the anomaly of the Jewish people, who had been fragmented into many sub-cultures, languages, territories and political loyalties, which had seemingly made its reconstitution into one land, one culture, one language, and one political entity unfeasible for a people which had for two millennia lost most of the attributes that make a nation. For unlike other peoples, who had continuously kept their territories and social system, and all they needed, like in the Balkans, the Middle East or the colonized peoples and tribes of Asia, Africa and the Americas, was to rid themselves of foreign occupation and its political and cultural tutorship and domination, the scattered Jews had had much history during those two millennia, but little or no geography. Their homeland territory had changed hands for many centuries, and they had forgotten the sense of being independent and politically proud of themselves, or of acting from their recognized turf and developing their own style of life, social and political structures, religion and language, and all that makes a modern country tick. Thus, the Zionist Revolution that was launched in the First Zionist Congress in Basel, Switzerland, in 1897, actually targeted, against all odds, the following tasks:

1. To create a territorial base for the implementation of the Zionist idea, preferably in the ancient Land of Israel/Palestine, although it was then under Ottoman occupation with an

Arab-majority population that had dwelt in the land since the Arab occupation in the 7th Century. The illusion that "a people without a land was claiming a land without people", was gradually emerging as the chief obstacle to the realization of Zionism. True, there had always been a small Jewish population on the land, even after the Second Temple's destruction by the Romans in AD 70, and in the aftermath of their subsequent massive massacre during their bloody uprisings against their rulers. In addition, a small trickle of Jewish immigrants had always fed that Jewish existence in the land, that had been alternately devastated and then rehabilitated by the successive Islamic regimes which ruled it, save for the short Crusader *inter-regnum*. But the Arab majority had prevailed there until the 20th Century when the state of Israel was reconstituted.

2. To encourage Jewish immigration into Palestine so as to create, against all odds, a viable demographic basis for the ultimate establishment of a Jewish entity, even if it was not a full-fledged state at the outset and even if not all its population was Jewish. Those were compromises that had be made to give any chance for the new Jewish entity to emerge and then grow. Indeed, in addition to the already existing trickle of incoming Jews, who arrived for the religious purpose of making a pilgrimage to the holy land, or of ending their lives by being buried in its earth, newly committed young Jewish intellectuals, mainly from Eastern Europe flocked to the land in order to implement the idea of return. The question of Jewish immigration to the land was so highly valued as a main component of the Zionist plan, that it was termed *aliya* (literally going up) alluding to the concept that moving to the holy land of Israel was a metaphorical ascent and upgrade, while the reverse trend of moving from it abroad was understandably termed *yerida* (going down). Hence *Olim* are those worthy who move to Israel while those who abandon it are

deprecated as *yordim*. The successive waves of immigration since the turn of the 20th Century until W W II, are all numbered according to their chronological sequence as *Aliya I, Aliya* II, etc. through *Aliya V.*

3. There was no point of returning to the land if the bourgeois life, or the traditional scholarly occupation, or the unskilled trades in poverty and deprivation of the Diaspora were transplanted there. It became necessary to restore normalcy to the Jewish social structure by turning on its head the abnormally reversed social pyramid where learning was at the top while farming, the military and the artisan menial work were negligible; so that Jews could become farmers in their land and artisans in their towns to sustain themselves, and learn to defend themselves by themselves. Hence the establishment of the first farming villages on a cooperative basis, which developed into *moshavim* and *kibbutzim*, the two forms of cooperative farming that remade Israel. That was also the genesis of Jewish self-defense when spontaneous associations like *Hashomer* (the Guardian or Watchman) became the precursors of the legendary *Haganah, Irgun and Stern group,* which were the base for the construction of the Israeli Defense Forces (IDF).

No wonder then that after Israel was established in 1948, upon the expiration of the British Mandate (1922-48), those three major and paramount requirements of Zionism (*aliya*, settlement on the land and security) remained the major tasks of the state, to which environing Arabs, especially the Palestinians who remained in the Jewish state, namely the 15-20% rate of the Arab population of Israel proper, have continued to object virulently, thus setting them apart from and in direct confrontation with the Jewish state they were inhabiting. For their sake and for Israel's sake in the long run, it would have been much safer and healthier to have completed their removal with the flow of outgoing Arab refugees. The

"humanitarian", "moral", diplomatic and public relations considerations that prompted the the lenient and generous policy towards
them which allowed them to stay, ultimately proved to their detriment, when after three generations of unsettled friction with the
Israeli authorities, their bitterness and rebelliousness only increased.
Even today, New and Revisionist Historians, and certainly Arab
politicians and Western moralists, who after they settled on Indian
and Inca lands and annihilated their cultures, started to preach
morality to Israel, still lament Israel's harsh and "inhuman policies"
toward the Palestinian refugees. They do not venture to analyze the
would- be fate of Israel had she agreed then to repatriate large por-
tions of the hostile Palestinian populations, when considering the
already impossible impasse Israel has been facing with its large and
indigestible large Arab minority. Naturally, the Arabs would have
elected to witness a Jewish defeat and disaster than suffer theirs in
the confrontation with Israel that they launched, and they were on
the verge of winning the 1948 war, but Jews have no reason today
to apologize for their survival and for the perpetuation of the Arab
plight in Israel, because their resettlement elsewhere had not been
completed then.

During the large wave of Russian Jewish immigrants to Israel in
the 1990's, numerous were the leaders of Arabs of Israel who pro-
tested against that influx of newcomers, at a time when Arab refugees were left rotting in deleterious makeshift camps for the fourth
generation now, waiting for their "right of return" which they knew
would never come true. That meant that the Israeli Arabs, like the
rest of the Palestinians, would like Israel to "repatriate" those long
gone refugees and their posterity now amounting to 4-5 million,
which would break the back of Israel. This sounds strange in light
(or rather obscurity) of Arab complaints about their "suffering" and
about the "discrimination" against them in Israel. For if it were so
bad, then why would they like to subject more of their brethren to
that oppressive treatment by Israel, while today they live in "liberty"

and "prosperity" in Arab countries' refugee camps? These contradictory remarks have been clarified and expanded lately, as Arab leaders, including the heads of Israeli Arabs, following Yasser Arafat in his time, have been clamoring for the "return" of all those millions of refugees, who are the descendants of the original 700,000 of 1948-9, and for their gaining full citizenship within Israel. The point is not that the PLO and Palestinians in general have been converted to the Zionist idea of boosting immigration to the land of Israel, and striving to increase Israel's population through the influx of Jewish immigrants, but this was an open and unsophisticated attempt to arrest at any cost the stunning and successful process of the growth, empowerment and reinforcement of the Jewish state. For, while they negate Jewish immigration as one of the foundations of Zionism, under the "humanitarian" argument of prioritizing the repatriation of Arab refugees instead, they challenge the rest of the elements of the Zionist enterprise like settlement, security, links with the Jewish people worldwide, democracy and economic development. They in the meantime benefit individually as nationals of Israel, from these elements, the like of which do not exist in the Palestinian Authority or anywhere in the Arab and Muslim world.

Aliya, i.e. Jewish immigration, is the central theme of the Zionist enterprise, for it has been the only factor which can somehow offset Arab natural growth and prevent the demographic takeover of the country by the Arabs, which would eventually put an end to the Jewish state that Zionism was created to foster. There is suspicion that this delicate balance might not be perpetuated in the long run, for the Arabs cannot wait to implement their demographic potential, either by letting in an influx of Arab refugees under the "right of return", by stemming Jewish immigration, or by neutralizing the Jewish identity of the state by adopting the destructive notion of " a state of its citizens", with the courteous help of some self-defeating Jews of the Left, who can no longer reconcile to the idea of the Jewish state, and are prepared to renounce the Jewish symbols of their

country and its Jewish character in order to make it palatable to the
Arabs. When one invokes the catastrophic consequences of such a
demarche, like Arabization of the state of Israel and the loss of the
Jewish majority, which would put an end to democracy, liberty and
economic development, and the country would get to look more like
Gaza than Tel Aviv, in its backwardness, poverty and corruption, the
Arabs and their Jewish aides rebel against this "racist" statement that
points to Arab inability to establish a democratic and open entity like
Israel's if they were to gain the majority. However, since the Arabs
have been unable thus far to produce any precedent among their 22
states and 380 million citizens where these achievements were
attained, mainstream Israelis have every reason to doubt their ability
to do so. Once upon a time we were told that the Palestinians were
different, and that if they should attain independence they would
establish a model democracy, but the disastrous experience since
Oslo and the establishment of the PA has shown that it is chaos,
bigotry, backwardness, violence, lawlessness, tyranny, and idleness
and reliance on international handouts that have predominated in
the Palestinian entity. Those who watched Palestinian developments
were far from persuaded that the Palestinian great promise was real-
izable. Nor were they convinced that the returning refugees would
bring with them any great positive innovation in government, economy or values. Nonetheless, the Arabs of Israel, like the rest of their
kin, seem to be more eager to bring Israel down to their own level,
if its cultural, technological and economic edge can be thereby eliminated, than to endure the eye-poking advance of the Israelis, even if
they themselves should suffer as a result the loss of all these advan-
tages, rather than accept their status as a minority in an advanced,
modern, orderly, prosperous, free and civilized Jewish society.

This sort of thinking is also linked to the adamant Palestinian
refusal to recognize the right of the Jewish people to self-determination and independence. Indeed, in the infamous Palestinian
National Charter, which has not been amended or abrogated as part

of their pledges to do so, in spite of Arafat's assurances to the contrary, Article 20 negates the national rights of the Jews to statehood, since "they are not a nation" and their dispersion among other nations is the best proof in their eyes of that. Palestinian desire to implement their "right of return", which is supported by some suicidal Israelis and ill-intending Arabs, is precisely calculated to dilute the Jewish population by inundating it within Arab masses, so that Jewish independence should become irrelevant. The Israeli mindless politicians who concocted the Oslo accords, did not pay attention to this essential detail in spite of the warnings they received. Therefore, during the Oslo negotiations, they never raised the fair, equal and reciprocal demand that in return for Israeli recognition of the right of Palestinians for self-determination they should have responded in kind towards the Jews. But Israel did not advance that demand, nor did the Palestinians volunteer to make that fair statement, therefore Israeli recognition of the Palestinians' right to the same remained unilateral, while they persist in negating the Jews' parallel and equal right by threatening Israel with Arab refugees who would render the notion of Jewish self-determination obsolete and unfeasible. Had the mindless Israeli negotiators insisted on this simple and matter-of-course recognition, it would have acquired the sympathy of the world while at the same time it would have rendered irrelevant that Article 20 of the Charter. Thus, as the Arabs of Israel and their kin outside of it refuse to accept their permanent status as a minority in the Jewish state, whose character they are seeking to dilute and then to erase, and they clamor for the right of return of their kin into Israeli territory, they declare outloud that Jews have no right to self-determination or statehood, while at the same time advocating the "inalienable and natural" right of Palestinians to the same.

The same applies to the Zionist component of the State, which the Arabs are also demanding to alter. Once again, those who concocted Oslo were oblivious of that fact when they recognized the PLO as the movement of national liberation of the Palestinians, but they did not demand reciprocation by insisting that Zionism, the movement of national liberation of the Jewish people be equally accepted by the Palestinians. Had Israel lodged that matter- of- course demand, it would have gained the support of the world and brought about the abrogation of the PLO Charter which vows in 15 of its 33 articles the elimination of all manifestations of Zionism (not of Israel) in Palestine. Instead, while Israel recognized the PLO, it continued to hear the Palestinians and other Arabs denouncing Zionism as "racism" and "Nazism". Israel's spineless leadership of the time had promised that it would ensure the removal from the Charter of all "anti-Israeli items' before peace was signed with the Palestinians, but that was never done, if only due to the fact that such items do not exist in the Charter, which only negates Zionism, while if Zionism were recognized as a condition for accepting the PLO, the latter's Charter would have been *ipso facto* rendered obsolete. Instead, Israel went into a long series of demands, supplications and begging from the Palestinians, who never budged from their negative position, and from the American intermediaries who were coaxed by the Palestinian double game which ended in nothing. Therefore, attacks on Zionism, by the Palestinians and Israeli Arabs, continue unabated, because naïve and spineless Israeli "peaceniks at any price" never raised the issue, and once again the Palestinians never volunteered to do it out of their own volition. Quite the contrary, as if de-Judaization of Israel were not enough in their list of recriminations, they now demanded its de-Zionization as well.

Settlement of the land has always been a major bone of contention between Israel and the Arabs, especially since the first Land Day was marked violently by the Arabs on 31 March, 1976. For a growing, prosperous and successful Jewish settlement of the land not only signaled to the Arabs that the Jews were indeed taking roots in their country, but that their enterprise was coming at the expense of the Arabs, even when it was done on state-owned land and not on privately–owned patches of soil. Furthermore, for them, an expanding Jewish settlement means that the Arab dream to implement their own "right of return", was necessarily evaporating once the arable land was all settled. Thus, even though the modernity of Israeli agriculture has increased manifold Arab productivity, by introducing new methods of cultivation, quotas of production, new seeds, new fertilizers and new machinery, the Arabs have a hard time seeing this as a blessing, as it revolutionized their traditional (and more primitive) agriculture, and also upset their slow pace of life and their societal structure, and reversed old hierarchies and family authority. Arab anger increases as they see new Jewish settlements growing around them, like the new *kibbutzim,* and the Galilee *Mitzpim* (observatories- nuclei for new villages or community centers), and since 1967 also in the West Bank and Gaza. For they regard as intrusive into their own lives those alternative modes of modern, open and attractive ways of life likely to tempt their youth away from their traditions. This is all the more so when new urban centers are built on the fringe of their own towns and villages (like Carmiel, Upper Nazareth in the north, or Arad and Dimona in the south), and the many urban and rural centers in the West Bank and Gaza, which are salient by their modernity and advance in the Arab environment and arouse jealousies among Arab youth, especially as they are mostly build by Arab construction workers. Very often, these new Jewish towns also take away from the natural and potential area of development and expansion of the Arab towns and villages, thus "choking" their plans of extending their perimeters into a suffocating halt.

Therefore, the Land Days, which were inaugurated on 31 March, 1976 and have been held annually in all Arab towns and villages ever since, often accompanied by widespread violence and in collaboration with other Palestinians in the territories, do not stand only as a symbol of joint Arab resistance to the confiscation of their lands, but also as an attempt to block the establishment of new Israeli settlements. In recent years, the Arabs threaten violence if Israeli police should dare to enter their villages to establish order during those demonstrations. Does anyone imagine where all that would end in terms of law enforcement if any gang of violent people should set the boundaries for security forces to enter or refrain from entering? The police, which is under constant watch by the Arabs, the media and Leftist politicians who want to please the Arab constituency on elections days, would rather not enter Arab villages under their jurisdiction, than take the risk of being censored for "disproportionate use of force", a phenomenon also well known in Marseille, Paris, Malmo, Antwerp and many other European and international cities where Muslim immigrants make the rule. Instead, it "negotiates" with the Arab village notables, as if public security were a matter of negotiation, and rather than suing them for disturbing public order, it releases joint communiqués with them stating that the Day "went on peacefully", praising "Arab restraint". Under this cover of official blackmail, the demands made every year by the Arab leaders keep escalating, and there is no telling at what point would Israeli police consider itself totally excluded from watching these events lest they escalate into violence. After the fact, it turns out that this police "restraint" has included ignoring the hoisting the flags of the enemies of Israel, like Hizbullah and Hamas, waving slogans: "with our souls and blood we shall rescue you, O Galilee!" (from whom, exactly?), supplemented by occasional calls:"Massacre the Jews!!". In recent years, the Land Day has been coordinated between Israeli Arabs and the Palestinians in the West Bank and Gaza, and both have showed the same "restraint" on both sides of the border, against Israel- their common enemy. These demonstrations of "restraint" have occasionally born fruit, for example when there was question of constructing a chain of settlements in the lower Galilee in the early 2000's in order to ensure Jewish settlement continuity amidst the Arab population, under

Ehud Barak's government, but the plan was scuttled to please the Arab voters before the elections.

The question of Jewish settlements has yet another aspect which has asserted itself as successive Israeli governments have constantly yielded in the face of Arab pressures. Under the headings of "preserving Arab heritage", or "restoring Islamic holy sites", a large-scale operation is going on in Israel to register, restore, retrieve and commemorate all Arab villages which were destroyed during the War of Independence, and pressure is exerted on the government to allow resettlement of abandoned villages like Ikrit and Biram on the Lebanese border, with a view of creating a precedent and then plead with the courts to apply it to all the rest. The Arabs know that the courts decide on particular cases brought before them, without any regard for long-term political and strategic considerations of survival of the state. The registration and commemoration procedures are not done by the Arabs for historical purposes of preservation and remembering, but are used as a tool to relive the past and revive it, to bring back to life a village that has not been around for more than half century, to lead children to a tour on foot of the site for indoctrination purposes, and to clean up and restore old cemeteries or mosques that are no more since they were destroyed during the 1948 War that had been triggered by the Arabs. This is the significance of the recurrent cry by Israeli Arabs of "rescuing the Galilee" from the hands of the Jewish majority. Another consequence becomes apparent when the present map of revival is linked to the "right of return" of the Palestinians, which the Arabs of Israel support wholeheartedly. For this means that the sites for the future resettlement of the returning Palestinians have been already pinpointed, marked and brought possibly under restoration, in preparation for absorbing the returnees. The fact that in the meantime a new life has grown on the same places does not in the least diminish from the Arabs' enthusiasm for implementing the right of return.

Security, both state and personal, which is the most sensitive issue for Israelis who devote much of their lives to it, is also perhaps the most objection-raising among Israeli Arabs in particular and Arabs in general. This does not refer merely to the immediate and personal level, where they feel they have no obligation to contribute their part in order to become full-fledged citizens, but also to the philosophical, and for Israel often existential, question of Israel's right to security. For them, Israel is always the "aggressor", even as she defends herself, because she is not entitled to defend what she got by theft, robbery and usurpation, oppression and discrimination. Conversely, the Arabs are always the victims, even when they attack, murder, ambush, sabotage and terrorize. The question of examining each case separately and analyzing its merits does not even arise in the Arabs' minds, in order to identify the aggressor and the victim, for in their eyes aggression is part of Jewish nature, while absolute truth is always on the Arab's side. Therefore, whenever Israeli Arabs, either as terrorists or as victims, feel constrained to react to any heinous act of terror perpetrated against their country, they would, like other Palestinians, at best condemn the act, not its perpetrators, as if it were a natural calamity. The perpetrators, even when they identify themselves openly as members of some Arab or Islamic group, would rarely be censured, for it does not stand to reason that Arabs, who merely defend themselves from Israeli aggression, could be accused as aggressors for their act of bravery and self-sacrifice.

Israeli security, as a concept, not only as a practical pursuit, cannot therefore be palatable to Israeli Arabs, and if they do not act consciously to defeat it, they would at the very least refrain from lifting a finger to implement it. Some years back, when it was question of night-watching by students on campus, Arab students, precisely those who do not usually lift a finger for the security of their state, refused to stand their watch, arguing that they had "no one to guard against", as if a prospective Palestinian terrorist had a way to distinguish between Jews and Arabs in the same dormitories that were to be defended. As far as they were concerned, Israel might as well renounce all its security assets, for every tank and plane that Israel buys not only deprives them from civil budgets, but it thereby also delays the return of the Palestinian refugees. As a result, any Druze who serves, or any other Arab who volunteers to the Army, be he Muslim Christian or Bedouin, is looked down upon and is considered a "traitor", who would be subjected to the wrath and hostility of other Arabs if it were not for the protection he enjoys from the state apparatus. Those few who are praised by Israel for volunteering to the security forces, are condemned as "collaborators" by the majority of their coreligionists, thus deterring others from following their example. So, in the eyes of the majority of Arabs, while those who are censured for their service are looked upon as abject turncoats, those who condemn them act as if they were the enemies of Israel. And when they are killed in battle, one can hardly find a Muslim cleric who would consent to lead a Muslim funeral for the defunct because neither he nor his family can mend the terrible sin of defending his country. Even worse is the situation of other Arabs (Like Lebanese or Palestinians) who assisted the IDF and were brought to the country to be protected from their kin, but Israeli Arabs would avoid them, boycott them, refuse to dwell in their neighborhoods and prevent their children from playing with the "traitor'" children. All this not only amounts very simply to saying that defense of Israel or contribution to its defense, will always be reprehensible, but that gnawing at its security and plotting against it in concert with its enemies, is the best manifestation of Arab national honor. What other country in the world would suffer in silence such a destructive and subversive behavior of its citizens, while clamoring for equal rights?

Security is also the general context in which Israel faces the Arab and Islamic worlds. The Arabs in Israel have watched the military power of their country, but they wish it were not operated against other Arabs and Muslims, and whenever they are faced with such situations, they are more likely than not to criticize Israel's military power rather than the conduct of their own compatriots and core-ligionists by usually justifying their stance by the saying that "the policy of force" will not succeed in the long run. They are cognizant at the same time, however, that had Israel been devoid of its military power, it would not have survived one day. They not only refuse categorically to lend any security service to their country, but they harshly censure those among them who do, and they castigate the Druze for fulfilling their duty towards the state. Unlike the pre-1967 years, when Arabs in Israel had served as volunteers in civilian jobs and donated blood during the wars, now any volunteer duty in time of distress to the country is considered a sort of "treason". Namely, the more advanced the process of Israelization of Israeli Arabs, the more reserved they grew about involving themselves in anything having to do with the security of the country. This is not only because they feel reluctant to engage in battles that were not essentially theirs (despite their protestation that they are "loyal" citizens of the country), or to participate in beating and defeating their own people, but principally because that would have made them unwilling partners in the glory of the IDF, the much admired force of defense to whom the country owes its very existence. For pious Muslims, there is also a strict ban to fight against other Muslims, particularly in the service of Infidel troops. They, on the contrary, would rather see the IDF defeated, or at the very least repulsed, maimed, humiliated and unsuccessful.

In recent years, criminality has increased exponentially within the Arab population in Israel, including "honor killing", and *lex talionis,* which recur in every Arab town or village with a frequency and cruelty that have become unbearable to the Arabs themselves. For the Israeli authorities that does not only expose, more acutely than ever, like among Muslim immigrants in Europe, the incompatibility between traditional Arab/Muslim traditional society and the modern Western civilization and concept of the rule of law, but that due to the double rate of criminality among the Arabs and Muslims, as in their midst in their host societies, the socio-economic burden of this conduct on the state apparatus is becoming unconscionable. Moreover, failing to take responsibility for any of their deeds and preferring to throw it on others, the Arabs in Israel, like their counterparts in Europe, accuse the country that pampers them and affords them much more than are entitled, of "depriving them of its protection". In other words, we are told, the country whose security they disparage and refuse to foster, owes its protection to them. Never mind that the obligation of a citizen to defend his country has at least an equal footing with the duty of a country to defend its nationals. For the Arabs, they unabashedly recognize only what they think is due to them, not what they owe to the country or to their other compatriots.

As envisioned by the founders of Zionism, this movement had a more messianic than nationalistic character, for its very name evoked the dream of an apocalyptic day when the people are released from exile and persecution and returned to settle in tranquility in the land of Jewry's heroic age.[12] However, the harsh requirements of a reality which imposed a painstaking process of building a modern state, a massive ingathering of people from the hundred countries of the Diaspora, revolutionizing the structure of Jewish society and returning Jews to the land and to the chores of state management, have all dictated slightly less idealistic measures than those envisioned. Thus, if we follow briefly the major milestones of the hundred years of Zionism, we will detect the directions of its development both as an idea and as a plan of action[13]. For although Zionism started off in Europe as an idea and a political movement, it soon became enmeshed in the geo-political history of the Middle

---

[12] Arthur Hertzberg (ed), *The Zionist Idea,* Atheneum, NY, 1979, p. 16.

[13] This timeline is based on the work of Joseph Goldstein, summarised in H. Erlich's, *Introduction to the History of the Middle East* (Hebrew), Vol. 6, pp. 200-209).

East in more senses than one: not only the beginning of the Jewish settlement on the land, and the contacts of the Zionists with the rulers of the dwindling Ottoman regime (Sultan Abd al-Hamid II and then the young Turks) as well as the beginning of the awakening of the Jews under Islam, notably in the Yemen, and the rise of a new leadership of the Zionist movement who not only talked or just visited the Holy Land, like Herzl himself, but moved permanently to live there, like Chaim Weizmann and several of his colleagues. One has to remember nonetheless that even before the official foundation of the Zionist movement in Basel in 1897, there was a degree of awakening which had shaken part of the old Jewish *Yishuv* from its old lethargy with the founding of Petach Tikva (literally the Gate of Hope) in 1878, which was to become one of the major cities in the country, though by 1880 only 25,000 Jews lived in the land, less than 10% of the entire Arab population of the country which hardly amounted to 300,000.

When in 1881 a series of pogroms were visited upon Russian Jewry, the largest in Eastern Europe, the "Lovers of Zion Association" was established in Petersburg the Capital, embracing the symbolic name of Zion even before the first Zionist Congress. It soon branched out into many other cities in the Czarist empire, prompting one of the intellectual fathers of the movement, M. Lilienblum, to publish his pamphlet: *Revival of the Israeli Nation in its Ancestral Turf.* That same year coincided with the beginning of the messianic-driven *Aliya* of Yemenite Jews which all the same served the Zionist purpose of settling Jews on the land. 1882 also signaled the establishment of the *Bilu* Association in Kharkov in the Ukraine, it being the acronym reflecting the same Zionist trend: "Let us go forward to the house of Jacob", although the Sultan (abd al-Hamid) rejected the plea of the new association to permit acquisition of land by Jews in Palestine. But that did not prevent its fervent members from beginning their thin trickle of *aliya.* In the same year, another intellectual figure of Zionism, Y. Pinsker, published in Germany his famous pamphlet, calling for an autonomous existence of Jews, entitled *Auto-Emancipation* and meaning a self-help trend of thinking which did not wait for others to accord autonomy to the Jews, but took the initiative by themselves and moved forward. Baron Rothschild, one of the wealthy Jews of Europe and their greatest philanthropist, whose family members branched out from Germany into England and France, declared in that year his support to the Jewish resettlement in Palestine, whereupon Rishon LeZion (literally the First of Zion, once again brandishing the symbol of Zion as their banner, now the fourth largest city in Israel with close to 300,000 inhabitants in 2018, comparable to the entire population of Palestine in 1880), and also the Rosh Pina (literally the corner stone) and Zichron Ya'akov (the Memory of Jacob, the Baron himself after his death), on the model of *moshavot*, the first collective farms in the land, which soon distinguished themselves with their high productivity and fines vineries.

The following years of 1883-4, and still one decade and half prior to the official declaration of Zionism, new *moshavot* were sprouting in Palestine, like Nes Ziona (again the symbol of Zion coupled with the double meaning *nes* which connotes both a miracle and a banner), Yesod Ha-ma'ala in the upper Galilee and Gedera in the south. In those years attempts were made in Katowic in Southern Russia, to unite all the movements which professed their love for Zion. By 1887, the number of Jews had increased to 34,000 out of a general population estimated at 450,000. The giant Jewish intellectual, Ahad Ha'am (literally "one of the people", a pen-name) published his epoch-making article: "This is not the Way", which viewed the Land of Israel as a mere revived spiritual center, Pinsker resigned the leadership of the Lovers of Zion and Orthodox Jews took its lead. The next year, two more *moshavot* were founded – Rehovot and Hadera, both destined to become cities in Israel. In 1892, soon after Theodor Herzl was sent to Paris by his Austrian paper, where he was to cover the Dreyfus trial which tormented his life and instigated him to found political Zionism, to compare with the intellectual Zionism which preceded him, an Ottoman edict forbade the Jews to purchase land in Palestine, a first major hostile response to Jewish settlement in the land and to the emergence of so many Jewish villages and *moshavot* which the Arabs viewed as a looming threat to their hegemony, in spite of the high spirit of innovation and progress they brought to the land, and the employment they provided to local Arabs, whose ranks were swollen by immigrating Egyptian, Syrian and Transjordanian work seekers. When in 1894 the Dreyfus Affair burst out in Paris, becoming the *cause célèbre* of the time and provoking bitter anti-Semitic sentiments throughout Europe, West and East, another *moshava*, Motsa, was founded near Jerusalem, expressing thereby the Zionist response to hostility and restrictions by purchasing land and settling in it.

Deeply shaken Herzl, by the course and the initial outcome of the Dreyfus trial and the conviction that demoted that Jewish officer of the French army, he proceeded to write his famous and celebrated vision of a future Jewish autonomous entity under the title *The Jewish State*, and he was joined in that endeavor by another prominent leader of the Lovers of Zion – Max Nordau, followed by David Wolfson. In 1896 Herzl was in Istanbul in his vain attempt to meet the Sultan and persuade him of the necessity to establish the coveted Jewish entity in Palestine under Ottoman sovereignty, but he was only able to be received in audience by the Wazir (a sort of Prime Minister) of the realm. At any rate, the *moshava* of Metullah, in the far north adjacent to the Lebanese border, was founded. The year after, the first Zionist Congress was convened in Basel, giving birth to the Zionist Organization, which was to take up the leadership of implementing the Zionist blueprint between Congresses. The Second Congress took place in 1898 and the Third, which adopted the constitution of the organization was assembled in 1899. The next one, the 4th, gathered in London in 1900, where the Jewish National Fund was created to mobilize all Jewish Diasporas to collect money for the purchase of more land, in spite of Ottoman prohibition. In that year, the number of Jews in the land reached 55,000.

Finally in 1901 Herzl met Sultan abd al-Hamid II, much in vain, but the Fifth Congress was convened and two more *moshavot* in the lower Galilee (Yavniel and Kfar Tavor) were founded. It seemed that the more rejections the Zionist movement encountered on the international scene, the more determined it grew to speed up *aliya* and settlement of Jews, in the belief that *fait accompli* on the ground was not only the only way to circumvent the political and religious difficulties posed by the Ottoman authorities and the awakening Arab population of Palestine, but also that in the long haul reality would prevail on the decision makers that be and facilitate the recognition of the Zionist enterprise. That far-reaching vision would take another half century to materialize, and the horrible *Sho'a* that decimated one third of the Jewish people by the Nazis, to finally soften the hearts of two thirds of the world nations who voted in November, 1947 in favor of creating a Jewish state in Palestine, based, *inter alia*, not only on ancient Jewish history and the misfortunes the Jews had encountered in Europe, but also on the reality of the Jewish pattern of settlement on the land, which by that date had reached the figure of half a million, out of the total population of two million in Mandatory Palestine, which included mainly the massive influx of Arabs from the surrounding countries and the much smaller trickle of Jewish immigration. But that intermediary half century was well used by the growing Jewish *Yishuv*. It established the Anglo-Palestine Bank in 1902, the year Herzl completed the writing of his *Altneuland* (literally the Old-new land) where his vision of the Jewish state was laid out in detail, which pitted Ahad Ha-Am's intellectualism against Max Nordau's practitionism, the one advocating the Land of Israel as a spiritual center for the Jews and the other pursuing the goal of settlement and building a state in the making. The latter trend won the upper hand after the

Kishinev pogrom against the Jews of Moldova and the rejection in the Sixth Congress in Basle in 1903 of the British Colonial Secretary, Neville Chamberlain's offer to found the coveted Jewish state in Uganda. One again, a new *moshava* was erected on lands purchased by Baron Rothschild on the seacoast down the hill from his previous Zichron Yaacov village.

Herzl pursued his diplomatic campaign, obtaining audience with the Pope in 1904, the year the pioneers of the Second *Aliya* (the first was of the Lovers of Zion in the 1880s) started to arrive to Palestine, which included David Ben Gurion and his companions who would create and lead the Jewish Workers Union, then the Jewish Agency under the British Mandate which represented the Jewish *Yishuv* vis-a-vis the British mandatory power, and finally would declare and lead the state of Israel in 1948. But that year also marked the death of Theodor Herzl, the founder and prime mover of the Zionist enterprise, at the young age of 44. The year after, in 1905, David Wolfson was elected in the 7th Congress in Basle to lead the Zionist Organization, and the first Hebrew Gymnasium opened its doors in Jaffa. In 1907 the 8th Congress which assembled in the Hague decided to open an office in Palestine to direct the entire settlement enterprise in the land, headed by the legendary Arthur Ruppin, the first expert-agronomist, who would help create the company "*Hakhsharat Ha-Yishuv*" (literally- in preparation for the *Yishuv*, the settlement of the land) for the purchase of more lands in the country, and the first self-defense Jewish organization Bar-Giora was founded. Jaffa, the main Arab city in Palestine at that time, which also hosted a Jewish minority, knew the first clashes between the two communities in 1908 that were customarily triggered by the Arab majority launching attacks on the Jewish minority. These events exemplified the major problems that were to be experienced by the Jews in Palestine and would guide them in the implementation of the Zionist blueprint: increase Jewish presence though *Aliya,* settle the land in as many as possible new villages and *moshavot* as the incoming immigrants and land purchases would allow, and securing their safety by self-defense measures. These issues and the gradual remedies that were devised for them tend to debunk the Arab narrative of "brutal imperialist Jews, who had no attachment to the land, invaded it by force and terrorized the poor and helpless Arab victims". None of the components of this depiction could be true in view of a tiny Jewish minority, under Ottoman and then British rule, who purchased land from Arab owners and landlords despite the imposed restrictions, and tried to defend itself from the Arab onslaught the best it could.

In 1909 the *Ha-Shomer* (guardian, watchman) self-defense association was created in Kfar Tavor in the lower Galilee and the first Jewish quarter outside Jaffa was inaugurated under the name of *Ahuzat Bayit* (House domain) which was to grow into the Tel-Aviv metropolitan area which has turned Jaffa into one of its neighborhoods. But in the same year the great Degania and Kinneret *moshavot* were established in the Jordan Valley on the shores of the Lake of Tiberias, another calculated pioneering measure to settle down in that fertile part of the country and watch the border with Syria and Transjordan. The famous Kibbutz Merhavia in the Jezreel Valley was settled in 1909 and the year after Wolfson was replaced at the 10th Congress in Basle by the practitioners on the ground who led the implementation of the Zionist blueprint: Ushiskin, Sokolov, Warburg and others. The first school for higher technological education, the Technion (which became over the years the MIT of Israel) was inaugurated in 1912, agronomist Aharonson launched the first Farm for Agricultural Experimentation, and the first health fund which insured the organized Jewish population of the country was announced. This was some of the progressive innovation brought in by the Jewish immigration into matters which had been totally neglected by both the Ottoman rulers and the local Arab population before that, and which continue to this day to benefit the Arab minority population of Israel, its whining against

Israeli "discrimination" against them notwithstanding. The Jewish population of Palestine reached 85,000 by the outbreak of W W I, out of a total of 700,000. In the war, the *Nili* group of young Jews from the *Moshavot*, who held high hopes of ridding Palestine from the Ottoman domination, organized a clandestine network of spying for the British who were preparing their forces in Egypt to defeat the Ottomans and take over the country from them. As a result, harsh measures were taken by authorities against the Jewish *Yishuv*, expelling the Jews of Jaffa and Tel-Aviv, either to Egypt or to other places in the country, bringing down their numbers to ca 57,000 by the end of hostilities in 1918. The takeover of Jerusalem by the British in 1917, and the simultaneous issue of the Balfour Declaration, which crowned the activities on the international scene of the Zionist leaders Chaim Weizmann and Nahum Sokolov, seemed to augur a new era where the Zionist endeavor was no longer a one-sided Jewish effort against all odds, but an open recognition by the British, who were the predominant power in the Middle East at that time, of the Jewish right to a homeland in Palestine.

CHAPTER THREE

The Claim to Equality and the Search for Democracy

The Arabs of Israel had never had the opportunity for independence and for putting to the test their proclaimed commitment to democracy, or to any egalitarian system in the authoritarian, patriarchal and hierarchical rule of notables that they had been accustomed to, both in their Arab space and in their Muslim world. They were groomed into those novel notions of government for the first time under the relatively liberal British Mandatory power, which encouraged and recognized official representations of the "native" populations under their rule, and more so by the positive example of the democratic institutions that the Jewish minority was erecting in their close neighborhood. It worked likewise not only for the Jewish Agency which represented the *Yishuv* vis-à-vis the Mandatory power, but also for the Workers Union (*Histadrut)*, the various Jewish political parties which were bitterly divided between a socialist trend and revisionist bourgeois groupings, and were themselves engaged in virulent struggles within each tendency due to the battle over the souls or such a tiny constituency; but they all usually acted on the democratically representative principle which was novel in the Arab space in general. Most of all was in Arab eyes the wonderous and incomprehensible collective and nearly abhorrent communist system in their eyes of the social organization in the *Kibbutzim*, a bit less so in the collective *moshavot*, due to the egalitarian principle which governed them.

By contrast, not only were the Arabs used to traditional authoritarianism in politics, but the farmers and other villagers (*fellah*) who were practically under the thumb of their absentee landlords, lived under an oppressive feudal system. Even when the British instigated the "election" of an Arab representative body to parallel that of the Jews, the Mufti of Jerusalem, Haj Amin al-Husseini who was hand-picked by the British High Commissioner to Palestine, Herbert Samuel, won also the position of the Head of the Supreme Muslim Council, and since 1936 of the Higher Arab Committee, which he would hold almost unchallenged until his demise and exile, all the while undermining and eliminating his rivals. Those were not exactly models of democratic representation that the Palestinian Arabs could learn from. Similarly, while the Jewish towns and villages were democratically electing their heads, whom they often replaced by taking turns among the members of the community, the Arabs notables in their villages or their hereditary chiefs who represented the dominant clans, continued to conduct the affairs of their communities.

One of the lone instances where semi-democratic rules were introduced to the Arabs of Palestine, was the Communist Party, led in common by the Arabs and the Jews of Palestine, where some familiarization with elections, political ideology, debate and partisan competition in the public arena were at first tasted, experienced and gradually adopted. Incidentally, after the birth of Israel, and the gradual familiarization by the Arabs of the democratic system into which they were being coopted, they absorbed the change at great pains, due to the notable, clan, and tribal rivalries and competitions that had survived in their societal milieu. The rigidly structured Communist Party remained the main model of representative politics that Arabs in Israel could contemplate, subject to their total enslavement by the *Comintern* and the Soviet indoctrination, which was for them sacrosanct. Even as late as the early 1990s, after the

Soviet structure had foundered, a delegation of the Communist Party, consisting mainly of Arabs, who attended the last convention of the Romanian Communist Party, returned to Israel full of praise for Ceaucescu and his "enlightened" regime, only to witness to its embarrassment, a few months later, his horrible demise and execution, together with his wife, by his furious populace in the public square of Bucharest.

It is therefore quite dissonant and bizarre to say the least, to watch and hear the members of the defunct Communist Party, now rebaptized *Hadash* (literally "new", an acronym for the Front of Democracy and Equality) and constituting the main component and leadership of the Joint Arab Party, should preach to Israel about democracy and equality and castigate the Jewish state, which has groomed them into democracy and given them legitimacy within its parliament in spite of their outrageous subversive statements against its very structure, legitimacy and policies. In fact, they now lead the minorities within Israel in their open combat against the Nation-State Law, which simply and legitimately restates by proclaiming in a basic law, adopted by a majority of its legislative body, the fact that it is a Jewish state. Refuting this proclamation, and battling virulently against it, is a clear statement by the Arabs that they ungratefully reject, lock stock and barrel, the very concept of the Jewish state in which they are accepted as privileged citizens with rights and benefits that they could not attain anywhere else. For they are in fact demanding that the dagger to stab to death the Israeli democracy and progress that they enjoy, should be handed to them, short of which they will accuse the democratic country where they thrive as undemocratic. Admittedly, this law should have perhaps mentioned the devoted Druze community, in contrast with the general Arab Muslim and Christian population, as constituting part of the Israeli nation and of the Zionist creed, in order to appease their fears and mitigate their sense of being ignored. But vis a vis the other minorities that are hostile to Israel, this law was undoubtedly timely and necessary to purge from their minds any illusion that they can ever overturn the basic Jewish and Zionist nature and goals of the State of Israel. The absurd struggle of the Arab parties for their unattainable platform, which only alienates them further from the Jewish majority and earns its suspicion and sense of mistrust, can only put them ultimately on the collision course with the Jewish state which may eject them as part of future peace arrangements with neighboring Arab countries.

The Israeli Arabs' misapprehension of what democracy and equality mean in a modern state, is arguably occasionally upheld by the Israeli Supreme Court which refers to the purity of the ideal law and interprets it liberally regardless of how the Arabs view it and strive to alter it, or how often they violate it by their illegal demonstrations, violent anti-Israeli manifestations, false accusations against their country and siding with its enemies, illegal construction and delegitimation of their country's legal system each time it is applied against them. They believe that democracy means to act as they please, including when disturbing public order or disregarding general rules that apply on all society, under the claim or excuse that "democracy protects the rights of minorities", or they have "no choice, because Israel curtailed their rights or put impossible or immoral restraints on them". And if the establishment or the law enforcement authorities act contrary to their wishes or expectations, they are accused of racism, discrimination, Islamophobia, apartheid and what not, and of overall undemocratic, or even anti-democratic principles. In sum, while Arabs in Israel are enjoying Israeli democracy at the same time that they blame it for undemocratic practices, at least they have internalized the principle of fair and honest elections, and barring occasional violent rejections of the results of elections in local Arab councils (like Kafr Manda in the 2020 elections),the like of which they had never experienced before they came under Israeli rule, Arabs in Israel probably remain the sole Arab public in the entire space of the Middle East, where fair and honest elections are taking place under Israeli legal supervision, where rigging is virtually unknown and the many complaints against Israel do not include accusations of fake or dishonest elections. Where else could they have found that within the vast Arab world?

The issue of equality, on which the Israeli Arabs have hinged their political slogans and platform, has two aspects to it: the internal and the external. The former concerns the question of the struggling Arab women for emancipation, higher education and free professional occupation outside their homes, a question where the libeled state of Israel has done much more than the Arab political parties, at times against their opposition, for the accelerated pace of change of old traditional practices. The external aspect regards the Arab battle for acquisition of equal rights within Israeli society, not only civil but also political, so as to ascend to a status of power-sharing with the Jewish majority which now rules almost exclusively. The rapid advance and modernization of the Arab society on both scores, in its daily mingling and friction with the Jewish public, has driven up the Arab standard of living, motivated the Arab women to join the work force and the institutions of higher learning, to shrug off the authority of their elders and notables, to venture into the high tech culture that makes Israel a start up nation, and to cause its youth to launch into the professions, both technological and otherwise academically inclined. At the same time, one has to acknowledge that those opportunities which make the Arab new generation of Israel the envy of their contemporaries in the rest of the Arab world, are not interpreted in their midst, or at least in their propaganda campaigns, as their good fortune that they can benefit from, due to their life in free, advanced and prosperous Israel, but as their heroic attainment in spite of the horrible discrimination and deprivation that they undergo in the apartheid regime they have to endure. During the coronavirus crisis of early 2020, far from thanking Allah for their enjoying the excellent medical care in Israel which ensured them the lowest rate of fatalities and the highest rate of recoveries in the world, they did not stop to boast about their vital contribution to the medical system in Israel, thanks to which it could function that effectively. They just forget that doctors, nurses and pharmacists in themselves do not make a medical system, exactly as a parked assembly of one hundred buses or airplanes does not make a transport or air company. Both need an organization and a living spirit to activate them, and that was the creation of the Jewish state into which they were coopted, not theirs. For, we did not see in other Arab countries, where the entire talent and workforce was Arab a comparable level of achievement.

The best manifestation of personal equality and human emancipation which has been the most dramatically manifested among the Israeli Arabs has been the quantum leap in the status of women, which was welcomed and boosted by many advanced spirits among them, but also shunned, blamed and at times scuttled by traditional and conservative diehards, especially among pious Muslims and tribal Bedouins, who could not bear watching their spouses out-smarting and out-advancing them in education, jobs, skills and the expression of free opinion. That tremendous emancipation of Arab women in Israel had been withheld for decades by the reluctance of traditional and clerical circles who fed on the mood and the current vogue in the rest of the Arab and Muslim worlds, and were in no state of mind to allow their position of tight control on their societies, especially of women, to slip out of their hand. Naturally, when the leaders of the Israeli Arabs, especially when they were dominated by the Communist Party, rarely demanded equality for their women, knowing that inequality existed in their midst, while their women were longing to gain the status of the Israeli women of the Jewish majority. When they clamored for equality it was a political and partisan issue that they raised, to challenge an equal status for their men in politics with the Jewish men who ruled Israel.

Naturally, before before Arab women in Israel discovered that they could make careers for themselves in Israeli professions and civil society, they looked with some yearning to their Palestinian female kin, like Lailah Khalid or Hanan Ashrawi who made names for themselves in the Palestinian hierarchy via their public struggles, something that was not available to Arab women in Israel. But when the doors were opened to them in education and professions, they flocked to break the invisible glass ceiling that had obstructed their path, to the point that in 2020, the thousands of Arab girls attending the best institutions of higher learning in Israel are outnumbering the numbers of their male Arab colleagues. This is one of the privileges that Arab youth of both genders in Israel enjoy over their Jewish compatriots in spite of their continuous whining about their discrimination; yes, it is a discrimination, but in reverse, for while Jewish boys and girls of their age group spent 2-3 in mandatory military service, in which they get alienated from classroom study while they risk their lives in combat operations and would rejoin civilian life only 3 years older, their Arab counterparts will have completed their first academic degree and launched either in the second or into the remunerating work force. In the meantime, Arab young women have completed their academic education and have possibly launched their working careers, and internalized several notions of science, knowledge, the outside world foreign languages, mastered the Hebrew language which will serve them in their careers, and got familiarized with modernity when they met other young people and shared with them common concerns of that age group.

But there is also a phenomenal transformation of some young Arabs, especially the young women among them, under the Israeli system of higher education, in which they endeavor to preserve their own Arab Student Associations which operate in Arabic and hang their Arabic posters in the University corridors, tends to immunize them from slipping too precipitously into the Israelization camp in which they are immersed, and cultivates in them the Palestinization or the Islamization trends, that not only keep them from growing too much apart from their Arab village affiliations, but on the contrary train them to enter Arab national politics, not as part of the Israeli mainstream but as proponents of the developing secessionism and separatism that are permanently brewing among them.

Particularly remarkable are the Islamic inroads among young Arab students, who not only insist on talking in Arabic and performing prayers as part of their busy schedule on campus, but also occasionally go out in noisy and provocative demonstrations for Islamic and Palestinian causes which often turn into clashes with Right wing Jewish students who cannot tolerate the growing daring of the Arab manifestations of their own national or religious concerns, assured as they are of the protection they enjoy for their right to demonstrate by both police and the university authorities. More young Arab women than ever before demonstratively wear the veil and other trappings of Islamic or Arab national clothing, so as to manifest in public their equal status to that of their male counterparts, just like within the Palestinian revolutionary society which they often take as their model. However, unlike Palestinian women, who in order to claim equal status with their men have been dragged into *Islamikze*[14] operations, Arab-Israeli young women elect to act in the domain of rhetoric and propaganda, often very viciously, but would rather pursue their careers and studies and benefit from the bounty of Israeli higher education which at the same time they also blame and condemn profusely.

The status of women in Islam has been a controversial topic for centuries. Muslims usually point to Islamic *largesse* toward their

---

[14] *Islamikaze*, the combination of Islam and Kamikaze has been coined by this author to designate what has been wrongly known in the media as "suicide-bombers", because there is no element of suicide in their operations but of dedication and self-sacrifice for the Islamic cause, just like their Japanese predecessors during the Pacific War. See R. Israeli, "Islamikaze and their Significance", in *Terrorism and Political Violence,* Fall 1997, pp. 96-121.

women, while Western critics are horrified at what they regard as female oppression, discrimination and exclusion[15]. While unwilling to go into a thorough discussion of this important issue here, I would like to focus or just point to the fascinating process through which Palestinian women have become *Islamikaze* martyrs in order to effect a breakthrough into their struggling society, a process that is a source of inspiration to their Israeli coreligionists. The paradox is that while self-immolating young women are glorified posthumously among the Palestinians and also gain renown among Israeli Arabs, which remains mostly unstated, there seems to be no noticeable change in the fortunes of the living women, just as the glorification of the dead *Islamikaze* males does not raise the status of the deprived by living youth. Anat Berko, in her investigation of the "Female Bombs" in Palestinian society, wrote with regard to the "cynical use done of the Palestinian women's bodies and souls by the operators who dispatch them to their death:

> I doubt whether this is a feminist value revolution, for this is a simple and direct exploitation of the "faithless woman, for [self-immolating] acts of terror, which are perceived as both easier of access for her to commit and less socially costly... The same applies to children, who can serve as "human shields" despite (or perhaps because) of their young age, and so both serve as "disposable bombs" in the service of terror, belying the horrifying immorality of making a societal allowance for such horror"[16].

There has been a serious controversy in Islam about the status of women. In one pole, ultra-conservative societies such as those of

---

15

[16] Anat Berko, *The smarter Bomb: Women and Children as Suicide Bombers* (Hebrew), Miskal, Tel-Aviv, 2010, p. 9.

Saudi Arabia, Iran and Sudan, require that their women be veiled and sheltered, either to protect them from the environing rapacious male –controlled society, or from their own irresistible lust and stereotypical "frivolity". In Saudi Arabia and Sudan a male *chaperone* from their first degree male relatives must accompany them when they go out, and they are prevented from mixing with other males or perform tasks like shopping, or schooling (and driving until recently) which might expose them to male scrutiny. On the other hand, we watch millions of emancipated Muslim women in other places, including Israel, who dress, think, behave and communicate every bit like their Western counterparts. Moreover, Muslim radicals who restrict women, recognize their value in their families, for raising children, and occasionally even in battle, which by definition requires mixing with males, foregoing the modest Islamic dress, and involvement in violence. How do we resolve these contradictions? Part of the answer lies in the concept of honor in Islam. The Arabic language distinguishes between male (*sharaf*) and female (*'ird*) honor. As in the West, man's honor relates to the deeds he performs and image he projects. His honor is redeemable only if he applies himself to maintain it, shelter it and retrieve it when lost. The woman's honor, by contrast refers to her intimacy, modesty and decency in dress, the preservation of virginity until marriage, gentle behavior and keeping aloof from male society, which is corrupt by definition. If she should fail in one of those categories her honor is forever lost. There is a linkage between the two branches of honor, however, inasmuch as the man's honor consists, inter alia, of preserving his women's honor, for letting it be smeared would inexorably expose the man's inability to protect what is his, be it women or property. That is the reason why usurpation on one's land by outsiders is often considered a violation of the honor of the owner, and then the land is said to have been "raped", "desecrated" or "violated". However, the place of the man as the protector of his women's honor posits him in a superior standing in relation to her, for while he can act to rescue his honor, she can only prevent its loss through abstention. Hence the many intellectual difficulties one encounters in dealing with women in combat duties, especially when those who have to make the decision are pious Muslims, who on the one hand cannot oppose martyrdom but on the other hand insist on safeguarding women's honor. Young emancipated Muslim women in Israel have transcended all that. For although episodes of murder of women to "protect family honor", or marrying off an adolescent girl against her will still occur in Israel, they know that they are protected by Israeli law against violence and polygamy, the avenues of education, while professions and social progress are open to them, and the space of freedom where they seek shelter affords them the unique opportunity to grow and prosper according to their talent, ambition and inclinations.

Many Muslim preachers in Arab societies, including in Palestinian and Arab society, sing the praise of their women and lament the corruption that the West introduces, notably the permissiveness that has filtered into Islamic societies by way of emulation, and through homosexuality which is considered a crime in Islam and imputed by some preachers to "the brothers of monkeys and pigs [i.e. the Jews] for whom, as for other Unbelievers this is a normative pattern of behavior". Permissiveness is linked to the status of women who, when "liberated" and Westernized become the worst agent of social corruption and disruption. For Muslim conservatives, the interest of the West in the rights of Muslim women signifies its determination to ruin that traditional order by hitting it at its soft belly- its honor. Honor meant that women are dragged into promiscuity and permissive mores, together with the debasement of men's honor who watch their women slipping from under their authority and exposing themselves as unable to protect their modesty and decency. One sheikh, for example, said: "the woman, being a double-edged sword, can be turned into the most dangerous weapon of mass-destruction", hence her being a target of most plots against the social order of the Muslim *Ummah*, it being understood that the West is often accused of using women, the weakest link in the Muslim social chain to detach Believers from their faith. Under the guise of compassion and protection of the rights of women, the West also leads astray men's Muslim women, who are not aware that Islam affords them a status of equality and allocates to them rights and duties that "accord with their nature and character". Their nature and character are, of course, determined by those same clerics who declare explicitly that permitting women to go out to the streets to rub shoulders with men and talk in public to persons who are not their protectors, and export parts of their bodies that are forbidden, lead to destruction and shame"[17].

Incidentally, the Jews take the brunt of those accusations, possibly because of their close proximity to Muslims in Palestine and in Israel Proper, and are considered as the agents of the Western drive to corrupt Muslim women, in addition to the anti-Jewish stereotypes among Muslims as being the people who spread corruption, guile, dishonesty, prostitution, rebellion, and destruction of societies in the world. Numerous are the quotations from Muslim sources during the sermons of clerics which "corroborate" Jewish corruption with regard to women. For example, they say that the first crime committed by the Biblical Children of Israel was to let their women go out adorned with jewelry with a view of rousing *fitna* (unrest and disorder), and were therefore punished by Allah.[18].Another preacher remarked that one could detect the clear link between the Western campaign against the "modesty and morality of Muslim men and women, and the Jewish schemes to destroy their humanity and make them look like beasts, namely

----

[17] www:al-mimbar.cc/alkhutab/khutba.asp?mediaURL=5473, accessed 1 February 2002.

[18] See Sura xvii (the Children of Israel), verse 4 which says: " And we decreed for the Children of Israel in the Scripture: Ye, verily, will work corruption on earth twice, and y will become great tyrants".

naked and exposed"[19]. Preachers also draw lessons from other cultures, like the Greek and the Roman, which have collapsed, in their estimate, due to "the corruption of women in their midst". They contend that while at the inception of those civilizations women were modest, protected and cared about their house work, both the Greeks and the Romans were successful and build vast empires, but when their women engaged in make-up and in frequenting clubs and public places, those civilizations were doomed. They infer from that example that since the enemies of Islam wished it to collapse irretrievably, they have decided to target the corruption of Muslim women. They find solid proof for their contention in the form of the "irrefutable *Protocols of the Elders of Zion*" and therefore they conclude that the enemies of Muslim women are the Jews, the Christians, the hypocrites, the secularists and the utilitarian types that flock in their wake. Great credit is due, therefore, to the young Israeli Muslim women who defy, or at least ignore this rhetorical onslaught on modernity and embark on their journey of emancipation and liberation. Credit is due equally to the open minded Muslims in Israel who disregard those warnings and have encouraged their daughters, sisters and spouses to pursue their course of liberty and equality within their society in spite of all these campaigns of scare and threats against emancipated young people.

Equality with Jews within Israeli society, on a base of democracy, however, is quite another affair, because in a heterogenous societal grouping that is divided and separated so deeply in its most basic conception of the nature of the state, its ambitions and goals, its operational modality, its beliefs and convictions, friction, suspicion and competition are bound to reign and no consensual social pact can be agreed upon to govern the relationship between government and governed. The gap is too wide to be bridgeable and there is no

---

[19] www.alminbar.cc/alkhutab/khutba.asp?mediaURL=2699, accessed 13 June, 1999.

way those so divergent philosophies, born out of long held preju-
dices and beliefs, and sustained by an insoluble Arab-Israeli conflict,
that constantly gnaws at the roots of any artificially erected structure of peace, understanding and reconciliation, as the past seven
decades of co-habitation (one dare not say coexistence) in the land
have driven these issues into an impasse. We shall revert below to
the Vision documents where the leadership of the Israeli Arabs has
boldly and unreservedly outlined its blueprint for the future of its
constituency. Here, let us draw attention to some of the practical
issues of discrepancy between Jews and Arabs that nourish the constant fear, friction and suspicion between them.

The Arabs demand, for example, their share in the political
power and in decision making. For this purpose they usually get to
chair some committees and sub committees in the Knesset, com-
mensurate with their relative partisan strength, which in the last
2020 elections has risen to 15 MKs (out of a total of 120).In 2016,
for example, the sub-committee on women's rights was headed by
Arab MK Toma, who holds the authority to decide when to convene her sub-committee. In that instance, the issue on the agenda
was the Israeli women who serve in the IDF. It was an odd situation, because Arab women, like their men, do not serve in the IDF,
and the entire idea, together with the culture of service for the
country, was alien to the Chairwoman of the Sub-committee, hence
her refusal to convene such a meeting. Thus, while the human
rights and equality champions in Israel could welcome the authority accorded to a Arab female Arab MK, yet they could not ignore
the fact that the topic was central to the Jewish MKs' concerns and
agenda, and they regarded their Chair's decision as an abuse of
power, which could only aggravate the tensions between the antagonistic parties. The consequences were grave, for what could happen if, for example, another Arab chairman would block a debate
on terrorism just because the terrorists are Arab or Muslim? Or
another would prevent budgetary allocations to the military just

because they were potentially directed against other Arabs or Muslims? That would be equivalent to the refusal of a member of the Senate Appropriations Committee to allow a military expenditure in the Pacific, just because he is himself of Japanese origin. There, the reverse has happened: legendary Senator Inoue, had lost his arm in the war against Japan before he was elected Senator.

This is only the tip of the iceberg. For in the name of equality and democracy, the Arabs in Israel have a long list of recriminations and demands down their sleeves, like the Vision Documents, proportional budgets to their demographic strength, a separate Arab university, which if accepted and implemented, would put Israel's identity as a Jewish and Zionist state into a question mark. Not incidentally, after they discovered their strength in the 2020 elections, one of their conditions for supporting a leftwing coalition for Israel was that it should renounce the idea of maintaining a Jewish majority in Israel, in order to allow them to achieve parity with it and then ultimately to take over the country. For example, the demand that they be recognized not only as equal citizens, committed to obtain their rights like Jews, but without committing themselves to the obligatory duties like the rest of their compatriots, or that they be recognized and accepted not only on equal rights an individuals, but as a corporate body, equal in rights, on a parity basis as the Jews, means turning the country into a bi-national state, like Belgium or Bosnia, a sure recipe for continued friction and conflict. Moreover, while they demand to express their Arab and Palestinian identity within such an altered state of Israel which would be no longer Jewish, at a time that Arab and Palestinian entities also exist elsewhere, they *eo ipso* deny the Jews' right to sovereignty, independence and statehood. The Jewish reaction is swift and immediate: not only do they doubt Arab fealty, and some Jewish groups even wish to eject some Arabs from the Israeli Parliament as a subversive enemy, and precipitate the process of Israeli settlement, even annexation, of the West Bank and the Jordan Valley.

The idea is to block any possibility that the Palestinians are not only denied their blueprint of taking over Israel, but that their aspiration to create a state in the Territories is scuttled so that it is not used as a launching pad in the future to undermine Israel. They learn the hard way that by depriving the Jews of their sovereign state, they also undercut their own aspiration to the same, both for themselves and for the Palestinians in general.

Arabs in Israel have also learned to play on the sensitive chords of some Israelis, by activating with hyperbolic exaggeration their claims of discrimination which as we showed, are not always justi-fied, and their long litany of recriminations which all tend to prove their victimization, thereby provoking the legendary Jewish self-flagellation and making their Jewish interlocutors take upon them-selves and their people the burden of guilt for a sin they did not commit, thus paving the ground for advancing more accusations and demands against Israel. Thus, all civilian issues, which seem innocent, naïve, inoffensive and merely touching upon human and civil rights that every decent person in other times, places and cir-cumstances would wholeheartedly champion, when presented to the Jews as a panacea for the solution of all problems between Arabs and Jews, if accepted and implemented, turn out when scrutinized more thoroughly, to be part of the patient and long term Arab scheme to disinherit the Jews from their land, undercut their rule, undo their huge achievements and take them over piecemeal. Their virulent demonstrations against the Nation-State Law are not merely manifestations of displeasure, conducted peacefully within the right of demonstration in democratic societies, but a blueprint to deprive the Jews from their state and to raise the remorse of the sensitive and humane Israelis who had long suffered themselves, to the plight of the "poor oppressed" Palestinian Arabs, the "victims of Israeli oppression and mistreatment" who now deserve sympathy and help. Admittedly, Jews in general are usually very suspicious of others and skeptical of their coaxing acts of entreaties, but their long experience has taught them the hard way to cling to their caution and to resist sweet talk.

Another issue that undermines the prospects of harmonization and cooperation between the Arab population and the Jewish majority, is the Arab tendency to evince a rebellious spirit and to refuse to accept discipline and instructions that emanate from the authorized leadership and the elected authorities, whenever they are displeased with the given situation. Cases in point have been "unsatisfactory" results of democratic elections like in Kfar Manda in 2020, reluctance to abide by restrictions during the Coronavirus crisis in Spring 2020, setting out to identify violently with Palestinians, Arabs or Muslims, violating urban planning blueprints, or rejecting laws that were adopted democratically by the Israeli Parliament, or any other issue they chose to rebel against. The result is that instead of acquiescing in the consequences of their acts and abide by the rules, they break into violent outbursts of violent dissent where they whine about their being discriminated against, oppressed and victimized all over again. The Land Day, the October 2000, disturbances, the demonstrations on Temple Mount and against the Nation-State Law, are current illustrations of this state of mind. It is never their act of shrugging the law and disobeying the authorities which concern them, for they constantly undermine the Israeli polity by either covering, and never denouncing, their youth who joined ISIS, al Qa'ida or other terrorist organizations, disturbing public order and endangering Israeli civil peace and public traffic, and seem constantly on the watch to welcome any opportunity to just burst into unrest and confront the security forces, in order to claim later that they were quelled by an excess of force.

The seemingly innocent Arab demand that Israel should become a "state of its citizens", which is upheld by many naïve and well-meaning Israelis as a way to accommodate the fake Arabs will "to be accommodated in their civil rights endeavors", is nothing more than a blunt attempt to strip Israel from its *raison d'etre* as the shelter for the entire world Jewry and from its national symbols, like its national anthem, its national flag and its Jewish character. Because that would mean that the country becomes a bi-national state, where the two national groups would reach parity, and without the consent of the Arabs no laws can be maintained like the Law of Return that ingathers world Jewry by *Aliya,* or new Jewish settlements can be created, and Israelis' self-defense capacities would be curtailed since the Arabs would not vote for one penny of defense budgets, preferring to lend priority to settle Palestinian refugees and developing Arab villages. Similarly, while their Arab towns and villages remain unattractive for Jews, due to their cultural, religious and linguistic environment, Jewish cities and villages must be, in their minds, open to Arab settlement which in the long run would Arabize them by their sheer numbers. Similar processes have began in Upper Nazareth, Carmiel and Afula in the north, Jewish towns that were established precisely to offset the local majority of Arab villages and towns in the Galilee, but now that process would be reversed under the protection of the Israeli Supreme Court, who ruled that Arabs have the civil right to settle anywhere in the land. That is fine in principle, but when one considers the deleterious long term effect on the slow takeover of Israeli cities by Arabs while Arab towns and villages remain impermeable to Jews, one can imagine the disastrous consequences for the Jewish state, an issue that does not come up in the Supreme Court's strict and cold legal considerations.

Such a long term process, boosted by the Arab support for the Palestinian "Right of Return", will by necessity create an Arab majority which will degrade Israel into a third rate country, like the environing Arab countries, where democracy, freedom, civil rights, prosperity, and the prevalence of science and technology would wane, and Diaspora Jews would be discouraged from coming, for they would be banned and priority would be given to Palestinian resettlement. Moreover, the Jews who had made the country flourish would begin a process of *yeridah* (going down from the Holy Land) once their Zionist dream was crushed and the Western diasporas becoming again more attractive, civilized and enabling Jewish thriving than the Jewish state in the land of Israel. Jews have all the reasons to fear such developments (or rather degradation), when they hear the violent Arab opposition to the Jewish nation-state, and Arab unreserved reluctance to partner with any Israeli leadership which upholds the maintenance of a Jewish majority in the land. Most obvious of all, when called upon to join and vote for the wide gamut of existing Israeli parties, the Arabs deem that call a conspiracy to deny them their right of assembly and to quell their very identity, i.e. another sort of "incitement" against them, a mantra that recurred in all the election campaigns of 2019-2020, and arguably helped mobilize their crowds in favor of the United Arab Party which kept increasing its power. In the final analysis this amounted to a clear and sound statement that the Israeli political system was not adequate for their political aspirations (the Arab representative in the Labor Party quit in disgust, while the Arab representative in the Left-wing *Meretz* was ejected from the list), and that they prefer to walk their own separate way, divorced from the Jewish majority.

One of the watersheds in this long process of alienation was crossed during the 2000 Arab Uprising in the North, which illustrated for a few days the fury and the imminent danger posed to both populations when the tensions and frictions come to a boiling point and explode in the face of all. Prior to that momentous explosion, complacent Israelis had lived under the illusion of the melting pot and the wishful thinking which convinced them of the "power of life and reality" that will have worked its effect on smoothing up the relations between the Jewish majority and the restless and rebellious Arab minority. However, it turned out that the Arabs had been on the brink for a long time, waiting for the opportunity to bring out their wrath, and they used the occasion of unrest in the territories to express their solidarity with their kin by airing out their frustration with the bitter feeling of discrimination that colored their existence. But the discrimination that they felt can be verified objectively too in one of three ways:

1. By comparing their socio-economic situation to that of Israelis. For example, they could show that Tel Aviv and Degania are more prosperous than Nazareth and Jisr al-Zarka, which is true, but it can also be proven that Nazareth and Abu Gosh are richer than Bnei Brak and Yeruham. It is also obvious that most Jewish Israelis live in a higher standard of living than the Arabs, but it can also be demonstrated that many Arab businessmen and landowners and many senior Arab officials and professionals, like judges, professors, and doctors make a much better living than most average Israelis, and that the ultra-Orthodox families among Israeli Jews are much lower on the socio economic scale than the average Arab villager or urban dweller. What does this amount to? That in every society there are wealthy and poor, educated and uneducated, employed and unemployed, lucky and unlucky people, connected and less connected people, and each individual achieves in a free society according to his/her intelligence, training, diligence, education and good fortune. If the average Jew in New York or Melbourne does better than his average American or Australian counterparts, the latter will not claim that they are discriminated against.

2. One can compare between what one receives from the state versus what he gives to it. The average Jew is on the giving side because he spends his life in military service and then many years of reserve duty, pays his taxes according to his income, participates and contributes to the country's joys, its democratic and free system, its high tech, scientific and technological advance, its foreign relations and international trade, its pros-

perity and welfare; the average Arab is on the receiving end, enjoying the most advanced social services, and the prosperity, democracy, stability, security and freedom, even protection from his own criminals, while at the same time refraining from lifting a finger in defense of the country which affords him all those goodies. Moreover, he shuns the few among his kin who volunteer to side with Israel, often fails to accept the results of free elections in his own villages, produces twice the rate of criminality proportionate to his numbers, and constitutes a security and economic burden on Israel by crowding its social services, by drawing social welfare benefits, demonstrating against his country and in favor of its enemies, and generating security hazards that threaten the very nature of the state, and what not. Let the advised reader decide who gets more than he gives to the state, the Arab or the Jew.

3. And the claim of discrimination by oppression can be totally crushed just by watching the incredible advance of the Israeli Arabs in their prosperity, life expectancy, rate of education, especially for their women in the top Israeli universities which open for them the doors of the choice high learning institutions of the world. Their villages are thriving, their agriculture producing manyfold what it used to prior to the rise of Israel, and professional and high-skilled labor, including high tech are open to them. They were groomed in democracy that has no parallel in the entire Arab space. They were pulled up in the space of two or three generations, to heights that are not paralleled anywhere in the Middle East, probably covering the equivalent of several centuries. If Israel had imposed quotas on their education, like the *numerous clausus* imposed on the Jews in the Christian world until recently, or obstructed the tremendous leap forward of their youth in the professions, they would have had a fair ground to complain, but the only domain that remains closed to them, by their own choice, is

the military, in which some of the most spectacular innovations were made by Israeli genius. They do not understand what they miss by not sharing with other Israeli youth, male and female, that marvelous learning and living experience of service to the country and forming life-long friendships and like-minded fora of discussion and brain storming.

In the unfortunate uprising of October 2000, the watershed that was crossed has for ever altered the way both populations viewed themselves as permanently dwelling on either side of the deepening divide. While there were heightened recriminations by the Arabs about their oppression and their yearning for equal rights, and again a sentiment of victimhood due to the 13 fatalities they suffered, which they qualified as, "murder in cold blood, which became a cause for a bitter divisiveness; on the official Israel side, typically, a Commission of Inquiry was established, which instead of indicting the Arab instigators of the unrest, who threatened neighboring Jewish villages and the traffic on the main highway that linked central Israel to its north, condemned the extremely restrained conduct of the Israeli police in that incident which in an Arab country could have ended in thousands of fatalities. For during the orgy of hatred, violence and destruction generated, unprovoked, by the unruly populace of Umm al-Fahem, openly hostile banners and slogans were voiced, fitting to enemies of Israel, not to its citizens, against the Jews and Israel under the "friendly" banners of Hizbullah and Hamas. The Commission, headed by a Supreme Court Justice, which was intended to coax the Arabs and gain their favor, only further intensified their hatred and recriminations because the Israeli actors in the incident were not punished for that "massacre"; but what the Jewish majority registered from that traumatic event was that the Arabs were not exactly "loyal" citizens as previously believed, that the gap separating them from mainstream Israel was only widening, and that more rocky relations with them were to be expected. These expectations were fully met in the three successive elections campaign of 2019-2020 when the hostile Arab parties showed their mettle and their political platform was revealed to the entire Israeli public.

Chapter Four

The Cultural Fence of Separation

When the political impact of the Joint Arab List in the 23rd Knesset became apparent after the March 2020 elections in Israel, its 15 MKs reiterated their demand and obtained, as part of their negotiations with the various factions to constitute the Committees and the sub-committees of the House, that a committee to tackle the grievous issue of Arab crime within their society be established. As its Chair was elected Dr Mansur Abbas, a member of the Southern Islamic Movement, one of the three components of the United Arab Party. But when the Coronavirus pandemic was declared in Israel and dealt with as a national crisis, while Arabs took it lightly at first and paid little attention to the government's strict instructions of self-isolation, many viewing it with suspicion as another conspiracy visited on them by Americans and Jews, the penetration of that malaise to Europe and the US, that they watched on TV and was reported to them by their many children studying in Europe, (as part of the oppression, poverty, deprivation and limitations imposed on them by Israel) they became convinced to take the matter seriously. But then, another cultural barrier emerged, that of the shame (*'eyb*) notion which prevented them from admitting their "weakness" of having succumbed to illness, and therefore for a while they still resisted either to yield to the government imposition of limitations like self-confinement or restricting inter-human communication.

But when they realized the mounting numbers of infected victims and fatalities among them, they finally yielded to the general requirements of caution and self-preservation. Taking advantage of the occasion, Dr Abbas announced that his Committee will not only deal with violent crime in his Arab sector, but with violence of all sorts in the entire Israeli society, due to the Corona malaise that plagued the country.

That seemingly well-meaning statement was obviously intended to signal that violence was not only the domain of the Arabs and that his Party was determined to take charge of the entire context of the Israeli national scope, and no longer exclusively of the Arab sector of society which had elected it. This seemed to fit as part of their vision of partnership in, and impact on Israel's decision-making, as they made clear during their negotiations with the Central-Left Blue and White Party with which they ganged up to oust PM Netanyahu from power, with little else common political platform to share. But that was only a small segment of the Arab political viewpoint and plan of action. Previously, as other Arab and Muslim minorities had operated elsewhere in the world, very different attitudes and conduct had been in evidence. For part of the friction between the Muslim and Arab minorities in Europe and in Israel today and their host societies arises from their Muslim attitudes toward the host state when it is Infidel, from the rule of law, which they usually hold in lower esteem than the tenets of *Shari'a* law, and from the social and family ties and loyalties that they cultivate among themselves and strive to inject into their host societies. On the most fundamental level, they experience a great difficulty in interacting with democratic values and state institutions that they feel are remote and impersonal and sanctify the individual and the secular while discounting the religious and affective links within the clans and families. For them, custom and tradition, social conventions and the culture of shame that is connected to the notion of honor, which are governed by personal relationships and the rule of the notables, and certainly religious law, take precedence over state law, and over the cold and impersonal rules of conduct imposed on them by the alien culture that surrounds them. For in their original despotic and chaotic countries they had been brought up on a quite different law and order, enforcement of which was not strict and what is viewed as criminal by Western standards often went unpunished. Hence the very different notions of right and wrong, just and oppressive, welcome and coercive, legitimate and unlawful, which make for the failed states they had originated from and the ensuing clashes between them and their Western societies that are governed by the rule of law. By contrast, the Jewish and other minorities in the West, that Israeli Arabs like to take as a yardstick to compare themselves with, have internalized their local customs, and acculturated to the local mores, legal standards and the requirements of modern society, and they quickly acculturated to their lands of asylum.

In the West, including Israel, we are talking of the people as the sovereign and the source of legitimacy, while Muslims in general tend to hold on to their ancient belief hailing Allah as the supreme and sole sovereign of the universe, and save for the most Westernized and open-minded among them, to brand any attempt to impute sovereignty to humans as a sacrilege, since it purports to posit man-made laws, which are transitory and fleeting by nature to be superior to the eternal, immutable laws that Allah Himself has ordained for all humans. Therefore, pious Muslim radicals, like the followers of the Islamic Movement in Israel, similar to the Muslim Brother activists in Europe, do not recognize most governments even in the Muslim countries in the world, and are particularly incensed by Arab monarchs who dub themselves sovereigns, for the only form of government acceptable to them is the Muslim Caliphate where the Caliph was the Vicar of the Prophet, not a sovereign in his own right. In their view, Allah has already dispensed to humanity the most perfect of codes of law (the *Shari'a*), therefore human presumption to substitute for it a better one is also a sort of blasphemy. In the West, social consensus is the fruit of political bargaining based upon a give-and-take process between political, religious, ethnic, linguistic and cultural groups or lobbies of particular interests, which recognize the relativity of truth and the need to balance various interests and beliefs in order to arrive to a social arrangement which governs the state institutions, like the rule of law and its enforcement. For without a common agreement on the state authority to enforce the law and the citizens to conform to it, friction and chaos will reign in the entire system.

Muslims, however, while on their own turf live in accordance with their traditions and mores, when they move into Western territory or hold on to Israel/Palestine as their country, they *ipso facto* enter into a wide array of conflicts with their host societies. The pious Muslims among them immediately encounter enormous difficulties in compromising or striking deals with their new environment. Moreover, since most of those governments are viewed as anti-Islamic, for they do not accept Islam as part of their legitimate system, then at times violence against them is encouraged.. MK Ahmed Tibi in Israel, one of the two co-leaders of the Joint Arab List, who is usually regarded by the Israeli media and the Left as moderate and reasonable, secular and pragmatic, who has never showed any identification with Islamic fanaticism, was interviewed on Israeli TV, where he is a frequent speaker, with reference to clashes between Israeli police and Muslim demonstrators on Temple Mount, the Haram al-Sharif in Muslim parlance, sometime in late 2019. Quite surprisingly, he upheld the proven false Arab/Muslim narrative about the primacy of Islam on the Mount that claims that Islamic presence and consecration of al-Aqsa had preceded the Jewish presence there which Islam refutes altogether. When delicately reminded of the facts of history and archaeology that contradicted his stated narrative, hoping to invoke his well-known moderation and secular approach to history and to facts, and the presumed

Israelization that his secular spirit was imbued with, he surprisingly countered by stating bluntly: "Well this is what we believe". Things can get even more exacerbated when Muslim and Arab minorities in the West and Israel declare their rejection of the Western system into which they have migrated or within which they have grown up, and proclaim their goal to substitute for it an Islamic one. Confrontations come to a head when active acts of defiance of the system or worse- acts of terror, are initiated by radical Muslims to signal their discontent with the existing social order and their determination to alter it.

The problematic Muslim view of Western democracies as not totally legitimate due to their ignorance of the Divine Law decreed by Allah, is precisely what has prompted many a Muslim leader in the West and in Israel to declare that his purpose is the introduction of *Shari'a* law into the country's system. One of the chief leaders of the Islamic Movement in its initial years in Israel, Kamal Rayan, unabashedly declared in a press interview:[20]

> The most important thing to everyone is himself, followed by his nuclear family, his extended family, his village, other Muslim villages and finally the state. After finding success in one circle, I move to the next, until I finally arrive to the biggest circle. There, I still need to advance, but the state disappoints me. I live in a democratic society, I study democracy but I see that democracy is not for me… In school, I learned materials for the matriculation exam and I mastered the details of the Bible… but I never encountered Arabic in poems on the Qur'an…, I am disappointed, so I begin to look for another framework and this is Islam.

---

[20] *The Jerusalem Post*, 10 March, 1989; see also *Al-Sirat* Weekly, 4 August, 1989.

Since then, Muslim leaders in Israel, except for their paramount chief, Sheikh Ra'id,[21], who has been permanently confronted with the law enforcement agencies and going in and out of jail, have learned to skate skillfully on the surface to avoid indictment by their public statements. Some European governments like those of Britain, Germany and France, have by leaning forward toward their Muslim immigrants given them incentive to further raise their voices against the existing Western order and clamor for more pro-Islamic legislation. Open statements by some of the Muslim spiritual leaders that they have come to change Europe, through the migratory influx, not to submit to its rule, not only make the existing order dispensable in their eyes, but they endeavor by demonstrations, the use of violence and acts of terror to hasten its demise and substitute for it the *Pax Islamica* of their dreams. Hence the frequent clashes on European soil between Muslim communities and the forces of order, of which other more docile communities like the Jews are the obvious victims. The issue under debate is not only the illegitimacy of non-Muslim governments, but the tribal and Muslim family loyalties that often run against the state authority, or when they themselves are atomized under the modernizing impact of the host countries.

The Muslim religion whose presence is evident at every mosque and street corner where Muslims have taken residence, both in Europe and in Israel, is also expressed within and by their community, family, clan, tribe or local charismatic leader. In Europe, the immigrants from the failed states in the Islamic world who knew more strife, tension, violence and disaffection, than serenity, order, predictability and freedom, cannot do better than import with them to their host societies their age-old customs and rules of conduct. In Israel, this lifestyle is innate and has been followed for

---

[21] See R. Israeli, *Islamic Radicalism and Political Violence: The Templars of Islam and Sheikh Ra'id Salah,* Vallentine Mitchell, London, 2008, especially Chapter four.

centuries, so in the rural areas where modernity has not always penetrated like in the cities, and given that Arab villages are almost always exclusively inhabited by Arabs /Muslims, they can more easily hide these abhorrent customs, except when police is called to interfere in case of murders. Embracing bigamy, or even polygamy within the Bedouin community in Israel, which tolerates among its membership the importation of young women from dispossessed families in Gaza is an open defiance of Israeli law. They and other Arabs in Israel also regard as a natural social norm forced marriages and "honor killings" in their family when women are accused of illicit pre-marital love affairs. Not a few of the recurrent acts of murder within the Arab villages and towns in Israel today are the outcome of this horrendous custom which Israeli and European societies are trying to combat. The Europeans try to struggle against these alien customs, but even though Muslim migrants in Europe constitute the lion part of interns in government jails, many Muslims continue to assert their right to follow their ancestral mores, and rather than being reformed or deterred by jail terms, they undergo a strong Islamization process while incarcerated before they return to their communities more committed to Islam than ever before.

The ramifications of these uneasy relationships are staggering:

a. It becomes practically impossible for the Muslim minorities in Europe and Israel, once they have entrenched themselves in their antagonistic attitude to the majority culture, to identify with their state and they often find themselves in hostile situations against it. For example, when their country is at war or in a tense relationship with other Arabs and Muslims, the Muslim minority members would often find themselves siding with their people and religion and opposing the country where they live. They would not celebrate a joyful achievement of their new nationality and would mourn instead their original culture's loss against it. They would not stand to attention when their adoptive country's anthem is played or its colors are hoisted, and they would instead wave the banners of their country's enemies, in an obvious taunt to it (Israeli Arabs hoist PLO, Hizbullah and Hamas flags in their demonstrations, and Algerian Arabs in Paris would boo the *marseillaise* when they attend a football match between France and Algeria and the two anthems are played).

b. Muslim minorities are likely to act violently against their country of residence in case of crisis or just discontent with its policies. Muslim terrorists in Europe have perpetrated many carnages in Paris, London, Manchester, Madrid and Hamburg; Israeli Muslims have occasionally committed acts of terror against the Israelis or left to adjoining Arab countries to join terrorist movements or to fight their Jihad wars against Westerners and Zionists, or aided Palestinian terrorists to operate within Israel, taking advantage of their familiarity with the place and freedom of movement.

c. Since they usually do not serve in the armed forces of their host countries, they miss one of the tools of integration into their adoptive societies, and they end up being alienated, feeling outsiders to the national experience and unable to identify with its joys and achievements during festive occasions or national holidays, like Independence Day or the Jewish holidays that have turned national and are observed everywhere except in the Arab neighborhoods. The contrast on those occasions is eye-poking. Neither do they grief over its failures and mourning occasions like the *Sho'a* remembrance Day, the memorial days of wars or in honor of the fallen, or the Festival of the Ninth of Ab when the two ancient Jewish Temples were destroyed (a history that they deny anyway), or on Yom Kippur when the country comes to a standstill.

d. The lack of regard by Arabs and Muslims for the welfare of the country of residence often facilitates its deprecation and paves the way to ideological crimes against it (murder, terrorism, smuggling, illegal weapons, undocumented immigration and propaganda against it that is facilitated by the democratic freedom of movement and action within it). This in turn can slide into regular and petty crime for economic gain, which is not viewed as offensive except when it is directed against the Arab/Muslim community itself, in which case the state apparatus is implored to help fight it, and then is blames for "excess of force".

e. One can see the deterioration in the quality of life in the host countries that is occasioned by concentrations of Arab/Muslim residents or migrants: noises, smells and chaos in the streets which are reminiscent more of African and Middle East environments than Western ones. French people who are scared to travel by metro by night, or are disgusted at the sight of broken beer bottles on the stairs of the Opera House in Paris (both the old, *Place de l'Opera* and the New, *Place de la Bastille*), or women in Cologne or Malmo who are terrified from gang raping by Muslims, reckon that they feel strangers in their own country. Foreign visitors who went to admire the art of Holland or Belgium, find an Arab and Muslim –dominated Amsterdam and Brussels, and look-disappointed- in vain, for the old European civilization they came to seek; or when Jews pray in the ancient sites of their heritage in Jerusalem and Hebron and are harassed by intolerant and often violent Arab crowds, are recurrent scenes in both places. And if anyone dares to make a remark to this effect, he/she is Islamophobe, racist, xenophobe, Arab/ Muslim hater and all the rest[22].

---

[22] For some updated data on these issues, see Murray, Douglas, *The Strange Death of Europe,* London, 2016.

Thus, once they establish themselves in their countries of dwelling and feel confident enough to leverage their new-found democratic freedoms to their benefit, they also feel that their previous unprivileged status, (in Europe the refugee status of the immigrants, their colonized past and their socio-economic standing; in Israel, their previous restrictions under military government and their deprivation from their exiled leadership, compared to their present new educated leadership and professional elite) allow them to act in contravention to the public order, in which they feel alien, even though this contradicts the unstated terms of their naturalization in their adoptive countries. This does not appear to them as violating any legal or moral code, for their yardsticks of justice, right, order, fairness or rightful conduct are the Muslim ones, and are unnegotiable. For example, it would not occur to them that in any conflict involving Muslims vs Infidels, their present country of residence, may also be right sometimes. If, for example, Britain battles against terrorism in Afghanistan and Iraq, or Israel against the Hamas in Gaza or Hizbullah in Lebanon, they thereby make themselves liable to a counterattack against them by other Muslims, including their own, who are the natural allies of all Muslims. This is what perennially torments Israeli Muslims when they cannot tolerate their country's battles against other Muslims or Arabs (be they Iran or Syria) even if needed to defend itself against terrorists or other military threats.

For when Muslims demand justice, they mean their Muslim justice, namely the return to what they believe rightly belongs to them, regardless of whether, what and how others might advance as a disclaimer in historical, legal, logical and human terms, for all these are irrelevant. First, Muslims must get full satisfaction, in accordance with their own sentiments and convictions, their rights must be publicly recognized, and only then might they show generosity and give back some out of their own volition, or as a result of coercion or force. Thus, the whole notion of compromise does not come into play, because if you believe that something is yours, you must obtain it first. Take, for instance, the troubling question of "honor killing", among Muslims. In Muslim countries, like Pakistan, Saudi Arabia and many others, they enforce that rule at their whim and no one can interfere. But among Muslim minorities in Europe and Israel, they regard that, just like forced or under-age marriage, and the right to rebel without incurring any sanction, not only as an extension of their special and inalienable cultural make up that is expected to find a full fledged and uninhibited expression in the democracies where they have transported it from Muslim lands. It is "their" women who are the issue, therefore what right do Western states have to interfere in their "private affairs", which concord with Islamic law? Muslims have retaliated by terror against Israel repeatedly and the West on September 11 and the other murderous attacks in Europe and America, in self –defense, they claim; so why is there such an over-reaction in the West to their acts of self-protection? It is only natural that Muslims of Europe or of Israel should send their "volunteers" to train in Afghanistan and Pakistan, or to fight in the killing fields of Syria, Iraq, Afghanistan, Libya, Yemen and elsewhere just as other Muslims everywhere do, in order to fight their enemies anywhere it is necessary.

This wide array of incompatibilities between the two mentalities and states of minds of Arabs and Muslims on the one hand and Jews and Westerners on the other, even if we do not submit it to value judgment of any sort, is so deep as to suggest their unbridgeability. The world of ideas, sentiments, values and beliefs is so different on either side of the divide, and the fields of tangency are so remote between them, that the noble temptation of aspiring to live together in harmony and full compatibility seems like a pipe-dream. Two entities which cannot mix, like water and oil, cannot hope to create a peaceful society. We saw that in the wars of former Yugoslavia, where the six former components of the federation fought tooth and nail against each other for separation and independence despite the 70 years of federal co-existence that held them together under one kingdom and then under one Communist state that could be maintained only at the price of suppression of their local nationalisms. Thus, if the Arab society in Israel is willing to undergo metastasis and embrace the national and political ethos of the Jewish majority, the chance will exist of narrowing the gaps until the social, economic, cultural, linguistic and national aspirations of all individuals merge into each other. However, as long as the Arab political parties maintain their separation and nationalistic aspiration to turn the country into a bi-national state, the clash between Jewish and Arab nationalists will become inevitable, as it happened in Bosnia, Croatia, Kosovo and the rest of the Balkans, or as the tension, friction and jealousies are maintained today, with less violence, between Spaniards of Madrid and those of Barcelona, the Brits of London and those of Glasgow or Londonderry, the Belgians of Wallonia and those of Flandria, and any other number of rivalries of this sort. There is talk that the new generation of young Arabs in Israel might be less tolerant of the traditional clan authority which tilts towards Arab national or Muslim religious secession from Israel, and more inclined to integrate as individuals within Israeli society, but this is an assumption that is yet to be proven in reality. For now, to the extent that Arabs have aspired to the equality that they clamor, their commitment to the survival of the Jewish state has remained questionable, for they have always demanded equal rights in the name of democracy, but they have rarely stood by their country's rights when in confrontation with other Arabs or Muslims.

Externally, the surrounding Arab and Muslim countries which live in their self-contained environment without the mitigating effect of a Western-like society in their midst or in their proximity, are likely to pursue their mode of living and their traditional societal system, as long as they tolerate or cannot rid themselves of the yoke of their despotic regimes- monarchical or presidential. That is nobody's business and the West's attempts to interfere in order to impose democracy and liberalism there, simply did not work, as we have witnessed in Iraq and Afghanistan, and before that in pre-revolutionary Iran. That was like sending a blind person into a dark room to look for a black cat that is not there. Therefore, Israel's and the West's attitude towards those countries ought to desist from trying to convert them to our mode of life, but warn them that their political and social systems are theirs within their own boundaries, and if they should attempt to impose them or their neighbors or threaten any Western country or its allies by its takeover by Islam, the West is there to react in force in self-defense. The massive influx of Muslims to the West these past few decades, like the massive surging of Arab and Muslim identity in Israel recently, has rendered this ambition more complicated to implement, while more and more European and Western lands are getting more and more like Israel with their social and political systems challenged by the vocal presence and the growing demands of a self-confident Muslim minority which regards itself, as of right, entitled to expect that its mores and traditions be heeded by the host societies, where they demand an increasing share of power. If the Europeans and Israelis should capitulate before these pressing demands, they will have brought upon themselves the suicidal democracy that is the headline of a book recently published by this author.[23]

In the case of Israel, another crucial element has to be added to the creation of the deep mental gap between it and its Arab/Muslim neighbors and that is the deep cultural contempt for Jews that has been cultivated in that world for more than a millennium and has become such a formidable obstacle for the Israeli Arabs to surmount as it has become part of their ingrained attitude to Israel. Admittedly, in some Arab countries' leaderships these attitudes have

---

[23] R. Israeli, *Suicidal Democracy: Israel's Future in the Arab Environment*, Strategic Books, TX, 2019.

begun to dissipate under pragmatic geo-political considerations,[24] but among the Arab and Muslim populace they are far from disappearing, continuing to generate hatred towards Jews and their creations, Zionism and Israel, in the Arab and Islamic Islamic worlds, which amounts to gross acts of libeling them with all manner of abominable crimes. Unlike Western countries, where libel suits can be sustained in court so as to restrain the spread of false accusations, in most Islamic lands these acts are encouraged by whatever authorities are in place, or simply ignored and allowed to pass. It is said that while victors write history books which celebrate their valor and the myths of their heroes, the losers write books of poetry, nostalgia and vindictiveness which mark their victimhood and reflect their self-righteousness in the face of defeat[25]. The latter, who belong to the category of the second-handers in Ayn Rand's categorization, and waste much of their time hating and stereotyping the "creators" who humiliated them by routing them, or by providing a counter example of success to their own impotence, must invent, propagate, instill and absorb a whole range of compensating devices to fill the gap that separates them from their rivals, from outright hoaxes and common lies, to conspiracy theories in which they end up believing themselves. In this fashion, not only their own cultural and scientific development is stifled, as their youth are indoctrinated at best, incited at worse, with few critical exceptions, to accept the fabrications as fact, but the adopted culture of stereotypes, and the digested patterns of hatred, hostility and violence end up forging new generations which will perpetuate the hatred, and make international disputes between the hating and the hated,

---

[24] See R. Israeli, *Paranoia, Inferiority Complex and Fanaticism: The Case of Islamic Attitudes Towards the Jews*, Strategic Books, TX 2018.

[25] See the magnificent examples brilliantly exposed in Wolfgang Schivelbusch's *The Culture of Defeat,* Picador, New York, 2001; and to expand upon the themes dealt with in this chapter, see Raphael Israeli, *Hatred, Lies and Violence in the World of Islam*, Transaction, NJ, 2014; and Raphael Israeli, *Old Historians, New Historians, No Historians*, Wipf and Stock, Oregon, 2016 .

such as in the Arab-Israeli conflict, ever more intractable.

Many definitions have been suggested for hatred: emotional, economic, social and psychological or, a combination thereof. The difficulty in differentiating between various motivations arises from the stunning fact that while the impoverished dwellers of the south American *favelas*, for example, express their resentment in increased criminal activities, they do not blow up buses and restaurants with their innocent users who have nothing direct to do with their plights, but the Palestinians and other Arabs and Muslims do. So, beyond the anger, deprivation, degradation, humiliation or the simple envy of the haves, there must be some additional causes which push people to hatred, acts of violence, and to manufacturing lies to justify their deeds, such as cultural upbringing, religious tenets and authoritarian rulers who serve as models to their ruled and encourage their acts. For example, when Teyyip Erdogan was the Mayor of Istanbul in the 1990's, and was incarcerated for religious incitement, anti-Semitism in the rest of Turkey was subdued and relations with Israel attained their peak or cooperation and harmony. But when he was elected Prime Minister in 2002, his anti-Israeli rhetoric caught up with his public and permitted the *Mavi Marmara*[26] affair in 2010. Similarly, the Shah of Iran had maintained excellent relations with Israel and the Jews of Iran flourished, but upon the advent of Khomeini, who dubbed Jews the "enemies of Allah", those attitudes were reversed overnight until under Ahmadinejad Iran and its Hizbullah operatives became the most virulent and violent enemies of Jews and Israel. Similarly, one cannot compare the dominant stature of Arafat at the helm of the Palestinians, as he was himself a revolutionary who dipped his hands in terrorism, to the more subdued conduct of Abu Mazen, his successor, who enjoys the comfort of his position but shuns

---

[26] See R. Israeli, *The Odd Couple: The Aberrant Relations Between Turkey and Israel,* especially Chapter Six, Strategic Books, TX, 2019

combat, and is content with iconizing PLO terrorists and murderers since the leader could no longer serve as the model himself.

Basically, as we focus on the Arab-Israeli conflict, and its ramification into the condition of the Arab minority in Israel, both of which have been increasingly metamorphosing into an Islamic onslaught against Judaism and Jewry (as part of their resentment against the West)[27], we are talking about two different worlds and worldviews that run so far apart of each other that they are bound to generate misunderstandings, fears, suspicions and hatreds which must find their expressions in rationalizations and in lie-manufacturing. One day of January 2001, at the height of the second Palestinian Al-Aqsah *Intifadah* (2000-2003), the Israeli press carried the picture of a procession in Ramallah, which paraded a donkey wearing a Jewish prayer shawl and sporting on its forehead a Star of David in the shape of a swastika, with Palestinian police standing by and applauding the parade. The Israeli public was deeply shaken, regarding this act of profanation and abuse as a continuation of the torching of the Jewish synagogue in Jericho and Joseph's tomb in Nablus, which had been conceded to Palestinian protection under the Israeli-Palestinian Oslo II agreement, during the initial stages of that upheaval. In all those cases, what transpired was a Palestinian determination, born out of frustration and hatred, and made explicit in violent acts, to express their hostility to Jewish religious symbols, knowing full well the hurt and anguish they would cause among the Israeli public. Conversely, the angered Israeli readership of the papers was reminded that, when in 1997 a young Jewish settler in Hebron had held up a poster in public, in which the Prophet Muhammed was reviled by the drawing of a pig in his proximity, she was duly arrested by the Israeli police, tried for anti-religious incitement and incarcerated for three years. Her outrageous deed, which rightly provoked Muslim rage, was duly condemned across

----

27

the board by Israeli politicians and clerics, who understood the sensitivity of such provocations. Israelis had therefore expected, in vain, to see a similar reaction of the part of the Palestinian authorities and their religious hierarchy. Moreover, Israelis had expected the Palestinians to protect those Jewish sites as they had undertaken in their Oslo II engagement under which Israel had withdrawn from those places. Those desecrations, committed while the Palestinian police was idly watching, finally helped remove the readiness of Israelis to evacuate any more territory or to put their faith in Palestinian commitments[28].

Little did both sides know, in those days when the *Intifadah* kept escalating, that Muslim anger would acquire a universal momentum, as the Cartoon Affair broke out (2005-6) sweeping Scandinavian countries and much of Europe into a campaign of apologetics which only increased Muslim rage[29], and brought to bear the Muslim conviction that while their faith is untouchable, and above any human attempt to denigrate it, other creeds, especially the Christian and the Jewish, must recognize their subservient status and accept it, and punish within their jurisdiction anyone who dared to defy, denigrate or insult Islam, threatening that any violation of that understanding would be taken as "Islamophobia" or racism, the most dreaded accusation in modern Western culture, and violently retaliated against accordingly. The fact that Iran, for example, a member of the UN, openly threatens to erase from the map another member-state (Israel), or that an Arab Spring-grown Muslim head of state, like Muhammed Mursi in Egypt, following his Holy Book, his preachers and spiritual mentors, called the Jews "descendants of monkeys and pigs", based on a verse of the Word of Allah, is beside

---

[28] See the entire story in R. Israeli, *The Oslo Idea: the Euphoria of Failure,* Transaction, New Jersey, 2012.

[29] See the general context of the affair, in R. Israeli, *Retreating from the Mirage of Multi-Culturalism?: the Cases of Holland, Britain and Israel,* especially Chapter Three, Strategic Books, Tx, 2018.

the point. For, as no one in the international arena persistently protests against those outrageous utterances by Muslim political leaders, some of whose countries have signed peace with Israel, Arab and Muslim individuals worldwide, including in Israel, can only get accustomed that hatred and contempt against Jews is a matter of course, acceptable in the world scene. This is illustrated by the fact that whenever a clash happens between Israelis and Arabs or Muslims, one is likely to hear curses, insults, libels and gross injuries against Jews. During the Corona crisis in Spring 2020, it was the Prime Minister of the Palestinians who accused Israel publicly for spreading the virus purposely among Palestinians, after he asked and received professional help from Israeli medical teams who trained the Palestinian doctors in these matters. At the same time, Christian churches are being attacked and burned throughout the Islamic world, and by Muslim terrorists in European countries, where these statements become accepted as routine and as proof for the Muslims of their validity. Outrage is rightly raised in the West, and more so in the Islamic world, only when some Israeli fanatics, who are prosecuted by law and rejected by public opinion from wall to wall in Israel, commit a criminal act of desecrating a mosque or a church, which the Islamic world takes as "proof" of the "incendiary nature" of the Jews and their state. In consequence, hostility increases, violence abounds, and Islamic "love to hate" (to borrow an expression from Bosnian Nobel Prize recipient Ivo Andric[30]), comes to its full-blown manifestation, on the footsteps of noted Muslim historical Jewish haters, like the Prophet Muhammed and celebrated writer Jahiz, or like modern time eminent clerics and Islamic thinkers like Hasan al-Banna, Sayyid Qut'b, Ayatullah Khumeini and Yussuf Qaradawi.

The phenomenon of poking a Jew in the eye in order to demean

---

[30] Ivo Andric, *The Bridge Over the Drina*, was translated and published internationally into many languages.

him by diminishing his national and religious symbols, has been seen publicly repeated in the entire Islamic world, when Israel's national flag and /or the effigies of its leaders are burned in demonstrations, usually in conjunction with American flags, thus establishing a ritual whenever and wherever dissatisfied Muslim mobs gather to air their frustration against Israel or the Jews. More ominously, even more "respectable" gatherings, such as the annual commemoration by the Egyptian Lawyers Association of the peace their country signed with Israel in 1979, have adopted the same ritual. After the change of government in Egypt, and other Muslim countries for that matter, in the wake of the Arab Spring [31], this phenomenon has worsened, as the Israeli Embassy (as well as the American) have come under some vicious attacks that can be connected with the escalating hatred towards the West in general, the Jews and Israel across the Islamic world in particular. Those Muslim crowds are "angry and frustrated" we are told, therefore we are asked to "understand" them.

Certainly, in a conflictual state of affairs, no one expects the parties to love one another or even develop empathy towards one another. However, even in a state of hatred where there is contempt and denigration of the rival (like the French and Germans through two world wars and the Americans and Japanese in the Pacific War), there must be some measure of respect for fact and reality, for otherwise one begins to project on the other one's own defaults and to indulge in such an exercise in self-delusion as to end up harming oneself and one's own interest. One remembers the first day of the Six-Day War on June 6th 1967, when the Egyptian leadership

---

[31] It has been the contention of this author that, unlike conventional wisdom which dubs it the "Arab Spring", though it has no signs or aims of Arabism, the Spring phenomenon in fact extends to enough non-Arab but Islamic countries, such as Turkey, Iran, Pakistan, Afghanistan, Somalia and even Mali, to merit the epithet of Islamic. See R. Israeli, *From Arab Spring to Islamic Winter,* Transaction, New Jersey, 2013.

bluntly lied to its own people and the rest of the world, claiming that its air force had destroyed Israel's, and its armies were advancing on Tel-Aviv, while in fact they lay in tatters. What did they gain from that, except for bringing shame and disgrace upon themselves? One may take the basic deficiencies of the enemy and inflate them so as to score propaganda points, but when one invents "facts" and "events" that never were, one necessarily creates a devil larger than life, in which case no accommodation is possible or desirable. Because then, one becomes irrevocably trapped in one's own rhetoric and instinctively abhors any settlement or reconciliation that the satanic rival who proved to be the upper-handed victor may offer. Then, the enemy becomes the culprit for any misery suffered, often leading to the Kafkaesque reversal of cause and effect, which generates the creation of lies, and provides the "rational" underpinnings of the "resulting" hatred. For example, Germans hate America and Russia for the destruction they wrought upon their country in World War II, but many of them tend to ignore that it had been that hatred on the part of their people, accompanied by aggression and untold violence, which had triggered the war and provoked that killing and destruction in the first place. Similarly, the Turks and Hamas hate Israel for its "killing of innocent Palestinian people" in Gaza, but they deny that it was their explosion of hatred and murder towards Israel and Jews which had produced Israeli retaliation in the first place, which they end up dubbing as "aggression". So are rationalized by Israeli Arabs their losses when they violently clash with Israeli authorities like during the October 2000 Uprising that was discussed above.

When the Arab countries, supported my most Islamic peoples of the world, in defiance of the UN Partition plan of 1947, invaded Israel the day it was declared, many expected an easy victory over fledgling Israel, whose tiny size, poor equipment and seeming flimsiness, did not augur well for her ability to withstand that onslaught. Instead, Israel was not only able to survive, but it also ended up controlling at the end of the war larger territories in Palestine than assigned to her in the Partition Plan. The depth of the Arab frustration and humiliation for their defeat in that war corresponded to the summits of their arrogant self-confidence on the onset of the hostilities, confident that the "despicable and cowardly" Jews were unable to conduct war, especially as they were so outnumbered and isolated in the world. But in those early days of 1948-9, and contrary to the later 1967 rout, when they understood their defeat and undertook to redress it, it was their refusal to take cognizance of the facts, and their persistent denial of the consequences thereof, which blurred their view and distorted their reasoning. In a culture of shame and phantasmagoria, where words replace action and wishful thinking reality, Israel's firmness and survival were ignored as non-existent, and the delusion set in as regards its imminent disappearance. Arab leaders promised their people that after the failing "first round", which was due to "corruption", "treason" and "faulty ammunition, the victorious "next round" was around the corner to redress all wrongs by eliminating the aggressive and delegitimized Jews.

And with each one of the five upcoming rounds of war and their resulting defeats, the Arabs felt that they had sunk deeper into helpless and inextricable hatred and wrath born out of humiliation, frustration and helplessness. For they could either try to elevate themselves to the level of Israel and then try to defeat it, or desist from their hostility and settle the dispute. They tried indeed a rapid process of development, but still according to UN charts, they keep at the bottom of the international heap, while Israel continued to make such a progress as to bring her to European standards, and to keep her per capita GDP 10 times higher than in the environing Arab countries. These achievements only deepened Arab and Muslim resentment towards Israel, for her very successes accentuated Arab failures and triggered more hatred. Their only recourse, then, was to destroy Israel, so as to remove the humiliation she caused, or to force her into such withdrawals and other concessions, under the pretense of a 'peace process', as to weaken her, disinherit her and delegitimize her into oblivion. The Arab citizens of Israel can be seen as assisting the rest of their Arab kin in those long-term endeavors by helping to undermine the Jewish state from within. Successful and Westernized Israel, like the West itself, is deeply hated and resented by the Arabs and the Islamic worlds precisely because it is too strong to defeat. It is in the nature of things that the backward and the poor should detest those to whom they cannot resemble, therefore, Israel and the West are always intertwined in their eyes. One can hear in campuses around the world that both are Neo-Colonialist, or Neo-Imperialist, enemies of Islam and of the Third World. In those demonstrations the Israeli and American flags are always burned in tandem, because for them Israel is the corrupting Western arm in the heart of the Arab and Islamic world, that does the ground work of undermining Islam, or corrupting its youth with foreign values, music, pornography and permissiveness. Hence their commitment to fight them both relentlessly and ruthlessly, even at the price of self-perdition.

One of the major themes used by the Arabs and Muslims to justify their hatred and violence towards Jews, Israel and the West, has been their claim that injustice was done to them (they demand a 'peace with justice'), as if justice were absolute and not in the eye of the beholder. Justice (*'adalah* in Arabic) is for the Arabs linked to the notion of balance between the two saddlebags on the camel's back, short of which the camel cannot march at length to cross the desert. Justice is also connected to honor, and the maintenance of honor hinges on the man's ability to protect his property and his women, and on his proven capacity to retrieve or redress them if they are lost or violated. Otherwise, his reputation is irretrievably compromised. Thus, one's honor is constantly on the line, and it is tested by a man's daring in the service of his honor. An Arab will not rest until the wrong done to him will be redressed and his property is recuperated. Then, justice is done, and one can go back to functioning normally. For example, only the killing of a woman who has desecrated the family honor can stop the process of family humiliation and permit its male members to return to normal. These deep-rooted rules of conduct, far from helping the Arabs of Israel to Israelize, on the contrary help deepen the gap between them.

Hatred towards the perceived wrong-doer to the point of wishing his/her violent elimination, becomes then the requisite retaliation against him pending the redress. Many Arabs in Israel sense the wrong done to them by Israel in their losses, defeat, destruction and displacement can only be redressed by recognition and admission of their *nakbah*, and compensation for what they forfeited, something that Israel is not about to do, hence the transmitted sense of bitterness about the past and yearning for a bright future that they continually feed to their new generations. And until that is done, hatred with its attending fabrication of lies, is constantly blasted against the bearer of injustice, namely the Jews, Zionism and Israel. For example, the Turkish provocative flotilla into Israeli waters in June 2010, which was geared to break the Israeli blockade on Gaza that was approved by the UN as legal, and used force to attack and maim the Israeli enforcers of the blockade, only remembered that its nationals were killed when they tried to use force to scuttle the blockade. They demanded apology and damages from Israel, who foolishly submitted to the pressure, thus justifying Turkish violent but illicit interference. By thus collaborating with the Turkish outrage, which disregarded the UN vindication of Israel's position, Israel permitted it to perpetuate the unjust unilateral concept of "Islamic justice", while the onlooking Arabs, including an Israeli Arab MK who embarked on the flotilla in defiance of her country and of the Israeli legal system, applauded Israel's humiliation for once.

The Iranians deny the Holocaust, organize international conferences to celebrate the "end of the Zionist entity", whilst it is alive and kicking, and registers world-recognized economic and technological advances. The Palestinians, like the rest of the Arabs, keep repeating that the Holy Land in general, Jerusalem in particular, with its inner sanctum, the Temple Mount, which has a recognized Jewish history of three millennia, has nothing to do with Judaism or Jewry, and that it is the exclusive patrimony of the Arabs and Muslims since they were occupied by Islam in the 7th Century AD. To erase the Two Jewish Commonwealths, covering the first millennium BC, they have also systematically Arabized the ancient Canaa'nites and despoiled the Jewish people of any history or heritage on its land. Since the land was Islamized by conquest, it became a *waqf* (holy endowment) land, never to be parted with or negotiated away. Hence, for them their "right of return" is not only a human and political need, but also a religious duty which imposes on them to struggle and pay any sacrifice, so as to snatch the land from its usurpers who have subtracted it from their dominion. This is particularly valid with regard to the *Haram a-Sharif* (the Temple Mount) which was the very site of the Prophet Muhammed's mystical nightly journey (*isra'*) and ascension to Heaven (*mi'raj*). Thus, only after this right of theirs is recognized and fulfilled, as a matter of course, may they evince *ex-gracia* generosity and allow others to collect some crumbs from their table. Until then, all means are allowable to retrieve the loss, by peaceful means if possible, through violence if necessary, for in any case its holy character prescribes *jihad*. When Ahmed Tibi reiterated that tradition in the ears of Israelis, via the Israeli media, with self-assurance about its validity, it is clear what he has in mind, as is evident to the Israelis the unbridgeability of the gulf between the parties.

The category of self-deception that blinds the perceptions of self-deceiving haters, has been dealt with in Dan Ariely's [32]seminal work, for whom self-deception is a useful strategy for believing the stories we tell, in the process fooling ourselves as we try to fool oth-

---

[32] Dan Ariely, *The (Honest) Truth About Dishonesty*, Harper Collins, 2012, Chap 6 "Cheating ourselves", pp. 141-162.

ers. He, for example, tells the story of someone trying to impress his date by lying to her that he is a pilot, but on his next flight as a passenger, he was already giving advice to the airline pilot how to land more adroitly, so convinced he became in his own delusion. Self-deception can either stem from a desire to maintain a positive self-image, or to gain the upper hand in a game of one-upmanship with a rival (for example when Palestinians ascribe to themselves descent from the ancient Cana'anites, so as to dethrone Jews from their claim of antiquity on the land). However, this self-sustaining pride and high morale emanating from the "old is beautiful" axiom, can be rather devastating when reality, science, history and truth come crashing in. Ariely also observed that:

> Human beings are torn by a fundamental conflict – our deeply imagined propensity to lie to ourselves and to others, and the desire to think of ourselves as good and honest people. So, we justify our dishonesty by telling ourselves stories about why our actions are acceptable and sometimes even admirable. Indeed, we are pretty skilled at pulling the wool over our own eyes[33].

Another useful definition of self-deception made by Willard Gaylin is the one covering the emotional aspect of hatred thus:

> A sustained emotion of rage that occupies an individual through much of his life, allowing him to feel delight in observing or inflicting suffering on the hated one. It is always obsessive and almost always irrational... The feeling of hatred is simply an intense form of anger, like rage... It starts as annoyance, irritation or pique and

---

[33] Ibid. pp. 165-6.

extends to its extremes in rage and fury…[34]

We have seen much of that definition applicable after the September 11 events, when throughout the Islamic world, throngs of people grossly exhibited their jubilation in public, while in New York, Washington and the rest of the civilized world consternation, pain and fear dominated the scene. Scapegoating, which is the process of putting the blame for the hatred on the shoulders of the hated, as was the Nazi accusation that put the responsibility of World War II on the Jews, and for the Twin Towers horrors on America and Israel due to the "humiliation of Islam", was a way to wash the hating parties' hands clean on the one hand, and continue to indulge in jubilation over the suffering of the hated on the other. The blames and accusations that Israeli Arabs hurl against Israel are certainly of this sort. Gaylin, who regards Jews as the quintessential scapegoats, views that as the reason for their continued demonization throughout history, and one might add to the present day, when Israel, the state of the Jews, embodies Jewish evil. If we add to that what Gaylin has correctly identified as the ability of Islam to "create hatred by converting normal populations into crusaders for a cause", then we have some plausible explanations for much of the hatred proffered today towards Israel and the Jews in the contemporary world.[35]

Jews have traditionally been the victims of stereotyping, calumny and violence, based mostly on manufactured lies stemming from hatred. The centuries-old blood libel, the *Protocols of the Elders of Zion*, the World Jewish Conspiracy, which have practically disappeared in the Western world, due to legislation which forbids racism and incitement, have unfortunately survived in the Islamic and Arab worlds, which due to its continued hatred toward Israel and

---

[34] Willard Gaylin, *Hatred, the Psychological Descent into Violence,* Public Affairs, New York, 2003, p. 34.
[35] Ibid. Pp. 224-5.

the Jews, has neither limited that gushing hatred in their media and official statements, nor done anything to eradicate those lies. The Hamas state in Gaza for example, in whose Charter it cites liberally from the *Protocols* and the other anti-Semitic nonsense, is also on record as vowing the destruction of Israel, in concert with Iran's regime to which it serves as a proxy, who together with his repeated vow to "erase Israel off the map" also indulges in anti-Semitic rhetoric and reassures the world that there was no *Sho'ah*, so as to deny the Jews, Allah Forbid, any international sympathy as victims, for the ultimate victims always remain the Muslims, the Arabs and the poor Palestinians who were wronged by Israel and the injustice done to them was never redressed. True, Jewish synagogues are still occasionally set on fire by Muslims, and Jews are blamed for excessive political and financial power, but the style of hatred has changed, due to Internet where it is no longer necessary to shoulder the direct result of it or to document it. So, lies and accusations can be spread instantly and widely, and no longer need state-controlled media to conquer the cyberspace. Suffice it to read in detail the horrors that unfolded during the UN-sponsored Durban Conference (2001), and the incredible amount of hatred generated by the Muslim participants and their supporters there, to realize how international that plague had become[36]. Two days after that Conference, September 11 happened. Certainly, that enormous horror had been prepared many months in advance and Arabs and world Muslims, including many of their adepts in Israel, rejoiced over it.

Of particular concern in our context is the rise of anti-Israel, anti-Zionist and anti-Jewish activity not only in and by the Arab and Muslim countries where these campaigns of incitement are often sponsored by the governments and their media and by the educational systems which they control, but also by the Muslim

---

[36] See Phyllis Goldstein, *A Convenient Hatred: The History of Antisemitism*, Facing History and Ourselves, Brookline, Mas, 2012, p.. 340-ff.

minorities in Western countries, which import with them to their host cultures their bigotry and hostile attitudes towards the Jews and Israel from their countries of origin. Indeed, after every clash between Israel and the Arabs, immigrant Muslims and their local anti- Semitic partners, particularly in countries whose governments criticize Israel, like France, Belgium and Sweden, join hands with local Right-wing extremists who hate Jews and Left wing fanatics who condemn Zionism and delegitimize Israel, attacking Jews and vandalizing Jewish property. Of course, the larger the Muslim community, the more daring and vicious is its onslaught on the Jews and Israel and its manifestations of hatred toward them. France, with its highest rate of Muslims in the Western world (some 10% of the population) has also registered the highest level of anti-Jewish violence in 2012. Jewish Commemoration sites, cemeteries and Jewish property were the targets of serious attacks, including fire bombing. In the Netherlands, for example, the apartment of a Jew living above a synagogue in Amstelveen, was broken into and set alight. But the increase of desecration of Jewish sites was also observed in Poland, which should have known better due to its World War II experience, and in Hungary and Italy. The Israeli Arab critics of Israel have not been known to condemn that anti-Semitic bigotry, quite the contrary, in conjunction with the European countries who also sanction Israel, they regard those events as part of the struggles they themselves lead against the Jewish state.

Chapter Five

Integration versus Alienation

Of all Western countries, Israel has been under the most strenuous predicament with regard to its minorities policy due to its mistakes in its past conduct towards its Arab-Muslim population, which in Israel amounts to ca 20% of its total demographic makeup, compared to the rate of 5-10% in Western Europe. Admittedly, the Palestinian Arabs in Israel vary from their Muslim coreligionists in Europe in two major aspects, each with its far-reaching consequences, and working in Israel's disfavor:

1. Israeli Arabs (mostly Muslims, but some 20% of them are either Druze or Christians) regard themselves, and for the most part rightly so, as a native population that had been taken over by a Jewish majority of immigrants brought about by the Zionist establishment in Palestine/the Land of Israel during the century of Jewish settlement there, just like the European immigration into the Americas which overtook and transformed the demographic face of the continent. The Jews, however, did not eliminate most of the native populations as the Europeans did in the New World, nor did they expel them during the wars that ensued, remaining with a large Arab population on their hands. Strangely enough, today, it is not the US, Canada and Brazil who are internationally accused of ethnic cleansing and of Europeanizing their conquests by force in

America of which they had alien colonizers, but Israel who has kept most of the preceding inhabitants, acquired much of the land by legal and gradual purchase, and was actually retuning peacefully to its original turf.

2. Unlike the other Western countries which face their Muslim populations' problems as one of their local demographic and cultural challenges, Israel has to tackle the issue under the heavy shadow of its prolonged violent conflict with the Arab and Muslim world, of which its Arab/Muslim population is an integral part. It would be as if during W W II, the German inhabitants of Britain, or the Japanese population of the USA declared their open support for the bitter enemies of their countries of residence. Can anybody doubt the would-be reaction of the British and American governments and peoples to such a situation? Nonetheless, Israel, in its naivete, goodwill and hope of integrating the Palestinian Arabs into the fiber of its fledgling society, embraced the mistaken road of multi-culturalism, pledging full citizen rights to its Arabs, and ignoring the rivalry, and indeed hostility, that their Islamic, Arab and Palestinian upbringing had conditioned them towards Jews, and then Zionism and Israel. The consequences for Israel were dire, for it turned out that since the remaining Arab minority claimed that it possessed the inherent right of standing for its own cultural roots and for resisting any attempt to assimilate it to its new Israeli environment, it refused integration and merger into Jewish Israel, especially under the dark shadow of the ongoing Arab-Israeli dispute. This kind of argument, universally ignored in the world today, except by some purist ideologues, but is advanced by the original Indian populations of North America, by the great native populations of South America prior to their Spanish and Portuguese colonization, and by the aborigines of Australia and New Zealand, who were almost annihilated by Western settlers and invaders,

and then their vestiges enslaved and pushed to the margins of the invading white-man societies. Indeed, while the Western governments which rule those areas today, and now often stand in the forefront of the protection of human and native rights in countries other than the ones they rule, often preach to others the immorality of occupation and exploitation of the occupied natives, Israel often encounters must castigation and condemnation on the international scene for its attitude towards the Arab-Palestinian minority in its midst.

Nonetheless, and against all available evidence and the lethal risks involved, successive Israeli governments have, in the main, usually abided by the principles of the Israeli Declaration of Independence, which guaranteed equality to all citizens in the fledgling Jewish state, without even emphasizing the duties to the state that all nationals were bound by. The outcome was not late to transpire, as the 20% Arab minority in Israel, which is for all intents and purposes Palestinian, and has been described for decades as "torn between its country (Israel) and its people (Palestinians)", has in deed if not always in word, made its anti-Israeli choice for the most part. Moreover, since the October 2000 uprising of Israeli Arabs, they insisted on being called Palestinian citizens of Israel, when they rose in solidarity with the Palestinian Second *Intifadah* (2000-3), breaking Israeli laws right and left, totally identifying with the Palestinians and only caring for the wellbeing of the enemies of Israel, not for that of their country and their Israeli compatriots. By identifying as Palestinians, their ideological and behavioral dilemma was resolved, and they have indeed definitely declared themselves for the Palestinian side of the conflict, consistently condemning their country, whose Knesset seats they occupy, and backing the cause of the Palestinians and of other Arabs and Muslims under all circumstances, no matter what is the issue at hand or its intrinsic merit. That outbreak of hostility, hatred and violence towards the State of

Israel and its Jewish-majority population was the culmination of a long process of alienation and radicalization of the Arab minority in Israel, that started with the Land Day of March 31, 1976, when the Arabs of Israel evinced their growing identification with their Palestinian brethren of the West Bank and Gaza, and declared that the Palestinization process of their collective consciousness had overtaken the flimsy Israelization that some Jewish researchers had optimistically imputed to their community.

During the October, 2000 Uprising of the Israeli Arabs, which ran simultaneously with the launching of the Al-Aqsa *Intifada* in the West Bank, they demonstrated violently in their villages, raising the banners of Hamas and Hizbullah, who were waging a devastating war of terror against their Israeli compatriots, and shouting anti-Israeli slogans like "with our spirit and blood we shall retrieve you, o Galilee" and the like. They in fact were stating that the Galilee, the heart of Israel, in which they were generously left to dwell in the aftermath of the 1948 Independence War, was in fact "enemy territory" in urgent need to be "redeemed". They also blocked highways, threatened to assault isolated Jewish settlements in their neighborhood, burned and destroyed private property, vandalized public property and even killed a Jewish passer-by. Viewed from the outside, it looked like a full-fledged rebellion against the authority of the state which took the intervention of its security forces to quell. In fact, the police was so lenient and hesitant, knowing the liabilities of any security force that caused casualties among civilians, that its two-day battle to reestablish order ended "only" in 13 Arab casualties, probably one-thousandth of what it would have cost had it happened in Egypt or Syria, or Saudi Arabia. Nonetheless, the only impression that the Arabs registered of those disturbances that they had triggered, was that 13 of theirs were "martyred", "assassinated" by the "brutal" and "murderous" Israeli police force, as if it were an enemy police force who provoked or triggered those terrible events. Never mind the violence and the threats that they expended against their Israeli compatriots during those days, in which all Israel held its breath to watch how the combined unrest of the Palestinians in the West Bank and of the Arabs in Israel was going to unfold. Many hidden fears were aired among Israelis those days, with people asking in wonder whether those were the "loyal" Israeli Arabs that naïve Israelis and successive governments thought were their peaceful neighbors and citizens. After the unrest was quelled, for many months Israelis did not dare to shop in their adjoining Arab villages, which they had believed were safe and friendly until then.

The virtual zombies who were emerging from among Israeli Arabs since those events, kept growing and their stature overshadowing their post-October 2000 efforts to calm the moods down, and they gained even more prominence in the eyes of the Israelis six years later, when in the Summer of 2006 full-fledged hostilities erupted on the Lebanese border against Hizbullah, which were baptized as "the Second Lebanese War", the First being the incursion of Israel into Lebanon 24 years earlier in 1982. On that latter occasion, Israeli Arabs could no longer lean on the pretext they had used in October 2000, to the effect that their hearts went to their Palestinian brethren who were "crumbling under the yoke of Israeli occupation"[37], hence their violent reaction then, for this time Israel was waging war against one of its most deadly enemies, Hizbullah, who was committed to its perdition and shouting on each of its gatherings "Death to Israel!!", following their Iranian sponsors' model. Israelis watched on the screens those scenes of death and destruction as Hizbullah missiles landed all over the Israeli north, and shuddered at the realization that within Israel, in their close neighborhood, and often via a colleague at work or on the school bench, hidden allies of those murderers among Israeli Arabs were

---

[37] Dan Shueftan, *The Palestinians in Israel,* (Hebrew), Zmora-Bitan, Tel-Aviv, 2011, p. 204.

manifesting themselves with a terrifying vengeance like true scary enemy zombies. Ultra-nationalist Palestinian Arabs, among them Knesset members like Azmi Bishara and Jamal Zahalqa, had already publicly celebrated during the preceding years down to 2000, Hizbullah's "victories". So deep and committed was the support for Hizbullah among much of the Arab public opinion in Israel, while their country was engaged in a deadly war against that same murderous organization, that even though some of the Hizbullah rockets and missiles, that were blindly shot at the Galilee, the same Galilee they wished to redeem in October 2000, had landed on Arab villages, they reacted leniently and forgivingly for the casualties and damage they ensued (in fact half the total civilian fatalities of Israel were Arabs). Of course, the Arabs in Israel knew that Hizbullah did not target them, but by understanding and forgiving its outrageous attacks they lent legitimacy to the killing of their Jewish neighbors with whom they share the Galilee, and they partook of Hizbullah's aim to terrorize Israel's population. In one case, two children were hit and killed in the same Arab family in Nazareth, for which the leader of Hizbullah apologized on cyber waves. The bereaved father responded by thanking Nasrallah for the apology and, as usual with Arabs who always accuse others for their plights, he put the blame on the Israeli government for the death of his two children[38]. What Israeli in his right mind would refrain in that horrific situation from seeing that bereaved father as an enemy, who would certainly be much more open to sacrifice all Israel and its Jews than his country's enemies personified in the Hizbullah? Think about American or British nationals identifying with the enemies of their countries and expressing content for the damages caused to their country by its enemies. What would have happened then?

As a result of all these nefarious developments, and sensing perhaps that the gap between the Jewish state and its stated goals, on

---

[38] *Fasal al-Maqal, Nazareth*, 28 July, 2006.

the one hand, and its Arab minority and its heartfelt aspirations, on the other, having grown unbridgeable, the political and intellectual elite of the Israeli Arabs decided to formulate a document of demands that they put forward before the Israeli public and government, signaling their "Vision of their Future" as a national minority claiming its share of the state they wished to topple, no longer as a minority of individuals who sought rights and equality within it, while at the same time undermining the existence, legitimacy and security of the country where they live and call home. They chose to publicize their thoughts and wishes under the sponsorship of the Supreme Follow-up Committee of the Arabs in Israel, which is made up of all the Arab Knesset members and of the Heads of the Arab local councils, who were thought by the authors of the document to represent all trends within their Arab community in Israel. This document, which symbolizes and expresses the break of the Arab minority with the official state policies, was in fact an indictment against the Jewish majority, a denial of its national rights and of its collective identity, and was directed to the hard leftist Israelis and anti-Israelis abroad who deny Israel's right to nationhood and wish to dismantle it. In this regard, the Arabs of Israel joined hands with the foreigners who delegitimize the Jewish state. However, while the authors of the document wished perhaps to offer it as a platform for a dialogue with the Jewish majority, its very extremist, provocative and uncompromising wording does not stand any chance to become such a basis for negotiation, given that no one wishes to discuss one's own liquidation. Therefore, it remains a propaganda manifesto which either overestimates the Arab capacity to enforce it or underestimates Israeli and Jewish ability to resist and reject it. In any case, all it did has been to heighten the Jewish majority suspicions towards the Arab minority intentions, and to put a big question mark, in fact a death sentence, on the multi culturalist vision that well-meaning Israeli successive governments had held until then.

That document, which has become a foundational summary of the condition and intentions of the Arab minority in Israel, can be summed up in the following[39]:

1. In its very introduction, the document clarifies that it represents the "Palestinian Arabs living in Israel, who are natives of the country, and its citizens", without mentioning Israel in any context, or the Jewish majority within which they live. They clearly see themselves, as we all suspected, "part of the Palestinian people, the Arab nation and the Arab, Islamic and human cultural space". They reject their Israeli appellation as "Israeli Arabs", and even emphasize that their Israeli citizenship was imposed on them, and was not their choice, when the Jewish state "occupied" most of the Palestinian territory;

2. As has been the wont of most third world countries, the Arabs of Israel present themselves in terms of "victims of foreign occupation and exploitation", without any reference to any responsibility of theirs, or to the bounties they enjoy in the Jewish state. The Jews are presented are usurpers, exploiters, killers and occupiers, while they, the Palestinians, are the fighters for freedom and for a "just peace", namely without Israel. Even Israel's democracy is disparaged because it does not guarantee their separate Arab and national identity. In other words, they wish to push the country to a Bosnian model where peace and tranquility prevail only after the Muslims became hegemonic[40]; and the democratic system they enjoy uniquely in Israel is disparaged as oppressive;

3. The entire tenure of the document is the illegitimacy of Israel, which is dubbed as a colonial and undemocratic state, carrying all the blame for the conflict with its neighbors and for the displacement of the Palestinian people. The entire Zionist

---

[39] Shueftan, op. cit. pp. 207-212.
[40] See R. Israeli and A. Benabou, *Savagery in the Heart of Europe: the Bosnia War (1992-5)*, Strategic Books, Texas, 2013.

enterprise and the revival of the Jewish people on its land are negated to the point that only their total and radical removal can remedy the situation;

4. Hence the struggle of the Arabs to annihilate the Jewish presence in Palestine since the 1940s, because the Palestinians totally reject the international attempt of 1947 to divide Palestine between a Jewish and an Arab state. For, unlike the position of the Israeli Arabs in the 1960s and 1970s, which had invented the formula of "two states to two nations", this document demands that eventually all Palestine should belong to the Arab cultural space.

5. While the wording of the document avoided to state explicitly the delegitimation of Israel, all the components that describe the Zionist entity and its relations with the Palestinians converge towards that conclusion. They are not talking about amendments in the present Israeli structure to redress their grievances, but advocate a total uprooting of the Israeli entity and replacing it with a "new democratic and Palestinian one", as if it were not a contradiction in terms, and as if there were in existence any Arab entity anywhere which functioned democratically.

6. The document rejects the democratic system in Israel, as if the Palestinians, or other Arabs and Muslims were able to establish a better one, and wishes to attain national autonomy and national rights for the Israeli Arabs which would make them collectively equal to the Jewish component of the state.

7. They want Israel to shoulder the responsibility for their *Nakbah*, namely the "disaster" of 1948-9 that had occasioned the undoing of their society and its dispersion, while they were the party, encouraged by the rest of the Arabs, which rejected the UN Partition Plan and invaded fledgling Israel in order to nip her in the bud upon its birth. This had caused the 1948 war

and their own misfortune, but they want others to bear the responsibility for their misdeeds.

8. After the Israeli Zionist state is dismantled, the Palestinians wish to establish on its ruins a bi-national state, where Arabs can elect their own representatives and manage their national affairs in all spheres of life. Education, should be independent and the Arabs should be free to teach that Israel is a "colonialist country", something that would necessarily encourage rebellion against it and the shaking off of its authority.

9. The document also demands the Arab right to veto all decisions made by the Jewish majority. That would mean that all security, Jewish immigration and land settlement decisions would be killed by the veto, so as to bring about the systematic weakening of Israel until the Arabs can overwhelm it demographically or try again to destroy it by force and take over.

This harsh view of the "Vision Document" by a scholar who researched the matter for many years before he reached his judgment, was not universally shared by all Israelis nonetheless. In the Israeli school system, which remained hopeful for peace and coexistence since the "peace process" was launched with the Egyptians in the 1980s, numerous were the leftist teachers and students who ran "coexistence seminars", trying to introduce those foundational ideas as legitimate materials in their school *curriculi*. Understandably, the partisans of this trend aspired to spread in their supposedly open and tolerant school system the views that were anathema to the majority of Israelis, to wit:

a. To legitimize the Arab view which sees Israel not as a Jewish state, but as "country of all its citizens", rendering the country into a bi-national state and ultimately an Arab one, where the political identity is temporarily "Israeli" until its demographic reality would compel it to change that designation.

b. To update the concept of "group rights" where a large Arab minority living side by side with a Jewish majority gains an equal standing with it.

c. To view Israeli society as a multi-national, no longer only as multi cultural, entity, so as to pave the road to the equalization between all its ethnic/religious groups and pull the rug underneath its Jewish and Zionist character.

d. To consider the status of Arabs in Israel in terms of human and group rights, once again to facilitate the subtraction of the Arab minority from Jewish hegemony and gain for it autonomy or even secession.

The very terminology used by the advocates of this approach, who view the Vision Documents as the "Arab minority taking responsibility for its future", puts its emphasis on a game of words which if examined in depth, justifies the judgment rendered by Shueftan above. For, in the final analysis, it expects and demands:

1. A change of government which would no longer reflect the Jewish majority but become an "egalitarian" one with a shared government that would perpetuate friction and unrest, like in Bosnia, Belgium and Lebanon, where Palestinian Arabs in Israel have their determining say and are able to settle future disagreements violently;

2. A constitution which would define the state as the joint home of Jews and Arabs, as if the two sides were equivalent, ignoring the fact that Arabs already had 22 countries and the Palestinians three entities (Jordan and the PA in the West Bank and the Hamas in Gaza), while a bi-national Israel would eliminate the only sovereignty that the Jewish people had in their land;

3. Autonomous management of Muslim (and Christian) institutions, so as to allow them a legitimate relationship with international Islam and Christianity which are often hostile to

Israel. (The Christians were introduced only to lend to the proposal a universal and anti- discriminatory aspect); and

4. Institutionalizing the continuous and unrestricted link between Arabs in Israel and the rest of the Palestinian people, as well as with the other components of the Arab and Muslim nation. That would be the means to return the Jews to their minority status and facilitate their melting into the greater Arab and Muslim identities surrounding them, so as to reinstate their ancient *dhimmi status.*

Thus, instead of aspiring to lift themselves to the levels of prosperity, technology, modernity and democracy that the Jewish state has brought to the region, the Israeli Arabs, like their compatriots across the border, prefer to drag Israel down to their own backwardness, poverty and chaos even if they should themselves sink with it in the process. The Document also demands that the historical injustice done to the Arabs be recognized, i.e. that they themselves bear no responsibility for it, and all the blame is to be laid on others even though it was they who triggered most of the wars in the Middle East and caused their own misery. And finally, they demand compensation for the lands that had been confiscated from them if they cannot be restituted to them.

The Israeli partisans of this lenient approach to Arab demands also remind us that in addition to the Vision Document that was initiated and embraced by the political and intellectual leadership of the Arabs in Israel, other Arab lobbies and individuals in Israel also advanced their own propositions, all essentially geared to achieve the same goals. 'Ad*ala (justice)*, for example, the Legal Center for the rights of the Arab minority in Israel, published a "Democratic Constitution" that incorporates and reflects their vision of their future in the Jewish state. The Chair of the organization, Marwan Dweiri, a respected academic, suggests turning Israel into a democratic, bi-national, bi-lingual and multi-cultural society, ostensibly geared to "create human rights, national equality and social justice", but actually aiming at dismantling the Jewish state that has already achieved all these lofty goals, precisely because it has ignored and escaped the prescriptions of this "constitution". When the Arabs in Israel watch today the chaos and the killings that the "Arab Spring" has brought to their world of dreams in the Arab space[41], they must be praising Allah for sparing them those misfortunes. An "Egalitarian Constitution for All" was also promulgated by a rival Arab organization, *Mussawa, (equality,* but not of duties only of privileges), which also advocates the rights of the Arab citizens of Israel, and was authored by another academic, Yussuf Jabarin, focusing on the collective rights of the Arabs, based on "full and equal partnership of the Arabs in Israel, including in the state resources, altering the state symbols to suit Arab aspirations, effective representation in the state institutions, and turning the country into a bi-lingual and bi-national state. In fact, these newborn advocates of democracy, who had never experienced any democratic rule in their world of dreams except in Israel, pretend to invent a new democracy the like of which does not exist anywhere. If they had succeeded elsewhere, they would be much more credible with convincing their Jewish compatriots of their good intentions, who are deterred by the idea of rendering Israel a state of quotas, like Lebanon, where office is assigned according to ethnic affiliation, not merit. Destructive is also the idea of assigning the state resources equally to those who create the wealth, serve their country and drive it upwards, and to those who only benefit from that prosperity, refuse to lift their finger for their country and constantly drive it downwards. Another Arab Institution, *Mada al-Carmel,* also promulgated a "vision paper", usually referred to as the "Haifa Declaration", which was calculated to constitute an Arab response to the similar "Kinneret Declaration"(2001) convened by Jewish intellectuals shortly before. This paper purported to

---

[41] See R. Israeli, *From Arab Spring to Islamic Winter,* Transaction, NJ, 2013.

set new standards of conduct within the Israeli-Arab community, between Israeli Arabs and the Palestinians and Arabs at large, and to redefine the identity of the Palestinian Arabs living in Israel. This version of reformed Arabs within the Jewish entity comes closer than all the others to a peaceful multi culturalism, but it unfortunately remains a utopian vision.

It is noteworthy that despite the Palestinian and Arab nationalistic orientation which all these papers inspire among Arbs in Israel, they also hint to a rebellion against the Palestinian leadership, notably the PLO, which had agreed in Oslo to recognize the Arabs in Israel as a domestic Israeli issue in spite of its public claim of representing "all Palestinians wherever they be". We can see in the post-Arafat era a retraction from that position in the fact that Abu Mazen's leadership refused to recognize Israel as a Jewish state, thus leaving the door open to the bi-national state the Israeli Arabs aspire to; and that in the negotiations for the release of Palestinian prisoners deal mediated by Secretary Kerry in 2013-14, Abu Mazen insisted on the release of several Israeli Arabs who had committed terrorist acts against Israel on behalf of the PLO. It is also interesting to note that these papers reflect the newly-gained self confidence of the younger generation of Arab leaders who were born, educated and trained in Israel, master its language, culture and politics and aspire to change the reality into which they grew up. This new leadership has also become aware of new trends in the world democracies where they can bash Israel for not following their ways, though they are also specifically aware of Israel's security risks posed by its Arab minority, which are unparalleled in other democracies. Be it as it may, while in the past, Western democracies tightly supervised and imposed restrictions on their native minorities, for fear of grooming a disloyal citizenry that may undermine their systems, towards the end of the 20th century, new winds have swept those countries, especially in Western Europe, where the massive Muslim immigration of first *gastarbeiter* and then refugees, has tempted those countries to regard the issue of absorbing Muslim immigrants as all-European, and therefore they accorded citizenship and equal rights to the newcomers. Outside Europe, like the US, Canada, Australia and New Zealand, and to some extent in South America, more rights were accorded, in line with the new trends, to the native minorities. Alongside with the change in the attitude of the hosting states, public services like schools, hospitals, the judicial system, police and the media, have learned to adapt themselves to the minorities, assuming that such a policy would ensure the loyalty of the minorities to the state, an assumption which has in the meantime proved unfounded. The new Arab leadership in Israel has seized upon these precedents and set them as models to emulate. They declared themselves "native minorities" which now were recognized worldwide as naturally deserving of rights, and started to clamor for their privileges which were formulated in all the documents cited above. In 1991 the European Security and Cooperation Organization adopted this approach, and in 1995 it was embraced by all countries which joined NATO or the European Union. The Israeli Supreme Court also implicitly accepted this policy when it adopted the plea of the Arab "civil rights" organizations to enforce the bi-lingual (Hebrew and Arabic) road-signs in all Israel, arguing that since the Arab minority in Israeli had lived on the land from time immemorial, it had the inherent right, unlike immigrant populations, to preserve its cultural characteristics[42]. But nothing was said in those judgments pertaining to Israel's security and to the debilitating impact that would have on the public safety of its citizens.

In view of all this, there is no wonder that the opposition to the "Vision Documents" has been almost universal among the Jewish public across the board. While Israel Harel, an *Ha'aretz* columnist,

---

[42] See Supreme Court Document 4112/99, *Adala* vs the City of Tel Aviv. Referred to in 'Alaa Mahajneh' article "The Arab Language and the Native Status of Arabs in Israel" (Arabs) in the *Adala* Internet Site.

who is identified with the Israeli Right, has expectedly seen in the document "an attempt to alter Israel's nature as a Jewish and democratic state"[43], other center and left of center political activists felt merely shaken by the tone of hatred that the documents radiated, and insulted by the suggested comparison between Israel and South Africa. For, they asked candidly, were the Arabs in Israel ever prevented to access Israeli courts of law, its Knesset, its public transportation, its schools and restaurants, or banned from mixed marriage or co-habitation with Jews as the *apartheid* laws in South Africa had demanded? To the extent that Arabs chose to live in their villages, go to their own schools in Arabic, live in their neighborhoods or refrain from mix-marrying Jewish spouses or serve in the Israeli armed forces, it was their own cultural, religious or political choice, not a law imposed on them by the state. Especially after the launching of the Oslo Process (1993), when talk began of "two states for two peoples", did the Jewish public begin to believe that Palestinians in Israel, who cannot bear the idea of being ruled by the Jews of Israel, could move freely to their national state, exactly as 1 million Jews had moved from Arab and Muslim countries into fledgling Israel upon its inception. But in view of the PLO and the Israeli Arabs' express opinion that while there is acceptance of two states, there is only one people, i.e. the Palestinians, (the Jews are denied peoplehood, nationhood and self-determination under article 20 of the Palestinian National Charter which was never amended), one expects an explanation to this seeming contradiction. But in fact it is not, in Arab eyes, since the state of Israel, which the Palestinians on both sides of the aisle refuse to recognize as Jewish, is intended to absorb the 4-5 million refugee returnees who, together with the already existing almost 2 million Palestinian Israelis, will constitute an Arab majority, if not immediately then in the long run; then, will be gone the Jewish state, its democracy, its prosperity and prog-

---

[43] Israel Harel, " Foes, not Friends", *Haaretz,*, 17 June, 2011, part II, p. 2.

ress, its openness and freedom. The Jewish public in Israel watches these processes and hears these claims, and is inescapably terrified by so many zombies who cannot wait to scale its walls by their swarming refugees, to undermine its territory over-ground and underground (via the tunnels from Gaza and the Lebanese border) from within, and to calumniate it abroad by the likes of *Mussawa* and *'Adalah,* and the leadership of the Arabs in general within the UN and among hostile nations, in order to delegitimize it from without, and to undermine and then take it over from within.

We have shown above that more than other hyphenated identities in multi-cultural societies, the soul of the Israeli Arabs contains such a variety of, and often contradictory, elements as to make their life nearly impossible. It is human nature to yearn for the stable, the known and the predictable, the certain and the familiar. Thus, in an environment in constant flux, where the most expected does not happen and the most unexpected often occurs; and where values are different and changes are rapid, conflict rages or threatens to burst out, and chaos can erupt at any moment, the Arabs in Israel have more need than the average Israelis for sustained comfort in the context of their multi-faceted identities. The Arab in Israel is indeed Israeli, Palestinian, Arab and Muslim (or Christian), all at the same time. While the Druze and some Christians have learned to integrate and be part of the state, sometimes at the price of alienating themselves from their Muslim compatriots, a process of estrangement between the Israeli Arabs in general and the state of Israel, has been perennially weighing on the minds of both the Jewish majority and the Arab minority. This state of mind has gained momentum since the elections of 2014 when for the first time all Arab parties in Israel have coalesced into one list, that has acquired a considerably aggressive tone, which compels all its members to align along the most extremist nationalists among them. For the elections of 2019, though, the United List has split into two different ones again: Ahmed Tibi with his *Ta'al* party, in conjunction with the Hadash (former Communists) Party on the one hand, and the amalgam of the other two factions (*Balad* and the Islamic Party) keeping together in an attempt to rescue the United List. But in the 2020 elections, realizing that their disunity had cost them many mandates, they reunited and indeed swept the large constituency that won them 15 votes, the largest ever, which emboldened them to advance more daring demands than ever, alluding without stating it openly to their Vision Documents which have gone into a semi-dormant state in view of the outrage they had rages among the Jewish majority.

A large part played by the Israeli authorities in the dismal failure of their long term policy towards the Arab minority. First of all, there are the political parties in Israel which seek the Arab voters on the eve of elections, only to forget their promises the day after. This has understandably driven the Arabs into political cynicism and also encouraged them to establish their own political sub-systems. They have come of age and learned something about participatory democracy, and about the full-rights slogans that they have heard so often, which in practice carry so many restrictions due to their abnormal situation and to the obsessive security hazards which constantly threaten Israel's existence. They got used to the state's custom of appointing token Arab officials or judges, just to prove that the Arabs are not discriminated against, but in fact that evinces exactly the reverse: for if Arabs could accede to high positions without being positively discriminated for by affirmative action, that would have shown that they truly became integrated. Arabs also got accustomed to the demand of loyalty by the state, but at the same time authorities are lenient towards those who overtly operate against it. For example, Ahmed Tibi, a leader of the Israeli-Arab community, later MK, served for years with impunity, as the adviser of Yasser Arafat, an avowed enemy of Israel, and his compatriot, Azmi Bishara, traveled repeatedly, against the law, to enemy territory in Syria, without the government indicting him. Calumniation

of the state and incitement against it by Arab MK's and other notables, have become a matter of course, and no one was seriously
indicted for trespassing the limits of law. This has brought Bishara,
the Head of the *Balad* Party, to transmit information about Israel
to his allies in the Hizbullah in Lebanon and to run away from his
post in the Knesset to hide in Arab countries before he could be
indicted for treason.

It has become routine that Arab leaders in Israel, far from accepting the rulings of courts of law, which usually protect their rights,
on the contrary, when their compatriots are indicted or convicted
for "ideological" crimes against the state, to vitriolically attack the
system and blame all manner of machinations against them by the
police and the courts. They consistently follow the line that they
cannot be wrong because they are themselves wronged, therefore
any accusation of encroachment on the law on their part is a mere
concoction against them in order to frame them and discriminate
against them. Since they are vociferous about demanding their
rights, but are not asked to fulfill their duties, they regard any call
upon them to respect the law as a nuisance or persecution, and
reject it with disgust. Therefore, the leniency by the Israeli authorities towards them, far from easing the tensions, on the contrary
triggers the contempt and confusion on the part of the Arabs, out
of the realization that their violence pays off, that no one would
take them to task and demand that they abide by the law, and that
if they should persist in their lawlessness, they are sure to win at the
end. That is the mechanism that allowed Bishara to spy against his
country, the Bedouins to set up illegal villages and then claim that
they are dispossessed when they are evacuated by the authorities,
the Arab Members of the Knesset to sit in the Israeli Legislative
House and act against its laws, Arab intellectuals to issue papers
undermining Israeli existence and sovereignty, and Arab political
and religious leaders to side with the enemies of their country and
deny the latter's right of self defense. Israeli citizens, who see and

hear, and are very alert to what is happening in their neighborhood, are increasingly skeptical not only about an acceptable settlement with the Palestinians, but in view of the total identification of Israeli Arabs with their brethren, that skepticism has been extending to their livability with their immediate Arab neighbors in Israel proper. These fears are haunting the Israelis, especially after the trauma of October 2000, more emphatically than ever before.

And yet, Israelis are constantly asking themselves whether the Arabs of the country are friends of foes? For, due to their increasing vociferousness and the international stature that they claim for themselves, which is fed by the rising national demands of the Palestinians, they came to be seen by the Israeli public as a tip of the iceberg, representing the wider Palestinian, Arab and Islamic circles which have not made much progress towards reconciling with the Israeli presence in their midst. These days are not merely of strife, terror, war, hatred and incitement against Israel, where terror and killings occasioned by the Arab Spring within, and by Islamic terrorism worldwide, have dwarfed the urge for peace and much more even the practical efforts to attain it. The international legitimacy given to the Palestinian demands, and to their Arab and Islamic allies, with some lateral support by intellectual and leftist circles in the West, cast much doubt on the very right to existence of the Jewish state at a time when Israel, more than ever before, is in dire need of its supporters in order to continue to defend itself. For, the thugs who rule countries like Syria and Iran, and the terrorist movements like al-Qa'ida, Hamas and Hizbullah which have shown their mettle in the world scene, are no longer hiding their intentions against the Jews, Zionists and Israel, and anyone who dares to support anything Jewish or Israeli in the West and within the UN organs, also finds itself under attack and condemnation. Arab and Muslim incitement and hatred against Israel and Zionism are propagated by the Arab and Muslim media almost without regard to the facts, to history or to the truth[44]. Even "respectable" Arabic newspapers that appear in the West, often take upon themselves to diffuse disgusting and libelous anti-Semitic propaganda of the worst kind that is often topped by cartoons or straight anti-Semitic statements by the Western press itself.

Admittedly, since pure anti-Semitism of the classical type is no longer admissible in the West for the most part, it all comes now under the guise of anti-Zionism. But the effect is the same, because if all nations of the world are entitled to self-determination, independence and statehood save the Jews, that simply amounts to an ant-Semitic belief that Jews are somewhat worth less than all the others. In that regard, the anti-Israeli Europeans share the floor with the Palestinians, Arabs and Muslims who do not relent from their anti-Jewish and anti-Israeli broadsides. So, for example, as soon as the al-Aqsa *Intifadah* was declared by the Palestinians in late September 2000, it was immediately seconded by a parallel and unprecedented upheaval among Israeli Arabs, in support of that unrest, and Western critics of Israel joined hands with the Arabs to demonize Israel on an unparalleled scale, so much so that it seemed that even the Israeli conflict with its domestic Arabs and Palestinians was being internationalized and exported to the public square all over the world. The main actors were Arab and Muslim new immigrants into Western countries who used the ambience of anti-Israeli sentiment and the impunity that they incurred, to step up their attacks against Jewish targets in the US, Canada, Western Europe, Russia, South America and elsewhere where the strong Arab presence could ally with local anti-Semites in an orgy of anti-Israeli and anti-Jewish bashing.

Previously, in all rounds of the almost one century -old Arab-Israeli wars, never was there any fear in Israel, even not a suspicion, that the Arab citizens of Israel, who had been naively treated by all

---

[44] See R. Israeli, *Hatred, Lies and Violence,* Transaction, NJ, 2014.

governments as "loyal citizens", would under any circumstances join hands with the enemies of their country. Quite the contrary, though most of them had never joined active combat in defense of their country against their people (except for the Druze and volunteers among Bedouins and Christians), they had at least shown a degree of identification with the distress of their country in times of war, and they often volunteered to fill in for Israeli civilians who left their jobs to join the military reserves in the "people's war" that they had to fight. They also often donated blood to the wounded and expressed their anxiety lest their country, whose fate they had embraced, should be harmed by outside malevolent forces. But now, things are different: Not only any volunteer work to aid Israel would be considered as "treason" by fellow Arab citizens, but the leaders of the Israeli Arabs would openly voice support for the enemy's positions and raise its flags, as an expression of what one of them, former MK Taleb al-Sana' called a "new brand of Arab leaders". For that reason when there was talk of substituting "national service" in civilian tasks for military service to the Arabs of Israel, they stringently raised their voices against the idea lest, Allah Forbid, they might be aiding their demonized country. Can anyone imagine German- or Japanese-Americans in the US, or Germans in Britain, acting similarly, during the dark days of World War II?.

This turnabout in the attitude of the Arabs in Israel towards their country, did not occur overnight, as it did not come as a surprise to observers who followed closely Arab affairs over the years. Nor is it solely the result of the two *intifadah*'s which have inexorably pulled Israeli Arabs closer to their kin across the border. It is mainly the consequence of long-haul developments related to the evolution of the Arab minority in Israel since its inception, to wit:

>   a. The watershed events of the 1967 War, which pulled together the Palestinians of Israel with those who dwelt in the occupied West and Gaza;

b. Israel's hard time and real danger that hovered over it during the 1973 War, when Israel was surprisingly attacked by Egypt and Syria and had great difficulties to check and repulse the Arab armies, at great human, economic and reputation cost;

c. The mental revolution that produced the first Land Day in 1976, and demonstrated to the self-confident Arabs that they could stand up to the Israeli rule, by violent means if necessary, and cause it to budge in their direction, for aggressiveness and self-assertion paid off more that docility and passivity;

d. The decline of the Communist Party whose members were mostly Arabs and stood for the "two states for two nations" stance that is no longer in vogue, weakened that conviction both in the world and among the Arabs, especially the Palestinians;

e. The rapid rise of the Islamic Movement in Israel, as best personified in the leadership of Ra'id Salah, who did not believe from the outset in any peaceful coexistence with Israel and rejected the Oslo arrangement lock, stock and barrel, following the lead of the Hamas in that regard, diminished the belief of Israeli Arabs in that peaceful avenue;

f. The eruption of the two violent *intifadah*'s (in 1987 and then in 2000), which have shaken the Palestinians in the West Bank and Gaza and more and more dragged the Arabs of Israel into the fray, and resulted in the unfortunate Oslo process, and has finally crumbled under the weight of its own irrelevance and unfeasibility, persuaded the Arabs of Israel, like their Palestinian brethren, that too many exaggerated hopes had been hinged on that "peace process" which actually never took off; and lastly

g. Part of the fiasco of Israeli policies towards the Arab minority in the country must have also been generated by the naïve beliefs embraced by successive Israeli governments who had basked in an ocean of illusions for many years, cultivated a double language to sooth their people who ignorantly followed them, practiced politics of ambivalence and avoided taking audacious decisions in time, in order to mend the situation before it blew in the Israelis' face both literally and metaphorically.

Prima facie, since the Arabs in Israel have achieved a high level of liberty, life expectancy, social services and standard of living, they ought to evince a deep vested interest in the country that allows them all these goodies. But in reality, things are different. For, in spite of the fact that when given the choice, most Arabs in Israel would rather stay under Israeli rule (maybe in the hope of taking it over some day), they at the same time enthusiastically embrace the ideal of the "right of return" of their kin to Israel, which if fulfilled would once again turn them into the majority in the country, and convert it into another Arab space like all the rest. At the same time that they clamor for full Israeli citizenship, they also recoil from any idea of taking up obligations and responsibilities like their Jewish fellow citizens. They would rather cultivate their own "autonomous" institutions, and some of them dream about cultural and social, perhaps even political, secession from the state, and promote separatist ideas, which though legitimate in a democracy, push them to adopt expressly hostile positions towards the state of which they are citizens. Hence the sometimes harsh reactions of the state which wishes (and this is also legitimate) to preserve itself and its nature as is, much to the chagrin of its Arab nationals. In this state of affairs, all the doubts, suspicions, questions and ambiguities have inevitably exploded into a deep-seated crisis that can hardly be bridged and smoothed over, compelling the Jewish state, seven decades after its inception, to rethink the situation in a creative, innovative and daring way, in order to avert the dissolution of its own founding dream. For it is now too late to take preventive measures to avert disaster, the disaster being here already, the alarm clock having been ringing and all the red lights blinking frantically. So, to stop on the brink, before everybody is swept into the abyss, only harsh, resolute and uncompromising measures which Israeli leaders do not have the courage to adopt, can save Israel in the long run.

A vast literature exists which depicts the development of the Arab population of Palestine, since the Arab conquest in the 7th Century AD until our days, and there is no point repeating all that. Even if we disregard here the more recent waves of Arab immigration into the country in the modern era, whose traces are left in clan names like *al-Masarwah* (The Egyptians) or the *Mughrabi* (North African) Quarter in Jerusalem, nothing can dwarf the even longer history of the link between the Jews and the land, which has been recorded and documented, though the Arabs continue to deny it as non-existent. Instead, they have been cultivating a non-sensical myth which has no grounds in history, relating the Arabs of Palestine to the ancient Cana'anites. So, as an anchor and a starting point of history, let us refer to the historic watershed of 29 November, 1947, when the UN decided to partition Palestine in view of constituting two independent (though inter-dependent) entities in the country-one Arab (not explicitly Palestinian) and one Jewish (not Israeli, since the Israeli state had not come into being yet). For the Arabs, it was the demographic and political reality of those days, namely the clear Arab majority in the land under the British mandate, which should have dictated any prospective solutions to the Arab-Jewish conflict in the land. Added to that are the newly Arab-manufactured claims and myths calculated to "prove" that Arab presence in Palestine preceded that of the Jews, and that exactly as the Jews had taken over the land in antiquity from the "ancestors" of the

Arabs, the latter are now entitled to "return" to the land wherein they have been dispossessed by Jews in the modern era.

What cannot be disputed or challenged, however, and indeed determines Israel's status regionally and internationally, and lends legitimacy to both Israel and Palestine, is the fact that on the eve of the UN Partition Resolution of 1947, about two thirds of the population West of the Jordan were Palestinian Arabs, and the rest were Palestinian Jews. If we add to them the Arab population East of the Jordan, which was part of the Palestinian territory that came originally under the British Mandate, then the proportion of the Jewish minority shrinks even further beneath that one third. This fundamental datum is crucial, because only when we conceive of the entire Land of Israel (Palestine in Arab parlance) as one disputed unit, is there any chance of negotiating the two-state solution and adopting it, thereby also resolving the unbearable plight of the Arab minority in Israel. The numerical data teach us that on the day the Resolution was adopted on 29 November 1947, the Jews numbered over half a million souls in Western Palestine while the Arabs reached over one million. Had the Arabs accepted the Resolution, most Jews and a sizable minority of the Arabs would have been included in the Jewish state, while the Arab state would have comprised most of the Arabs and a small minority of Jews.

But that was not to be. The Arabs countries around, seconded by the Palestinian Arabs, rejected the Partition Plan and invaded the Jewish state on the morrow of its declaration on May 15, 1948. During the battles that ensued in 1948-9, the Israeli territory was expanded at the expense of the Arab one that was never declared independent. As a result of the war that was launched by the local Arabs, with foreign Arab aid, over 80% of them were uprooted from their towns and villages in the territory that was apportioned to the Jewish state, partly through their removal from the fighting arena by the warring parties, partly by their voluntary flight in the hope of returning with the victorious Arab armies that vowed to destroy Israel, and partly under the sheer fear for their lives in combat zones. Only some 130,000 of them remained in Israeli territory. Those numbers were reinforced by 30,000 more who returned at the end of the fighting, by virtue of the Armistice agreements, that temporarily settled the pending problems between Israel and the Hashemite Kingdom of Jordan which has, under British tutorship, taken over the West Bank of the Jordan and annexed it to the Kingdom, that was itself based on the East Bank. That Eastern part of Palestine, which had been torn away from the Mandate over Palestine turned into a separate Emirate of Transjordan, and then into the Hashemite (hinting to its Arabian origin) Kingdom of Jordan. Thus, at the end of the war and as Israeli borders were temporarily crystallized, there were within Israel some 160,000 Palestinian Arabs. One fifth of them were not permitted to return to the villages they had left during the battles, either because they were irretrievably demolished, on purpose or incidentally, or were considered a security hazard by Israel (like Ikrit and Biram in the Galilee, adjacent to the Lebanese border). So, most of them converged on other existing villages and towns, for unlike the adjoining Arab countries who put the Palestinian refugees in "temporary" camps, where they have been rotting for the fourth generation now, Israel did not establish any refugee camps for Palestinians. The uprooted Palestinians during the war had therefore no choice but to settle permanently in existing Arab towns and villages.

The most salient example of this sad process, which involved immense human suffering, but moral responsibility for which has to be shouldered by the Palestinian and Arab leaderships who rejected partition, is the city of Nazareth, a flourishing town in the heart of the Lower Galilee. It had been an important town since the Crusades when it was the seat of the Archbishop of the Galilee, through the Ottoman period (1500-1918), when it served as the main launching pad for the Turkish and German forces on the eve of the crucial Meggido battle in World War I, and up until the

British Mandate which made it a district town and a base for its garrison in the north of the country. When combat broke out in 1948, the Arab Liberation Army headed by Kaukji, which invaded from Syria to assist the Palestinians, made Nazareth its Headquarters, and launched its attacks against Jewish settlements like Mishmar Ha'emek. As a result, a major exodus of Arab villagers from the entire area made its way to Nazareth which was considered safe under the Kaukji forces. In July 1948 the Israeli Defense Forces mounted the "*Dekel*" operation against the Arab invaders and liberated the entire Lower Galilee from their control. In those days, when the fate of fledgling Israel was hanging on a thin thread, Prime Minister Ben Gurion found the time to order the establishment of a city management board in town, directed the troops to avoid friction with the local Arab population and to prohibit any harm to the holy places of all religions. Then, the entire population, like the rest of the Arabs who remained in Israel, was put under temporary military government pending the normalization of life in the country.

During the war and immediately subsequent to it, some 10,000 refugees assembled in Nazareth, thus increasing its population by 50%; and being for the most part Muslims, helped tilt the religious balance of the population to becoming evenly divided between Muslims and Christians (while previously it had been an overwhelmingly Christian town), in preparation for turning it into a Muslim-majority town since the 1970's. In the general context of the population movements during the war and in its aftermath, contradictory data are often cited. Some say that since ca 90% of the refugees who left Israeli territory were Muslim, the remaining 10% (amounting to 60,000 at the time in some estimates) were Christian. Others contend that since the rate of Christian refugees who left the country was considerably lower than the Muslim average, the proportion of Christians among the Arabs who stayed in Israel was as high as 20%. Be it as it may, the total numbers of the

Arabs in Israel in 1961 amounted to 247,000, and the proportion between Muslims and Christians was maintained in the main. But since 1967, the rate of Christians dropped considerably, as many of them emigrated to Western countries, or as the dramatic rise in their standard of living in Israel gnawed considerably at their fertility rates, or as the annexation of East Jerusalem by Israel brought within its boundaries great numbers of Muslims. In the 1990's, the rate of the Christians dropped to 12%, though their absolute numbers almost doubled- from 60,000 to 110,000, thus sending them back to their original rate among the general Arab population, before the refugee problem set in. This means that the Muslim population has grown much more rapidly, especially due to its high fertility rate, but also by reason of the welfare and health services provided by the state of Israel, which prolonged their life expectancy (from 50 in 1948 to 75 in 2000), and as a result of the annexation of the East Jerusalem population to Israel. In the beginning of the 21st Century, their numbers grew to more than one million and a half (more than six-fold since the birth of Israel), and their rate in the general population was around 20%, almost as in 1949 after the Armistice agreements, when the borders and the movements of population stabilized, and Israel began to absorb the trickles of Jewish refugees from Arab countries. At that time survivors of the Holocaust in Eastern Europe also streamed to Israel, even before the great waves of *aliya* (=going up, as Jewish immigration to Israel is dubbed), started to flock to Israel from North Africa and then the Soviet Union and Ethiopia. There is no more blatant disclaimer of the "ethnic cleansing" of which Israel is often accused by the Arabs, than this simultaneous dramatic growth of both the Jewish and Arab populations in almost the same proportions.

All Israeli governments in the past have repeated the myth of the "loyalty" of the minority in Israel, save for the small numbers among them who are occasionally caught in terrorist or other hostile activity against it. This exonerating statement has naturally not only relieved the Arabs from the embarrassing burden of proving their loyalty, but even justified in some ways their automatic alignment with other Arabs in every case of confrontation with Israel. The problem is with this bizarre interpretation of the notion of "loyalty", not as an active concept which has to be proven every day anew, but as a passive assumption that is valid, unless proven false. In other words, anyone who does not place bombs in the public square is "loyal" to Israel according to this concept. One may assume that many Arabs would have liked to blow up public places or to pelt rocks and Molotov cocktails on Israeli passers-by, and if they do not customarily do it, it is simply because they lack the guts to take the risk, knowing that they are under scrutiny by the Israeli security apparatus which they must resent and they fear the punishment if they are caught. But as it is, many hundreds among them have murdered Israeli soldiers and civilians, or behaved violently against police, or obstructed public traffic, or posed bombs and car-bombs in Israeli cities and streets, or collaborated with outside Palestinian terrorists, or incited against their country and its citizens, or volunteered to fight for Jihadi causes abroad. In any case, all in all, they have acted with malice against their state and in a much more strident way than anything known in liberal democracies. Today, much of the "work" of killing and hostile attacks against Israelis are committed by Palestinians from the territories, while Israeli Arabs applaud them without limitations. That "loyalty" is not even akin to that of ultra Orthodox Jews, who do not respect the moment of silence in commemoration of the Jewish and Israeli dead, either in the Holocaust or in Israel's wars with the Arabs, despise the national flag, avoid military service, and declare openly their anti-Zionist attitudes, but are nonetheless held as "loyal" because they do not sow terror around them. The difference is that at least the *Haredi* Jews do not encourage or sympathize with terrorism, do not rejoice over the death of Jews and do not actively undermine the state of Israel. Despite that fake "loyalty" attributed to both dissident populations, the state is exceedingly liberal, lenient and permissive towards them, in disregard to their obstructing roads on Sabbath or to other occasions of protest, burning tires and garbage containers, attacking vehicular traffic or otherwise demonstrating without license when they please.

Loyalty is also an active concept involving voluntary shouldering of the responsibilities and obligations of citizens towards the state and not only enjoying the benefits of its generosity, which both of those dissenting populations elect to dodge. For otherwise, in an ideal world, loyalty means accepting the country and its inhabitants' values, identifying with their goals, learning their language and culture, partaking of their national holidays, respecting their symbols, serving in the state's armed forces and defending it in times of war. The Arab population in Israel (like the Jewish Haredi ultra-orthodox) does not meet most of these yardsticks, and that is understandable, as neither the Arabs could be expected to be Jewish, nor the Haredi Zionist. But at the same time, Israelis ought to shed their illusions regarding the "loyalty" of their Arab and some of their citizens, and the Arab minority ought to desist from its demands to full rights as full-fledged citizens when they know that they are not and cannot be, nor do they display any will to become. The obsessive notion of security in Israel also encompasses internal security in the country which safeguards all citizens from all dangers domestically. It is noteworthy, that whenever the state confiscates private property for public use (roads, military training, development, etc), or seeks to enforce urban planning laws, which are openly ignored by the Arabs in Israel, or wishes to re-assert its property rights on state lands that had been illicitly taken over by Bedouins, violent clashes become inevitable as the police tries to enforce law and order. In such cases, leaders of the Arab minority, including members of the Knesset who should know better than that, taking advantage of their immunity as MK's, openly take the lead of law-breaking, often confronting the security forces, and then complaining that the police acted with "excess of force". This signifies that not only do the Arabs refuse to partake fairly of the heavy burden of the overall security like all other citizens, but they also impose another burden on the strained security forces who have to deal with them as a security hazard domestically.

The Arabs of Israel are also not content with the special links between Israel and the world Jewry either. They complain that while the Jewish state would rather encourage more Jews to immigrate to the country, by virtue of the Law of Return, it rejects the right of Palestinians, the native inhabitants of the land, to return to their land under the "Right of Return". They realize at the same time, however, that the Middle Eastern conflict is not about "justice" or "humanism", but about history and nationalism. Historically, the land had been inhabited by two Jewish Commonwealths for an entire millennium BC., and more recently it was the Arabs who rejected the UN resolution for partition, and attempted by force to eliminate the fledgling Jewish state. When they failed in their endeavor, their pride was hurt and they cannot forgive Israel for having won successive wars, despite the fact that it has been vastly outsized, out-resourced and outnumbered by the Arabs. Since the Arabs had triggered the war, Israel has consistently refused to take responsibility for it and for the refugee problem that ensued. Nationalism, because this land, which was destined to satisfy the needs of both nations for statehood and self-determination, has in fact become an arena of rivalry, where the exclusivists, who want everything for themselves at the expense of others, have lost so far, while the compromisers, who showed readiness for partition and for peaceful neighborliness, have won at the end. That scenario l has duplicated itself during the armistice times of 1949-67 and thereafter on Temple Mount, the Tomb of the Patriarchs in Hebron or in other areas of potential friction (the Joseph Tomb in Nablus, the Jericho Synagogue or Rachel's Tomb near Bethlehem), where Arabs refused to share and wanted everything for themselves, have always lost. This is a state of affairs the Arabs cannot bear.

Tiny Israel, which only miraculously and at a great cost emerged victorious from the 1948 war, was still deemed by the Arabs after that war as a fleeting episode. They have in fact incessantly readied themselves for another round of combat, and another, feeling that the little, weak, besieged and fragile Jewish state did not possess the requisite vitality to survive in the long haul. They have also realized that the Jewish people worldwide supports the new state, not only when at war but also in constantly reinforcing its ranks, lending to it financial aid and sustaining it politically. Above all, the Jewish Diaspora constitutes a large pool of potential immigration, to which the Arabs remain inimical by definition. It is then evident, that though the Arabs pretend that they have no quarrel with Jews as such, but only with Israelis and Zionists, they confuse between the three and use them interchangeably. They have always cursed the Jews and damned the Zionists when fighting against Israel, condemned the Jews when they fought Zionism and Israel, and despised and hated Israel, the product of Judaism and Zionism. No wonder then, that they have adopted the war cries of "Slaughter the Jews!" even prior to the inception of Israel (e.g. the Hebron Massacre of 1929, the Hadassah Convoy slaughter of 1948), and up until the October 2000 Uprising of the Umm al-Fahm Arabs in Israel. The political platforms of Arab and Islamic movements, like the PLO and the Hamas, their political speeches and religious sermons, school textbooks and daily small talk, are all replete with the negative and hateful interchangeability between Jews, Zionists and Israelis. Hence the permanent war that they constantly wage against all three, wishing all three eliminated.

Even Israeli democracy, which affords the Arabs the highest degree of liberty anywhere in the non-Western world, has been under fire by discontented Arabs. This is bizarre, *prima facie*, because it is precisely this minority, which is protected by Israeli liberal democracy, in which the court system acts a as watchdog for its rights, has been the most vocal, violent and destructive in its attacks and accusations against this system. They constantly accuse Israel of not being a "true democracy", as if they had known any better elsewhere, of racism, apartheid, incitement and discrimination, thus demonstrating that they have never internalized the meaning of democracy, and that by condemning it they in fact indict themselves by exposing themselves as having misunderstood its functioning and the philosophy behind it. One cannot obviously blame them for misunderstanding the significance of democracy, but one is certainly entitled to remonstrate them for refusing to learn from what they misunderstand. For they have ample opportunity in Israel to learn and internalize what it means, having enjoyed the unique opportunity in the region to absorb and experience its blessings. But instead of being grateful for its teachings and for their good fortune as Israelis, and attempt to improve themselves so as to deserve its benefits, they are trying to bend it to their needs and to teach the Israelis its "true" contents as if they had invented it, and not been immature novices who try desperately to absorb its principles, without much success. For some of them, Egypt and Syria are models of democracy, and some of the greatest preachers of "true" democracy among them have returned from visits to the capitals of those murderous regimes, as before from Communist Eastern Europe, full of praise for their "democratic" systems, which though "republican" have been often transmitting power from father to son, thus producing such innovations as "republican monarchies". At the same time, in Israeli democracy, which for the first time in Arab cultural history, has granted them the right to vote and be elected, they have perpetuated for years the tyranny of the Bolshevik regime in their Communist Party, under its various forms and appellations. Alternately, they often practiced much of the system of the rule of the notables in their villages, over the meritocracy represented by the young and educated among them who have grown up in the Israeli system. In either case, they choose empty slogans and irresponsible rhetoric over responsible civil activity, and sometimes give more and more precedence to their obscurantist religious sheikhs over secular and modernizing leaders.

If a serious dent has been lately eroding those patterns of behavior, it is only due to the blessings of the Israeli democratic culture which they absorb in Israeli campuses, through the free media and the market places where they mix with others, and thanks to the legal and political systems which imbue them with these values. Naturally, they constantly deny that they have learned anything positive from Israel, but as much as they refuse to acknowledge the benefits that the Israeli system has bestowed on them, they gradually convert to them, though they still have a long way to go. For now, they act and speak as if democracy only means gaining larger budgets from the Israeli government, participating in elections, demonstrating violently in the streets and abusing the parliamentary system, using force against the law-enforcement agencies with impunity, violating the laws of the land at will, obtaining from the courts judgments that please them and expressing their wishes without hindrance, capitalizing on their expectations that democracy must allow anything to happen under its permissive aegis. They do not understand that democracy also means preserving law and order, fulfilling security and civil obligations towards their country, defending its institutions against trespassers, at times subjecting desires and liberties of the individual in favor (or in defense) of the public interest, educating all citizens to loyalty and civil standards of behavior. They do not comprehend, for example, that they cannot expect extra-treats by the state to their youth, if the latter demonstrate against the very existence of the state on campuses and in the streets, hoist the flags of the enemies of their country, refuse to serve in any security capacity, and drag their feet when it comes to levying taxes or participating in national efforts that do not serve them directly. They cannot conceive a situation where, when they refuse to fulfill any duty towards the country and constantly side with their country's enemies even in a state of war, they cannot be permitted to have the deciding vote in their country's affairs with which they do not align themselves. When they demean the courts' judgments, incite their public against the law in their speeches and sermons, pelt policemen and passers-by with rocks and throw Molotov cocktails at passing traffic, launch violent demonstrations and kindle arsons in woods and cultivated fields, that can hardly be dubbed good citizenry.

In democracy, the citizens take part in the creation of the public good, assuming that the welfare of the public and of the individuals in that public interact and are inter-related. But the Arab public in Israel has been cultivating the assumption that public good means the welfare of the Arab public, while the welfare of the state as a whole has never been their concern. That means in practice that in their political, social and other activities, they focus on their sectorial (Arab, Palestinian, Muslim, National, communal) interest only. For example, the leaders of the Arab public in Israel have never been caught "red-handed" showing any concern for Israel's economy, security, tourism, unemployment, development, trade deficit, water problems or the reserves in foreign currency that are vital to Israel's standing in international markets. They only worry about those issues as they regard their Arab sector, or other Arabs and Palestinians. When some Arabs served in the past as vice-Ministers in the government, they were always in charge of Arab affairs in their office (health, education, religious affairs etc) while they seldom evinced any interest in the whole country in those domains. For them, service to their public, and only to it, was the very *raison d'etre* of their public function. But they are quick to blame any Jewish Minister or Vice Minister who, in their minds, discriminated favorably Jews over Arabs in their domain of operation. Even the "affirmative action" accorded to them under the Rabin Government (1992-5), in which favorably discriminatory budgets were showered on them, to improve their education and lend support to Arab local councils, was undertaken by Jewish Ministers under a clear government policy. But the government had a general consideration for the needs of the country, and decided to favor the Arabs in specific areas in order to help them overcome the long years of backwardness. But it would be unthinkable that any Arab minister would or could overview the general needs of the country and provide for the entire population on a basis of balanced and sound policy, nor certainly lend priority to the Jewish sector when that was warranted.

Evidently, the freedom of organization in Israel allows the Arabs to establish parties and found associations as they wish, which they would certainly be unable to do in the Arab countries they admire. For example, in the "democracies" or Jordan and Egypt, not to speak about the tyrannical regimes of Syria and Iraq's Saddam, Islamic parties as such are or were forbidden, and in the latter no party other than the ruling one could run for elections. In Israel, by contrast, 6 Islamic mayors were elected in Arab towns, and the Islamic Movement has delegated two of its leaders to the Knesset. But this does not prevent the Arabs in Israel to whine about "oppression", "discrimination" and "obstruction of free opinion" in a country that is tolerant to the point of taking up tremendous, some say suicidal, security risks. But the elected officials among them do not comprehend the degree of destructiveness, for themselves personally and for the state as a whole whose citizenship they claim, that the system they cultivate implies. For they alienate themselves from the foci of power, by the very fact that their election to anti-establishment, and often to anti-state bodies, relegates them to the margins of Israeli society and politics. Secondly, their identification with the anti-state margins make the Jewish majority suspicious of their schemes and designs, shun any association with them and prefer to unite the Jewish left and right rather than depend of their votes. Thirdly, the elected Arabs have no chance to deliver what they promise to their constituencies, for they will always depend on the goodwill of Israeli governments whom they customarily criticize and despise. If they had elected to act from within the existing establishment, and if they had shown interest in the general problems of the state and not only in their own court-yard, then their influence and political value would have increased tenfold. Unlike the sectorial and isolationist positions adopted by the Arabs which bring them no benefit, all successive Israeli govern-ments, with varying degrees of success, have acted to promote the welfare of Israeli Arabs and integrate them within society. Had the Arab leadership in the country collaborated with the authorities in this regard, out of a constructive approach geared to hasten integra-tion and cooperation rather than criticism and vindication, then this would have no doubt eliminated the present sentiment of alien-ation that has been cultivated by their present leaders.

Democracy is not applied only in the central government, which is far remote for most citizens of the country, but primarily in local government of which every individual partakes. In the Arab sector, the democratic process of electing the Mayor personally, and the members of his municipal council according to party lists, has trig-gered a revolution inasmuch as young forces have, to a large extent, superseded the traditional rule of clans and notables. The Islamic Mayor of Umm al-Fahm, for example, who was elected by 80% of the votes, could have therefore no longer needed to be elected only by his clan (one of four), or by the supporters of his movement alone. His energy, modesty, dedication to the town and its popula-tion and total devotion to the service of his public, won him repeated election by the sheer power of his popularity, efficacity and charisma. It is evident that he, and many other young leaders like him, who were tutored under Israeli democracy to lead and serve their constituency, have brought a sea change in the Arab local government in Israel, made it more representative, less corrupt and less nepotism-driven, more effective and more responsive to the electorate, than at any time before in Palestine and Israel. But the revolution is far from complete, for there survive now two types of local government: the old model of notable and clan rule, who whine about their "discrimination" and "oppression" by the authorities, while in fact their administration is defective, corrupt and unable to raise the requisite taxes to finance itself; and the new and young administrators, typically represented by the Islamic Movement, who thrive in their new role, act instead of complaining, get their citizens to contribute their time and money and bring about progress and development to their villages, without demonstrating against the central government or begging for its reluctantly disbursed budgets and then blaming it for their own failures.

The "Vision papers" were not the only blatant documents written by the Arab elites to delegitimize Israel, for many other organizations, which can operate freely only in the liberal and democratic Israel they wish to dismantle, are piling up one anti-Israeli document after another, under the guise of "human rights", "decolonization", "legality", "peace with Justice" and the like[45], which not only contribute to the trends of Palestinization of Israeli Arabs and their secession from the state, but are spread to international bodies and augment the delegitimation of their country in the world. These new trends, which have grown after Israel had foolishly allowed the PLO leadership to come into the Territories and foment incitement and rebellion there, had not always been there. Following the events of October 2000, only when the close to two -million (20% of the total) strong Arab community of Israel rose in rebellion against the Israeli authorities, in support of their brethren who had declared their Al-Aqsa *Intifadah* in the territories, was a commission of inquiry set up by the Israeli government to investigate the root

---

[45] See, for example the *Mussawa* Report of November 2006, written by Yussuf Jabbarin, which under the pretext of producing a n "Egalitarian Constitution to all", in fact advocates collective national rights for Israeli Arabs. 12. The latest was a book in Hebrew, *The Hidden and the Obvious with Israeli Arabs,* Jerusalem, 2016.

reasons of the uprising and the tragic killing of 13 Israeli Arabs which resulted thereof. This author was asked to appear before the Commission as an expert witness, and as a result has set out to summarize his analysis in various publications[46]. They all lead to the inescapable conclusion that all the efforts and attempts at multi culturalism deployed by Israel had been in vain, much like in other countries, due to the Islamic arrogant upbringing, which when heeded does not permit Believers to submit to the rule of Infidels. In this situation of a continuous and intractable conflict, where there are no prospects for a settlement, and in the face of demographic developments and the ambition of the Arabs, including Israeli Arabs, to see the Palestinian "right of return", implemented, the pressure on Israel to choose between its Jewish character and its democratic regime might impose on it an acute dilemma and an urgent need to make momentous and dramatic decisions.

---

[46] See the two-volume report of the Orr Commission to investigate the October 2000 Arab Rebellion, that were published in 2001.

Chapter Six

The Claim of Racism, Incitement and Apartheid

Without any doubt, the most recurrent theme one detects in the long litany of Israeli Arab complaints and whining against Israel is that they are discriminated against institutionally by the establishment of the state of Israel, regardless of their vastly improved condition within Israel compared to all other Arabs in the Middle East space. We have discussed above several economic and social aspects of discrimination and we have noticed that some of them are of the favorable kind, from which they draw benefits, like the exemption from military service, while many of them are self-inflicted due to the many measures of separation and hostility that they evince towards the Jewish majority. In this situation, those who behave like enemies or foes in this skin-thinned society, which has just survived the Holocaust and is now threatened externally with annihilation by other Arab enemies and especially by the blood-thirsty and hateful Iran regime, cannot expect to be treated kindly by those who feel threatened by it from within. And yet, most Israeli public, and certainly the law system, usually tackle fairly and generously the Arab population and stands for its civil and human /rights. We did not hear about any attempt by these Arab-Israeli citizens who are eager to integrate and to achieve equal rights, to denounce the calumniations and threats of other Arabs and Muslims in international forums to blacken Israel's reputation and heap on it abominable libels. Quite the contrary, leaders of the Arab Joint List who attended the UN General Assembly in 2019, did not travel there to lobby in defense of their country, whose representatives they avoided, but instead met with the Palestinian delegates, the chief instigator of the anti -Israel libels and calumniations there. In this chapter we shall deal with the most recurrent specific derivatives of discrimination which have become part of their daily litany of complaints and accusations against their country, in whose socio-political system they claim they wish to integrate, but against which they do not relent from propagandizing and inciting. Those domains are: Racism, Apartheid, and Incitement. The first two are interrelated and we shall debunk them jointly, the third must be turned in reverse and hurled back at the Palestinians as we shall document below.

Racism and Apartheid

The other day, when I exited from a live radio and TV interview in the Israeli Broadcasting service in Jerusalem, I was assigned the same taxi with a leader of the Arab Joint List, who was my interlocutor in the panel debate a few moments early, where he had repeated his anti-Israeli racism and apartheid mantra. While we were waiting to depart, I engaged him saying: "now that your Arab audience is not present to applaud you, can you tell me where do you see racism and apartheid in this country?"I elaborated at length about the meaning of those terms and about the obligation of every public figure to refrain from making irresponsible and untrue statements, which although they may win politicians a few votes in the next elections, they certainly will ruin in the long run his relations with this society. Yes, I said, Israeli society, like most societies has been afflicted on the popular level by manifestations of racism, towards the different in color, like the Jews of Ethiopia whose skin stigma is what differentiates them from others, like Blacks in America and Africa immigrants in Europe who are not always looked upon favorably by the biased populace. But to generalize in this fashion on the same Israeli establishment who went to great lengths, expense and risks to fly to Israel, tens of thousands of Jews from Ethiopia in the 1990s, more often than not clandestinely, and dub it "racist" is simply a distortion of reality. No one reluctant to take such a step on a vast scale, running into its hazards and into the difficulties of absorbing all those new comers into Israeli society and economy would venture and invest so much ingenuity, take so many risks and improvise so many unconventional ways to import to its turf immigrants he dislikes or shuns.

The commonality of Jewish culture between Israel and all Jews of the world, and the commitment of the Jewish state to world Jewry, is what has made possible the assembly of Jews originating from 100 different countries into the Jewish state, turning the ingathering of the Jewish Diasporas into the country's main purpose and historical destiny. Its success to bring in in the few decades of its existence, more than half or world Jewry (7 out of 14 million) is the best evidence of its dedication to this mission. Certainly, some Ethiopian new immigrants have felt discriminated against, either by Israeli parts of the populace or by police, and that is usually imputed to their skin difference. But all new waves of newcomers to Israel: North Africans in the 1950s and 1960s and Russians (including Ukranians and Central Asians) in the 1990's, have encountered this sort of "racism" in their time. It is natural that in a country of immigration, the new wave of migrants pushes upwards the previous one and takes its place, until the next wave inherits that stage of novices and suffers from the stereotypes, biases and stigmas that had characterized the previous one. So, the issue of "racism" is not specific to the black Ethiopians, but to all newcomers until they are absorbed within the organic tissue of society.

The generalization that we hear from Arabs in Israel and elsewhere about the Jewish state being racist, is even more absurd, bearing in mind that Jews are not a race, although the Nazis dubbed them so (and an inferior one at that), in order to facilitate the application of their racist theories differentiating between their Aryan *ubermensch* and all the rest. This sort of race theory is abhorred by and in Jewish lore, and is unthinkable in any Jewish or Israeli society. For one thing, one encounters Jews in all colors and shapes, from clear blond complexion in Eastern Europe, to dark black color in Africa. Such a multi-color society, united by a millennial tradition and culture, hailing from the ancient Hebrews of the Davidic Kingdom down to the modern state of Israel, cannot be called racist. It is certainly no more racist than the American or European societies which confront this sort of social frictions emanating from prejudice and bigotry. Arabs are the last to complain about racism, given that in their tradition blacks were held in low esteem, and it was they who dominated much of the slave trade until recently. Their wealthy rulers always coveted white women into their harems and the feminine white complexion won much praise in Arab poetry. Above all, scientifically speaking, the Arab ethnicity, just like the Jewish, is categorized under the Semite "race", having in common the Semite languages of Hebrew and Arabic, and the average Arab today looks not much different from a Jew. Looking at the two types walking the streets of Jerusalem, one would have a hard time distinguishing between them, save if they wore each their traditional differentiating clothing. Therefore, Arabs dubbing Israelis racists, just as their immigrant compatriots or coreligionists call their European host societies, as an expression of hostility and alienation, has absolutely no intrinsic validity to it. It is simply a way to air frustration or to smear a rival with stigma in the multi-cultural and multi-colored societies where we live.

The Arabs can certainly claim that they are disliked by Israelis, but that is not racism. They are not disliked because they are Arabs, exactly as Jews dislike and abhor Nazi Germans, not because of their Aryan origins but due to their abuses against the Jews. Arabs, notably Palestinians, who have sent their operatives to blow up Israeli families in their buses, restaurants and malls, or Israeli Arabs who have committed hostile or terrorist acts against their country, cannot be expected to be adored by Israelis. The French and the British never liked their German enemies (they dubbed them *Boches)* nor have the Americans showed much sympathy for the Japanese during the Pacific War, following Pearl Harbor or while they were killing thousands of Americans in the war. Even when the Americans dropped the bomb on Hiroshima and Nagasaki which many have seen as a racist act, for the simple reason that it was never dropped on any European nation, it was a false accusation. The Americans had indeed termed the Japanese with a disparaging "japs" during the war, but as soon as the war was won, both Germans and Japanese became the best allies of the West. Conversely, due to the unfolding Cold war, it was the wartime allies Russians/ Soviets who were now targeted for stereotypes and bigotry. Similarly, although Jews of Islam have flocked to Israel carrying in their luggage the deep contempt and hatred to them by their Muslim masters in North Africa and the Middle East, they did not join the war front against the Arabs with hatred, as a racist manifestation. They disliked the Arabs for their enmity towards Israel, their attempt to destroy the Jewish state and their constant undermining of it. How can anyone call that racism, anymore than any other hostile rivals can encounter an enemy which they detest, simply because he is the enemy?

It is "racism" which generates apartheid, as pre-Mandela South Africa had been disgraced by much of the world for being the epitome of both racism and apartheid, and Israel was conveniently accused of allying with that abhorred regime. Therefore, without attaching much importance to deep comparative analysis, it has been easy and expedient for Arabs in general and Arabs of Israel in particular, to add the smear of "apartheid" to blacken the reputation of Israel, even though a nation cannot apply apartheid without racism, because the latter is the prerequisite of the former. As a result, the Arabs easily tucked the one upon the other and hurled them routinely together as a matter of course in order to disgrace, discredit and demonize the Jewish state. It was even geographically convenient for the Arabs to emphasize during the international conferences of the African Union, to show at the two edges of the Continent, Israel and South Africa plotted against all Africans. This calumny has been diffused in campuses around the world by the champions of BDS, baptizing one day in their annual calendar as an "Apatheid Day", without having any idea what racism or apartheid meant, and without bothering to verify the validity of their libelous insult. It is easier, after all, to be critical than to be correct. A black south African leader who visited Israel recently and watched its open democratic society, mocked openly that anti-Israeli libel and dismissed it totally as emanating from total ignorance. Posing the same questions as I did to my Arab interlocutor following that join panel on radio and TV in Jerusalem, made that accusation ludicrous and unsustainable:

    a. In apartheid South Africa, colored people could not, under the law of the land live in the same neighborhoods or buildings, nor travel in the same buses or other means of transportation; Have not many Arabs in Israel moved to the mixed cities of Haifa and Acre? And have not many Arabs moved to new Israeli cities in Upper Nazaretn (Now Nof Hagalil) and Carmiel in the Lower Galilee? And have not individual Arabs, in the thousands, bought or rented apartments in those Jewish cities?. Has anyone prevented them from doing so, and have the Israeli courts deprived them of their protection when they faced scattered objections to their wishes? All this, while one is hard pressed to identify a single reverse case where Jews have asked or were permitted to dwell in the exclusively Arab villages;

    b. In apartheid, no colored person could sit in the white Parliament. The Arabs in Israel not only occupy 15 seats, from which they defy the majority rule, but they even challenge the basic laws of the country and seek its delegimation, knowing that similar moves in South Africa would send them to jail.

   c. In apartheid inter-racial intermarriage is forbidden by law. Do Arabs know of such a law in Israel? Aren't they aware of the Israeli girls who were married to Arabs, converted to the Muslim faith, moved to their villages and raised their children as Arab/Muslims?. Has anyone banned them from doing so in spite of the hostility and tensions existing between the two populations in Israel today?

   d. Apartheid countries prohibit social mingling between races, while in Israel, in most work places one can find Jews and Arabs, working shoulder to shoulder.

Propaganda tolerates minor deviations from the truth if the purpose is to diminish and denigrate the enemy. But blunt lies the like of which only Nazi propaganda was capable of, become so obvious and refutable in our world of communications, where paradoxically the media provide immediacy, that anyone engaging in them is likely to be found out and exposed and discredited in minutes, save when one who does not let facts and reality alter his "religious" ideology or set views, and prefers to ignore what contradicts them. This happened in the most blatant and humiliating way to President Abdul Nasser during the 1967 War, when he reported on the phone to King Hussein that his troops had destroyed the Israeli Air force and were on their way to Tel-Aviv, while in fact they lay in tatters in the most disastrous and devastating rout in their modern history. What did he gain from that? Just mockery and demeaning by the Arab populace, which forced him to stage an act of resignation from his post, which he was "begged to abrogate" a day later. Arabs of Israel know in what fortunate situation they live, and when they embark on these smearing campaigns against Israel, they are well cognizant that it is a pure libelous propaganda, designed to compensate their "lost face" for the defeats they undergo once and again.

Incitement

The most blatant and frequent accusation by Israeli Arabs against Israelis in general and especially their leadership, which is used widely and skillfully manipulated in election campaigns, is the claim of "incitement" against them. This is bizarre because their entire experience in Israel follows the general Arab practice of libeling and calumniating the Jews, Zionism and Israel, which is regarded as legitimate "criticism", but when Israelis, and especially their leadership, repulse their abominable defamations and libels, then accusations of "incitement" are hurled against Israel. We have seen above the false condemnations of Israel by the Arabs with regard to discrimination, racism and apartheid, which they think are legitimate, but when one shows how those unjustified recriminations amount themselves to racism, then they are branded as "incitement". For example, when PM Netanyahu described the Arabs of Israel as "flocking " to the polls during the 2015 national elections, aiming that as an incentive to his followers to do likewise, lest his party's votes were outweighed by Arab votes, an outrage of "racism" and "infamy", and a charge of "incitement" were hurled at him. And he, instead of confronting them and charge that their subversive and often hostile attitudes toward the state did not justify voting for them by any Israeli voter, he stood in humility before them and apologized for a sin he did not commit. For if a Labor or Democratic voter in Britain or America had warned likewise his compatriots from the danger of voting for the Tories or the Republicans, that would be considered totally legal and part of political struggles between political parties. Donald Trump did as much, or much more, in his campaign against Hillary Clinton in 2016, in his aggressive, demeaning, humiliating and diminishing campaign against her, but no one attacked him for incitement of his rival, especially after his tactics proved successful. Those are dirty tactics, all right, but that is politics.

The Arabs in Israel draw much of their incitement in reverse against Israel from their Palestinian and other Arab brethren, and from some of the abominable curses and defamations that are heard daily in the speeches of Ra'id Salah and his disciples in the mosques and gatherings of the Islamic Movement throughout the country. Arab Knesset members, who honor Palestinian terrorists who have murdered Israeli civilians and their children, and were elected against the will and political commitment of a majority of the Knesset members, could not be ejected from the Israeli Parliament which they despise and wish to undermine, only due to the Israeli Supreme Court blockage, because the super liberal Justices, who give priority to civil rights and freedom of speech over the security and wellbeing of their country, even when its honor and respect are threatened, actually act against public opinion beyond what other Western democratic countries would tolerate. The Justices always claim that they much consider proportionality in their judgment and always weigh freedom of speech and dissident acts or libels by politicians, even the most abominable ones, against the actual or potential damage that they cause to Israel's security and sovereignty. But what gave them the assurance that they would always excel in weighing security damages actual or potential, better than the far better experienced officials who are no less considerate than the judges?. Some of the latter have never heard a shot fired nor seen a round hurt anyone. How then could they be so sure when they exonerated the Israeli Arab Knesset member, who embarked on the Turkish *Marvi Marmara* ship, which illegally penetrated Israel's waters and confronted violently the Israeli Navy which imposed the maritime blockade, and resulted in nine Turkish fatalities and other Israeli casualties?. Moreover, if we mention the irreparable damage caused to the relations between the two countries and the huge reparations Israel was made to pay to the aggressive Turks, who were accompanied by the recalcitrant Arab Israeli MK, one in his rights senses can understand how the super-lenient judges came to their verdict. Israelis were again incensed, not only by the outrage caused by the Supreme Court, but again by PM Minister Netanyahu for yielding to Ankara's demands and instead of confronting it and make it shoulder the guilt, paid compensations for a sin Israel did not do.

The most frequent and most insistent Arab accusation of "incitement" hurled at PM Minister Netanyahu against the Arabs of Israel is precisely the domain which they find the weakest in their long litany of complaints, because at close scrutiny one finds that Arabs of Israel incite the Israeli public against its government and libel the Israeli public in general much more, and much more seriously and frequently than the other way around. In the elections of 2015, Netanyahu in effect called upon his voters to rush to the polls, because the Arab voters, who avowedly pledged to dislodge him from office, were "flocking" (or "streaming") to the voting stations. The Arabs immediately manipulated that straightforward and legitimate prodding of his constituency as "racism", an "attempt to delegitimize" Israeli Arab voters, and called upon their constituents to flock indeed in order to outvote the Likkud party in their areas. If a Democrat or Laborite had warned during elections his constituency to crowd the urns in the US or Britain, in order to outvote their Republican or Tory rivals, would that be considered an incitement? Donald Trump had done worse than that to Hillary Clinton in the 2016 elections in America, by demeaning, libeling, humiliating and diminishing her, yet no one claimed that it was incitement. Because in open democratic societies those are the rules of the game. It is inconceivable that when the Arabs accuse Israeli pollical parties by all sorts of accusations, and hurl at Israeli political leaders all manner of allegations, that is considered legitimate "criticism"; but when the defendant refutes those allegations it becomes "incitement".

And once again, instead of the Prime Minister refuting straightforward those accusations and sending them back to the accusers, citing the endless incitement by Israeli Arabs against the Jewish majority, he again foolishly apologized to them, thereby gaining only more hatred and contempt on their part, they taking the apology as a vindication of their claim to their status of permanent victims of Jewish racism and incitement.

Israelis do not need to be prodded by their government to protest and refute the incitement of Israeli Arabs against the Jewish state, its government, its Jewish majority and the false allegations of discrimination, oppression and the like. Israelis are well informed and they monitor in the free press reports the abominable Palestinian libel against Israel for allegedly spreading the Coronavirus, they watch the recurrent Arab demonstrations against the Nation-State Law which is one of the basic laws of the state of Israel (would the US or Britain countenance demonstrations against their constitution or common law?). Israelis are also aware of the Arab opposition to any party in Israel which supports a Jewish majority in the land (that is virtually all the mainstream Zionist parties), and other abominations that Israelis consider a plain and direct incitement against the foundations of their state. Aware Israelis, who realize that the Arab claims of incitement are aimed to intimidate them and make them feel guilty, but stand as firmly against any alteration or amendment in the Jewish and Zionist foundations and symbols of their country, do not need any encouragement to repulse those demands in disgust and to do it loudly and clearly, which would amount to "incitement " for the Arab propaganda. So be it, and it will be done. The Arabs are sometimes sustained in their complaints by naïve or oversensitive Israelis who cannot bear their dear state of Israel to be reproached, criticized, blamed or threatened. But life goes on, dogs will always bark as the convoy of hope and creativity proceeds, and in the final analysis the convoy will get to its destination.

Israelis watch and listens to what the Arab stations around say and show, and what the findings of the vast research done in Israel on Arab matters reveal. We learn, for example:

1. That the Palestinians, including in East Jerusalem where the curricula were amended only recently under Israeli rule, teach their children that the map of Palestine includes all of Israel, and the Israeli cities of Jerusalem, Haifa, Acre and others are Palestinian cities. Palestinian adults have absorbed long ago these ideas, since they and the Palestinian authorities have fallen into their own propaganda trap by internalizing that nonsense and believing in it; but when the same is bequeathed to children through school teaching, there is no chance in the world that the idea of two states could penetrate into their hearts. That constituted pure incitement against the Israeli state and its borders and inhabitants as far as the Israelis were concerned. No protest was registered among Israeli Arabs to mend the situation, as when they remained indifferent when the PA pursued its acts of terror after undertaking in Oslo to renounce violence and settle all problems peacefully, or bombarded and killed Israeli civilians with weapons that were banned from the West Bank and Gaza in the first place; but when this reproach is made to them, wondering about their indolence, they usually retort that they do not interfere in PA affairs, contrary to their open obligation to identify as part and parcel of the Palestinian people, as they had done during the Land days or the *Intifadahs*; but when Israel retaliated against Gaza, the Israeli Arabs suddenly woke up and regarded themselves as part of the "aggressed" people who were their kin;

2. The Palestinian kids are taught at school that not only is Palestine designed to replace Israel, but even in the entire map of the Middle East Israel does not exist. Instead, its area is defined as "Arab lands conquered prior and subsequent to

1967"[47]. The Israeli-Arab resistance to the Jewish majority in Israel, its violent opposition to the Nation State Law, and its rejection of the Jewish and Zionist foundations of Israel seem to have no other purpose than corroborating and coordinating the attainment of these goals with the Palestinian educational system. There can be no more blatant incitement against Israel than this subversive sort of "education" that talks peace and coexistence but readies the next generation of Palestinians for the long protracted war ("armed struggle").

3. Arabs in Israel not only engage in crime in their villages, the result of their culture of shrugging responsibility for anything they do and throwing it on others, but they refrain from participating in the welfare of their community, do not lift a finger to defend the country that they claim must protect them, resulting in increasing rates of crime in their midst. Their criminality not only keeps police busy beyond the proportionate rate of the Arab population in Israel, but they also have the nerve to incite against it by claiming that its efforts to fight crime are inefficient. Though their culture of lawlessness is at the root of their criminality, they impute it to those who are trying to combat it. It finds expression in:

a. "Honor killing" in their families, which only brings dishonor to them' as young women are murdered right and left, despite (and perhaps due to) the great quantum jump in the self-assertion of Arab women thanks to the encouragement that the blessings of higher education has provided them with. Yet, the blame is put on the Israeli authorities who should be blessed for the progress they have triggered, often much to the dissatisfaction of part of the Arab leader-

---

[47] *Modern Arab History and Contemporary Problems,* Part II for Tenth Grade,, No 613, (Ramallah/Gaza, Palestinian Authority p. 66).

ship which prefers to keep women docile and submitted so that they can be killed and silenced systematically;

b. The feudal system of notables in the Arab society did not completely vanish by the democratic order introduced in local elections in Israel. There are places, like Kafr Manda, which did not accept the outcome of free elections in 2020, with families and clans continuing to rival bitterly each other and fire at each other, resulting in violence and crime. They simply cannot accept that bullet cannot replace the ballot, and they throw the blame on Israel. That is pure incitement against the society that has shown them democracy and progress instead of recognizing their immense debt to the enormous advance that was effected by the state of Israel. Instead, they accuse Israel of "not lifting a finger" in the Arabs' benefit; what finger did they lift to eradicate crime in their midst?.

c. There is an enormous amount of criminal activity among young Israeli Arabs, the double of their rate in the population, and also translating into the numbers of incarcerated interns in Israeli jails, just like in the jails of Europe. Part of it emanates from "ideological" motives, such as contraband, stealing weapons, falsifying papers, driving without permit and such, which are committed not necessarily for economic benefit but sometimes as a way of defying Israeli laws and rule. Once again, blaming the Israeli authorities when they are themselves impotent to arrest these trends in their society, they engage in incitement against Israel instead of being grateful for the goodies they benefit from in this generous, well-ordered and civilized society among which they dwell.

d. Arabs forget that a pact exists between democratic societies and their rulers, that it owes them protection, from inside foes and outside enemies, while they owe her to mobilize their forces to defend her from her enemies and foes. But when they side with her enemies against her every time she happens to be in confrontation with them, how can she be expected to run to their defense when they are in danger? We do not live in a society of overlords where Arabs are expected to fight and shed their blood only in their domestic criminal battles, while the even more dangerous outside defense circle from which they benefit is reserved for their Jewish serfs to risk their lives for. And yet, they deny that they are protected by Israel and blame incessantly its failure to protect them. How absurd can things get?

e. Not only do not the Arabs lift a finger for their own protection, let alone for the defense of the country that they claim theirs, but they do everything to disrupt the functioning of that defense system, by harassing and humiliating those few among them who volunteer to serve, by refusing even to fill civilian duties, like nursing, as a service to the state, or fill in for key workers in essential public functions whose tenants are recruited in times of emergency. Shunning these vital functions that any citizen in other countries performs willingly, and even attempting to disrupt them, is an open challenge to the system that is worse than incitement, because it doe not only encourage people not to lift a finger to the nation's survival, but actually does it on its own.

4. Palestinians live out of handouts from the West, yet this is what they teach their children about the failure and the impending collapse of that civilization, of which Israel views itself as part. The denigration of the West, a view that many Arab and Muslim countries share, amounts to more than an incitement- it is a threat, preparing Palestinian kids to take

over from the declining West and Israel. A Palestinian textbook for 11th graders notes[48]:

In the present period ... of unprecedented material and scientific advances,... scientists in the West are perplexed by the worrying increase in the number of people suffering from nervous disorders, and the statistics in America in this matter are a clear indication of this (p. 3).

Western civilization had flourished, as is well known, as a consequence of the links of the West to Islamic culture, through Arab institutions in Spain, and in other Islamic countries where Muslim thinkers and philosophers took an interest in Greek philosophy...(p. 4).

Western civilization, in both its branches -the Capitalist and the Communist- have deprived man of his peace of mind and stability, when it turned material wellbeing into the coveted goal..., his money leading him nowhere, except to suicide (p. 5).

There is no escape from a new civilization which will rise in the wake of the material progress, and which will continue to lift man to the highest spiritual life... Is there a nation capable of fulfilling it... There is only one nation capable of discharging this task, and that is our nation... No one but we is able to carry aloft the banner of tomorrow's civilization (p. 12).

We do not claim that the collapse of Western civilization and the transfer of the center gravity to us will happen in the next decade or even in 50 years, for the rise and fall of civilization follow natural processes, and even when the foundations of a fortress become cracked it still appears for a long time to be at the peak of its strength....

---

[48] *Outstanding Examples of our Civilization for 11th Grade* (Ramallah/Gaza, Palestinian Authority).

Nevertheless [Western civilization] has begun to collapse and to become a pile of debris... We awoke to a painful reality and to oppressive imperialism, and we drove it out of our lands, and we are about to drive it out of the rest (p. 16).

5. With regard to Jews, Zionism and Israel, the incitement is blunter and more direct, as it appears in another primer in Palestinian and Arab schools[49]. Though this material would not be allowed in Arab schools in Israel, and was eradicated even in East Jerusalem where Jordanian curricula prevailed until recently, it has been shared by Arab nationalists and Islamic circles all around the Middle East. One textbook of this sort explained:

One must beware of the Jews, for they are treacherous and disloyal...

Racism: mankind has suffered from this evil both in ancient and in modern times. Satan, has in the eyes of many people, made their evil actions appear beautiful [to them]. Such a people are the Jews[50].

The clearest examples of racist belief and racial discrimination in the world are Nazism and Zionism...

Israel's mean, brutal, inhuman, fascist, racist, genocidal, ethnic cleansing wars --- the Jewish gangs waged ethnic cleansing against innocent Palestinians... large scale and appalling massacres, saving no women and children...[51]

It is mentioned in the Talmud: " We Jews are God's people on earth. He forced upon all the nations and races of the world to serve us, and he spread us through the

---

[49] *The New History of the Arabs and the World,* (Ramallah/Gaza, the Palestinian Authority).
[50] *Islamic Education for 8th Grade*(Ramallah/Gaza).
[51] PA TV, 14 May, 1998.

world to ride upon them and hold their reins. WE must marry our beautiful daughters to kings, ministers and lords and enter our sons Into the various religions, so that we will have the final word in managing those countries. We should cheat them and arouse quarrels among them, so they can fight each other. Non Jews are pigs whom God created in the shape of men in order to be fit for service to the Jews, for God has created the world for them…

6. And finally, the religious ritual which is always present, beyond national, ethnic and individual hatreds. Every pious Muslim in the world repeats 5 times a day the opening *sura* of the Qur'an (*Fatihah*) which is an essential part of the prayer, either individually in solitude or in community in the mosque. A key verse *(ayah)* figures in that so-often repeated prayer which regulates the life of every Muslim, because anything else that happens during that day between the prayer times only intermittently fills the intervals between the prayer times which are the essential, as if all the daily schedule is arranged in function to the time left by the prayer. During the recitation of the text of the prayer, the key verse is that which proclaims the Muslims as "those who have benefited from the Grace of Allah, unlike those who attracted His wrath and those who have gone astray". The former are the Jews according to the most authoritative *al-Jalalayn* commentary, and the latter are the Christians. Both are bedeviled and demonized, but much more so the Jews, because to incur the rage of Allah is far more incriminating than "going astray", out of ignorance or oversight. These words are Allah's, therefore they stand beyond any refutation or denial, they are immutable and eternal. It is easy to imagine the horrendous idea that an Israeli Muslim who goes to the mosque or prays in private, five times

a day, like other pious Muslims worldwide, makes of his Israeli neighbors whom he also perceives as his oppressors.

On another level, on Friday prayers at mosques, almost no Imam escapes the temptation to cite the Qur'anic verse which states the animal origin of Jews who descend by Allah's orders from "apes and pigs". The abomination which is also attributed to Allah's own words, hence their eternal validity, not only stains the Jews by the abhorrent symbol of the pig, which Muslims also detest, but also implies that they are not humans but of the animal kind, interacting with them exactly like the Nazis who imagined them as disgusting rodents, who can (or must) be disposed with. These are plain words or blood -chilling racial, religious, ethnic and genocidal incitement, which though imposed from above by religion and not man-made, they are repeated more or less enthusiastically every day by all Muslims, not least the Arabs of Israel, especially the Muslim radicals among them of the Muslim Movement, north and south. Such a repeated daily ritual cannot help condition the negative and hateful view by the pious Muslims of the Jewish neighbors he encounters wherever he turns.

The Jewish majority in Israel, has established a flourishing advanced and prosperous country, lifting up with them their ungrateful Arab minority into levels of prosperity, education and progress unknown in the Arab world. Yet, these Arabs wish Israel to shed its Jewish and Zionist character and to renounce their Nation-state Law and its Jewish symbols to please them and make the state of Israel a "country of its citizens", so as to melt in the long run into the Arabs populations and acquiesce in its own disappearance. Why? Because it is so successful? Are the Arabs suggesting a better model which could turn Israel into the like of Jordan of Yemen, or better yet- Gaza? They can simply forget it and they better begin to disengage from the pipedreams they have been cultivating in their midst, taking Israeli democracy and leniency as license to subvert it and liquidate it. Their only recourse is to replicate the lived experience of the present author, that will be detailed in the Summary of this volume. He is the scion of a converted family of Berbers in Morocco, whose roots there go centuries before that land was invaded and conquered by Arabs/Muslims from the Middle East, exactly similar to their own claim that Jews from the West have invaded their Palestinian land and taken it over.

Along the years, Morocco was Arabized and Islamized so that the ancient Jewish minority felt persecuted and oppressed, similar to what the Arabs of Israel now sense in Judaized Israel. They understood that the world had changed and the fundamental fact of an Arab North Africa could not be altered. Therefore, they abandoned their 2000 year patrimony and left, mostly to Israel, but also to other Western countries, and they have for the most part made a new start and reconstructed their lives there. So can the Arabs of Israel chose to reshape their lives in one of the 22 Arab countries, while enjoying the advantage of melting in their own culture and language, a benefit that the Jews who were constrained to leave Morocco (and the rest of the Arab world) did not enjoy. They will suffer hardships and heart-breaking experiences for a generation, but then they relieved their lives for ever from the frictions and fears that had afflicted them and basked in the delight and bliss of living in their cultural environment. Naturally, the Arabs of Israel will opt to stay and struggle in much better and opportune conditions than those offered to the Jews in Morocco; they can be adamant and decide to struggle for the bi-national state that they can and will never obtain. Thus, short of accepting reality as it is, as I had accepted the reality of Arab and Muslim Morocco as long as I lived there, they will erode their own forces in a hopeless battle for something they cannot achieve and they will end up miserable in their bitter and uncompromising dissidence rather than integration into Israel, enjoying its many benefits and shouldering its duties as deserving citizens. I suppose that they will regard these words as "incitement" too, but their lot will not improve as a result.

An interesting parallel, and possible debacle, can be drawn from the experience in Czechoslovakia of the Sudeten Germans. There too, it was a relatively limited territory, where the dissident German population, which regarded itself as Bohemian, found themselves living in the new state of Czechoslovakia after W W I when the Austria-Hungary Empire was dismembered, like the Arabs of Israel when the Ottoman Empire and then the British Mandate were dissipated and the new Israel was created. The crisis was triggered in 1938 by Pan-Germanic demands to annex that area to emerging Nazi Germany, in contrast with the Arabs who remained in Israel after 1949, who regard themselves as part of the Palestinian people to which they claim affiliation and aspire to connect. The German *diktat* was imposed at the Munich Conference in 1938 through the betrayal of France and Britain, who hoped thereby to bring peace to Europe, but instead precipitated disaster on the continent, including on themselves, while the rebelling German minority, who did not know to count the blessings of their existence under the Czech liberal democracy, ended up being exiled into Germany to unite with their German folk. Pan Germanist Czech politicians had raised the German question, and a conflict had built up between Czech and German nationalists since the 19th Century where while the German speakers wished to participate in erecting a German nation-sate, its Czech speaking population insisted on keeping Bohemia out of such plans. But with the growing nationalism of the early 20th Century, at the end of W W I, the Germans of Bohemia asked for the right of self-determination, which aimed at joining the German speaking territories with Weimar Germany. But that was not to be and the Sudeten remained part of Czechoslovakia. The American delegation to the Paris Conference determined that it was best for the Germans of the Sudeten to remain part of undivided Czechoslovakia, much as the Partition Resolution of the

UN left large Arab minorities within the prospective Jewish state, which constitute today the hard core of the Arab minority in Israel.

German minorities remained restless and several of them attempted to proclaim their union with Austria but failed, due to the Czech refusal to relinquish lands inhabited by Germans in their state, despite the fact that in 1921, they accounted for 90% of the population, which amounted in total to almost a quarter of all Czech populations. There claim was territorial- namely that Bohemia had always been part of the Bohemian crown, the predecessor of the modern Czech state. In fact, the St Germain Treaty of 1919 confirmed this thinking, though some German groups continued to strive for a separation based on ethnicity. It is fledgling Israel's determination to keep the Wadi Ara Arab populated region within Israel after it was redeemed from Iraqi occupation during 1948-9, which contributed a large part of Israel's Arab population (The Triangle) to the Jewish state. The same rate of about 23% Germans in all Czechoslovakia, headed by Konrad Henlein (the Czech Ahmed Tibi of those days) continued to clamor for separation, and then the Great Depression broke out and the German regions of Czechoslovakia were particularly hurt due to their export-oriented industries of Jewelry and glass. Against that background of unemployment and extremist groups, German irredentists grew, like the Sudeten German National Socialist Party (SdP) that gained popularity among the Sudeten Germans, something strikingly similar to the Arab Joint List in Israel today. The increasing aggressiveness of Hitler (which could be compared to Nasser or Saddam Hussein, or ISIS in their time, or to the Ayatullahs in Iran and their Hizbullah proxis in Lebanon), prompted Prague to prepare for war to protect itself, but Hitler advanced his position as the advocate of all Germans (like Saddam, and then the Ayatullahs for Palestinian Arabs), after he achieved the *anschluss* with Austria (Saddam in Kuweit, Iran in Syria and Yemen, ISIS in Syria and Iraq). Thereafter, Konrad Honlein agitated for autonomy in his district, and in

April 1938 declared the *Karlsbader Programm* which demanded total equality of the Germans with the Czech people (like the Arab Vision Documents,and the Joint List's rejection of the idea of a Jewish majority in Israel, after their gains in the 23rd Knesset).

Only the debacle was fortunately different:The frightened and spineless Czechs yielded to the cowardly Franco-British capitulation. Chamberlain's personal messenger to "mediate" between the parties was doomed to failure, for the Germans made outrageous demands, like the Arabs of Israel today, which could not be accepted by any sane political party. But unlike the Czechs who yielded because they did not trust in their power to resist and to fight, Israel has wisely rejected both the Vision papers and the aborted attempts of the Joint List to seize the balance of power in Israeli politics and decide the fate of the country to its whim. The demands made by the Sudeten Germans were: To transfer the Sudeten to the German Reich, to organize a referendum in the German-majority district to approve that annexation, to convene a Four power conference (which would include the cowardly powers who had signed Munich), and create a federal Czechoslovakia in which the Sudeten would constitute an equal part (like the various proposals of federating Israel with Jordan and Palestine so as to outweigh it in an Arab majority). President Benes rejected those demands and declared his choice to fight rather than to surrender. But in the end, after the British and French yielded to Hitler, the Germans walked in without a shot. The outcome was that in October, the Germans invaded Czechoslovakia itself and subjugated it, except for the Bohemia-Moravia enclave which retained its nominal autonomy under the Nazis. The day of reckoning and revenge arrived when defeated Germany had to repatriate millions of its nationals who were expelled from Russia, Poland, Czechoslovakia and elsewhere.

The Israelis should learn that lesson lest its grows on them into a national tragedy, remembering that suicidal democracy leads to the sort of disaster that the Jewish people cannot afford to undergo once again; the Arabs in Israel should learn that better to make peace with the reality and make the best out of living in a free and prosperous society, than playing intransigence to its extreme and then losing everything and becoming third generation refugees all over again.

CHAPTER SEVEN

Israeli Arabs in the Web of Palestinian, Arab and Islamic Nationalisms

The United Arab List, which purports to represent all segments of the Arab public in Israel, and has indeed gained ca 80% of their vote in the March 2020 elections which enabled it to appear in the newly elected Knesset with 15 self-confident MKs, has made history in Israel by its very unprecedented new capacity to impact the Israeli complicated and divisive inter-party and entire political system, down to its very ability to put together a government to rule the land. Due to its composition of Arab nationalist, former Communist and Islamic components, that hodge podge medley of divergent political convictions and orientations, they could so far only rally around the negative purposes of dethroning the Israeli Prime Minister whom they hated and demonized. They could also prevent the formation of an Israeli government unless their outrageous demands are accepted and heeded, but they will have to crystallize in the long run some positive elements of a common platform which would conform to the Israeli narrative of the Arab-Israeli dispute, and to the basic political requisites of the Jewish-majority Zionist state, if they stand any chance to survive as one united and solid Arab bloc that plays by the rules of Israeli politics and by the overarching rules of the Jewish and Zionist state of Israel. In other words, if and as long as the Israeli Arabs let themselves come under the influence of various Arab and Muslim tendencies, which divert them from their

Israeli nationalism and Identity, they will look like a chariot harnessed to three studs which are prodded to race in three different directions, namely they will exhaust their energies to stay in place and mark time.

If the incompatibility between Israel and the Arab world makes so difficult, almost impossible, to attain unity of purpose and of values between Israel and its Arab population, even much less in their *modus operandi*, how much more so when it comes to resolving the insoluble Palestinian issue in this zero-sum game, where every party's win is the other's loss, and vice versa. The tenets of liberalism that impose on every democracy to take risks to its very existence while consecrating the principles of freedom and democracy at any price, pose the very weighty question of the desirable ladder of priorities, in case these principles contradict each other, for example when honoring the one-man-one-vote principle means jeopardizing the very democratic principle when a majority, for example, of pious and fanatic Muslims like ISIS, aspires to take over power and also declares its commitment against democracy. What is more important and what is better: democracy or the rule of the majority? This is not only applicable for addressing the problem of a rebellious Muslim minority internally, but also for dealing with external issues. For a liberal and democratic country cannot ignore the right of self-determination of others, is not supposed to occupy others' lands or treat them otherwise undemocratically. But then, what does one do when these lofty principles run counter to others in the order of priorities of a nation? Britain occupies Northern Ireland and the Falkland Islands, one as part of its national territory, the other as a colony; what democratic rule can justify this state of affairs? Israel is accused of occupying Palestinian territory in the West Bank and Gaza, but what if surrendering it to any Arab authority jeopardizes its very existence, as has happened after the withdrawal of Israel from Gaza has brought upon her a shower of missiles which sends its population to shelters and its children to a permanent state of post traumatic disorders? And how did the Arabs come to rule that area if not by conquest, occupation, forced Arabization and Islamization, in the first place, etc? And what about the claim to proven historical, archaeological, religious, ethnic and native rights on those sites that stand at odds with the Arab and Muslim claims to the same, which the Arabs of Israel also live by?

In an attempt to act as fairly and as liberally as possible, in a democratic spirit that has been alien to the world of Islam since its inception, Israel has been implicated during the decades of its dispute with the Arab and Muslim worlds[52] in confronting them firmly despite their uncompromising attitude, at the same time that it tried to handle the domestic question of its Arab population which has become inseparable from the general issue of the Middle East Conflict. For, it was the Palestinian problem which initially dragged the Arab world to war against Israel and provided the territorial aspect of the dispute, and it was the rise of Arab nationalism which confronted Jewish nationalism (Zionism) and emphasized the national and ideological angle of the struggle, before Iranians and other non-Arab Muslims injected into it the religious element which made it intractable. In this state of affairs it became impossible to negotiate the unnegotiable and the conflict has been driven into an impasse. Trying to tackle by liberal and gentle means of negotiation and compromise this difficult situation, so as to manage or resolve it as long as it fell within negotiable quantitative political issues, before it escalated into the sphere of qualitative and absolute religious creed, clashed with the tyrannical and definitive doctrinaire rejection of the other by the Arabs and Muslims.

Israel's desperate attempts to provide an agreed solution has been manifested in the variety of options it brought up for discussion and consideration, which were always met by the absolute rejection

---

[52] See R. Israeli, *The Intractable Dispute: Why the Muslims and Arabs Are at Loggerheads with Jews and Israel*, Strategic Books, TX, 2019.

of any avenue of this sort. The all-or-nothing approach of the Muslim world, which closes itself up to any reconciliation and concession, except when a mortal danger obliges it to do so (like today's Saudi Arabia and the Gulf States which face the Iranian threat) remains at the base of the evasive solution that was never found. The Arabs have been hostile for the most part toward Israel, except for the hopeful cracks in that attitude in this past decade, as was explained above. For the Arabs it is a matter of accommodating a neighbor, but for Israel it is a matter of survival in its natural environment. How much more so with the Palestinians who not only resent Israel and reject it lock stock and barrel, but also aspire to replace it. Hence the importance of understanding their national ambitions, in spite of the gloomy prospects of bridging over the widening gap between them and Israel's existence. The dialectic of their relationship has indeed become a zero sum game: either the one or the other, as things have transpired during the prolonged, and vain Oslo Process[53]. For what was acceptable for the one, turned out to become during the prolonged negotiations far beneath the minimum that would satisfy the other.

As one watches the Arab and Islamic world scene, one is dazzled by the almost universal vista of chaos, lawlessness, failed governability, disregard for human life, and a medieval-style cruelty when dealing with enemies and rivals, domestic and external. These unpleasant issues are not often discussed openly, only due to the self-imposed censorship in the West whose politicians, diplomats, officials, scholars and journalists have been cowed by the exactions of political correctness and terrified by "Islamic terrorism", whose name they do not even dare to pronounce. Even Turkey, which has long, and wrongly, been considered a model for the successful combination of Islamic moderation with modernity and democracy, is apparently sinking back into autocracy and a crisis of legitimacy of

---

[53] R. Israeli, *The Oslo Idea:the Euphoria of Failure*, Transaction, NJ, 2012.

power, due to its return to the old standards of Islam. We are often told by politicians and others, who are sycophantic at worst, ignorant at best, that Islam, like Christianity, is basically "a religion of love and peace", and that whoever acts contrary to those lofty ideals simply distorts the true meaning of the faith. But the challenging questions insistently emerge and refuse to die:

a. If so many Muslims participate in acts of terrorism, and they do it while invoking Allah's name, how can we say that they are "distorting" Islam?

b. If the Islamic crowds usually support these acts of terrorism, especially when directed against non-Muslims, where does that instinct of tolerating death and violence originate from?

c. While Muslims in general boast about their tolerance of other faiths, how come that they have historically endeavored to dominate and debase, if not to eliminate them in the vast areas that they conquered and continue to dominate?

d. What makes young Muslims whose families had migrated to the West, in order to supposedly improve their livelihood, flock back to the arenas of Islamic action, usually against Western nations whose shelter their parents had sought?

e. What is it in Islamic countries that makes them ungovernable at worst, subjected to monarchical or other authoritarian regimes at best, as the condition for their stability and survivability, temporary as they may be?

f. Why have Muslim countries consistently occupied the bottom of the scale in the UN reports of development, despite the fabulous petro-dollar wealth of some of them?

g. Why is the Muslim world so prone to violence, domestic and external, that most of the world terrorist organizations act from there or were born there? Is it only a problem of the legitimacy of the rule in those countries or some other common denominator which governs them?

h. Why is it that most unrest in the world occurs in Muslim countries, and most contemporary wars have been fought within them or on their borders?

i. What makes the populations of Islamic countries seek to emigrate elsewhere, while few, if any, outsiders wish to move therein?

j. Why has the West been hesitant to tackle these questions and confront them, rather than choose to conceal them from the public eye, like David Cameron's government in Britain, which commissioned recently an investigation of the Muslim Brothers with much fanfare, headed by eminent diplomat John Jenkins, and then ignored and hid its recommendations from his constituency and then resigned from power?

Hard and pertinent questions indeed, which become even more acute for us when touching upon the life, conduct, attitude and future of the destitute Palestinian people that we shall try to tackle in the following pages. It is true that not all Muslims are made of the same mold. As a comparative parable, we know in the setting of liberal democracies, that political parties come to life only during elections. Until then the hardcore membership maintains the structures of the organization, initiates and leads its activities, propagates its causes, recruits new membership and keeps it alive; but basically, all members, the hardcore and the grassroots, share the ideology and platform of the party, and act for its advancement. No one claims, that because there are various degrees of involvement and activity in any party, from the leaders, MPs, activists down to the voting constituents, who represent the "silent majority" of the rank and file, the party is split into different factions. Factions do occur in politics, but not necessarily based on the depth of engagement to the party's ideals. Islam in general acts and behaves the same way. It has a billion and a half constituents sharing the same ideology of the centrality of the Qur'an, the Prophet and the unity of Allah, finding in the daily execution of the same Pillars (*Arkan)* of Islam, incomplete and imperfect as they may be, a sort of validation of their membership in the universal *Ummah*. And like in political parties, there are often in Islam wide gaps between the stated ideology and the real world of practice, giving rise occasionally to various reformers and revivers who wish to take their followers "back to the roots". The activists among Muslims, whom the media and politicians, and some misguided scholars, like to dub "militants", "fanatics", "extremists", or "radicals" and "fundamentalists", or more fashionably- "Islamists", did not create an alternative faith, they are simply striving to implement the principles they were universally raised on, like the idea of the Jihad, hailing the activists who are out there trying to do it in person, and rejoicing whenever a spectacular feat, like September 11, "succeeds". The most devoted in this hardcore of activists, are those who are committed to sacrifice themselves in the process, and are held admiringly as *Shahids*[54] *(martyrs)* by their coreligionists, and derogatively as "suicide bombers" or "terrorists" by the rest of the world.

We observe within the Arab world an obsessive preoccupation with suspicions and fears of "schemes" and "conspiracies" mounted by others against them; a projection on others of their own disabilities, hidden wishes and unfulfilled dreams; violent counter attacks against the perceived schemes or enemies in order to justify their own bigotry and hatred; lending negative interpretations even to the most innocent events that occur around them; a persistent reluctance to trust others in general, and particularly for fear that anything divulged to them may be used negatively against the

---

[54] See R. Israeli, *Dying as a Shahid: Martyrdom in Islam,* Strategic Books, TX, 2018.

afflicted. In the gloomy days of the worldwide spread of the Coronavirus, as a case in point, many rumors and suspicions run across the Arab and Muslim worlds that the virus was the concoction of the US and Israel; maybe for that reason, many Arabs/Muslims in Israel were embarrassed to wear masks for protection or to otherwise admit that they were sick or might have contacted the disease, for that would mean that they yielded to the evil machinations of their enemies and were weak enough to succumb. In that culture of shame, to show weakness outwardly was the most humiliating and derogatory manifestation of one's stature and honor. These traits are more common in cultures and societies that have a propensity for emotionalism, superstition, fanaticism, hyperbole, unrealistic personal or collective ambition, egotism, and a complex of self-election. Since many of these characteristics are hereditary and transmittable by the reigning cultural environment, it is understandable how an entire nation, cultural or ethnic group can be "infected" by them, and can build up what anthropologists hate to call a "national character". Nonetheless, we all resort to the common usage of such stereotypes as "rich and greedy like…the Jews", "beautiful like…the Greeks", "thieves or misers like…the Romanians or the Scotch", "prompt and precise like…the Swiss, or the Germans", "murderers like… the Nazis and the Mongols ", "corrupt and fanatic like …Arabs, Muslims", etc.

Certainly, we all tend to detect these attributes in our rivals, enemies and any individuals or collectives we tend to debase or dehumanize. This case study of Israeli Arabs however, which is based on historical documentation and lived experience of many years, and not merely on untested assumptions or accusations, will try, to the extent possible, to substantiate through concrete examples, all the claims advanced here. Conversely, and quite surprisingly, a series of recent and iconoclastic articles in the Saudi media, which were hitherto the leading anti-Semitic loudspeaker in the Arab and Islamic world, show that hatred, racism and annihilationist desires towards others, can be turned around or at least mitigated. If such newly written articles[55], which have exhibited a remarkable courage of their authors, have been trial balloons to test public opinion, and especially the views of the severe and puritanical Hanbali (*Wahhabi-Muwahhidun*) clerics who guide the Saudi government, before a concrete shift is effected in the public policy of the Saudis, this will have marked a truly revolutionary shift in the Islamic world. For it is certain that, if and when this trend firms up, and Riyyad is followed by other Arab capitals in the Sunni world, this would be a sign that some moderate Arabs and Muslims have come to regard the benefits that can be drawn from a partnership with Israel and the Jews, as by far outweighing the "dangers", or the loss of face, of making up with the sworn Zionist enemy. For, this daring move, if and when it happens, will be triggered by a wave of rare self-criticism in the real world of Islam, before it evolves into any positive relations with Jews and Israel. This kind of self-criticism is precisely what happened in Saudi Arabia in the Summer of 2016, and is hoped to be duplicated in the rest of the Arab and Islamic world, first of all among Israeli Arabs who are usually influenced by what goes on around them among their kin and coreligionists.

It is evident that, if there should occur a reversal in Saudi policies, that should prove that hatred, contempt and enmity can be turned around, if and when pragmatic considerations so necessitate. For when Arab and Muslim propaganda blacken for years the faces of their unrelenting enemies whose conduct was demonized internally and in the main international arenas[56], it becomes difficult, nay impossible, to reverse course and present the sworn rival of yesteryear as a worthy partner, even when the leadership wishes to do so. In this regard, Arab and Muslim leaders are the first victims

---

[55] See R. Israeli, *Paranoia, Inferiority Complex and Fanaticism: the Case of Islamic Attitudes Towards Jews,* Strategic Books, Tx, 2018, the Introduction.

[56] See R. Israeli, *Hatred, Lies and Violence in the Islamic World,* Transaction, NJ, 2013.

of their own propaganda which had for decades delegitimized Israel and promoted hatred and contempt of the Jews. But in view of the Iranian Shi'ite and nuclear threat on the one hand, and the retreat of America from the Middle East on the other, Israel remains as a viable option for a new order in that area, if the Arabs read the writing on the wall and take real steps to heed it. So far, the Palestinians being impervious to and imperturbable by this kind of reasoning which is not theirs, have not been affected by it. Their nationalistic sentiment stems from other sources from which Israeli Arabs also draw their inspiration.

We tend to regard nationalism as a militant movement that articulates the link between man and a particular land, what we usually call a "patriotic feeling," in Arabic *wataniyya (watan=* homeland or motherland). But there are more meanings to nationalism: a policy of national independence, a policy of rescuing industry and other economic assets from the hands of foreigners (by nationalizing them), a chauvinist feeling of narrow and exclusive identity to set us apart from others, or a doctrine that lends precedence to national values over international ones, and even provides a particular interpretation of national character and national values. Sometimes, this nationalism can come to be personified in the figure of a charismatic leader (e.g., Gamal abd al-Nasser, Saddam Hussein, Yasser Arafat, the prominent 20th Century leaders of Egypt, Iraq and the Palestinians, respectively). Nationalism is also a matter of identity. People seek their roots, and desire to locate the origins of their being in an attempt to determine who they are, particularly in this cosmopolitan world of ours where values and consumer goods have become universalized. At times, people look for a traumatic event or moment in their collective past (a revelation, a myth, an act of heroism, a founding father, or some historical cataclysm) that helps explain how in the remote past that happening had turned an inanimate material culture, or a haphazard collection of individuals into a culture, a religion, a people, a history, an ethnic or national group.

In the search of those links to the past, real or imagined, people often create their own mythology that lends depth to their history.

The genesis of Palestinian nationalism can be situated in the 1920's when the disintegration of the Ottoman Empire, which until then encompassed the entire Arab world and constituted the major focus of its Islamic identity, gave rise to Arab nationalism in general, based on cultural, religious historical, ethnic, territorial and linguistic affiliation, under the all-inclusive appellation of *Qawmi-yya* (qawm= tribe), which assumed a descent from ancient common ancestors originating from Arabia. However, while that definition paralleled the emergence of modern Turkish nationalism, which inherited the mantle of the extinct Empire, territorial, ethnic, dialectal and historical circumstances further established local and regional differences between, say, Morocco and Syria, Iraq and the Yemen, Saudi Arabia and Libya, and also gradually detached Palestine and the Palestinians from the idea of constituting Southern Syria. Hence the development over the years of local/territorial nationalism (the *wataniyya* mentioned above*),* which has come to divide the Arab nation into 22 separate and independent states, all members of the Arab League. Indeed, during the 1920's and even further down the years, many Arabs, including those who dwelt in Palestine, believed and articulated their strong identification with the idea of Greater Syria, which was thought as the most appropriate Arab entity to inherit the Ottoman rule in the Middle East. Only when the Middle East was divided, after World War I between Britain and France, and new entities were carved out of the defunct Empire, did a sort of European-style nationalism begin to take root in the Arab world, combining both territorial and ethnic identity into separate nation-states which have perpetuated that differentiation ever since. Syria and Lebanon came under French influence, while Iraq and Greater Palestine (including what is now Jordan) went to the British. As in other Arab lands, local national movements arose in all those countries, including in Palestine, which was allotted to Britain as a mandate by the League of Nations, with a view of building a "national Jewish home", without however, hurting the local Arabs' interests. The British, for their own perceived interests, then severed Eastern Palestine from its western part, in order to establish the Bedouin Emirate of Transjordan (later the Hashemite Kingdom of Jordan).

In view of these developments, a Palestinian national movement was declared, mainly founded and led by the young Mufti of Jerusalem, Haj Amin al-Husseini, a heir to the long-established Husseini notable family in Jerusalem, a sworn rival to the other leading Arab families of Jerusalem, like the Nusseibeh's and the Nashashibis. Often, against the counsel of his rivals, he and his followers frequently acted violently both against the British mandatory forces and the Jewish Zionists who were building their national home, supposedly under British sponsorship, as promised in the Balfour Declaration of November 1917. As explained above, nationalism can arise from situations of defining oneself as different and separate from the others. The British colonialists and the Jewish Zionists were amply used by Haj Amin as such walls against which rising Palestinian nationalism could rebound. He insisted that no Jewish entity could set foot in Palestine, hence his extreme opposition to Jewish immigration to the land, even after the Nazis came to power and the Jewish exodus from Europe desperately sought lands of refuge, chief of which was Palestine.

Muslim anti-Semitism and the Rise of Palestinian Nationalism
Husseini's fanaticism was augmented by his close association with the Muslim Brothers in Egypt, who were established in 1928. Suffice it to record here that the Muslim Brotherhood was created by Hassan al-Banna, who had all kinds of ideas that he introduced into Islam. He did not generate or invent a new Islam, but he updated it, so to speak. For example, he revived and added to the Islamic routine usage two major terms, which injected perhaps a new life

into the very operation of modern Islam. He addressed *jihad*, the holy war, which had been taken before by many Muslims around the world, as a spiritual striving, as an aspiration to be a better Muslim. That's precisely what it means, for *jihad* connotes an aspiration, self-strengthening or making an effort, which can also be intellectual, not necessarily military. From now on Hassan al-Banna said that, as of old: "*jihad is* an instrument in order to battle against the enemy." The problem is to identify who the enemy is. And the enemy is, he said, first of all the British who were occupying Egypt, and secondly the Jews who were coming to colonise Palestine, and who were battling against the local Arabs, Muslims, and Palestinians for the same land, and therefore Muslims were duty-bound to help the Palestinians against the Jews. And the second term was *shahid* or martyr. He said that whenever a Muslim dies in this battle it's not just death as when others are killed in other combats. This is the death of a martyr, because then the fallen Muslims are assured to go straight to Paradise. Therefore, not only were people who volunteered to the Muslim Brothers not afraid to die, they were eager to martyrize themselves in battle for the cause of Islam and in the Path of Allah, and so take the short cut from this tormenting life into eternal Paradise in the close entourage of Allah.

When Hassan al-Banna spoke of those terms, he revived a terminology which had not been operational since medieval times, when Islam was great and victorious, except in World War I when the Ottoman Sultan, at the instigation of his German allies, called for a Jihad against the British, without much effect. He was impressing upon the Muslims of Egypt that: "We are under the obligation to help other Muslims", that is to say those in Palestine; and not only to wage *jihad* against the Jews and the British, but also not to be afraid to die, because those who die are assured of their second life in Heaven, in the after world. Now one can understand how the Nazi Germans picked up the same ideas realising that this was the great occasion they were looking for, quite a great opportunity to penetrate the Islamic world. They had been trying to create in Egypt an office for propaganda, for their own cause, though the whole idea was dismissed at first in public opinion, showing how Egypt was ill-prepared for a negative anti-Semitic propaganda towards the Jews at that time. But here the propaganda machine of the Nazis in Egypt and later on in Palestine, together with the Muslim Brothers in Egypt since the 1930s, combined with the efforts of the Mufti of Jerusalem, Haj Amin al-Husseini, simply changed attitudes in the Middle East towards the Palestine and Jewish problems, whose consequences we suffer from to this very day. The Germans, who understood exactly what it was all about, jumped on the opportunity to tell the Arabs, and Muslims in general, that as a matter of fact both Germans and Muslims shared a common ideology. Both of them wanted to eliminate Jews, for both of them thought that Jews were treacherous in character, and so on, therefore, it was only natural for them to join their efforts and to collaborate in their elimination.

Against this background, we can understand that as soon as the war broke out, the Mufti of Jerusalem, Haj Amin al-Husseini was invited to Berlin. He established together with 60 more Arabs and other Muslim broadcasters and translators, a broadcasting service, which operated from Berlin until the very end of the war. And in the middle of the war, when more and more German divisions were needed for the eastern front, as Stalingrad went awry and the whole situation in the war front started to deteriorate, the Germans became very short on manpower, and therefore they resorted to the 38 divisions of *Waffen-SS* that they recruited to fill the ranks. *Waffen* means armed, the armed SS. The SS was created initially as a police unit, some kind of elite unit, and later they were needed for battles, for selected battles. Therefore their numbers and their tasks expanded from three battalions of police at the very beginning, into 38 divisions of fighting troops at the end of the war. Most of them were German, but since they ran short of recruits they started to enlist others: Lithuanians, Ukrainians, Romanians, and of course Yugoslavs and Albanians, and so on. So, in 1943, the concerned Nazis flew especially the Mufti of Jerusalem – who was settled in Berlin –to Bosnia, with the task to convince the Muslim population there of his newly-adopted militant Muslim Brother ideology, which he had embraced as a tool to achieve his goals in Palestine, and which prescribed that it was good to fight against the Jews who deserved elimination, and the British because they supported the Jews, and that if one fought that war, it would be considered *jihad*, and any casualty would be regarded as a martyr, hence his automatic salvation is guaranteed to eternity when he goes to Heaven to dwell in the vicinity of Allah. The Mufti went from place to place in the large Muslim agglomerations of Bosnia, especially the cities where in 1941 the imams of the major Muslim communities of Sarajevo, Tuzla, Banja Luka and Mustar had issued *fatwa* decrees, a sort of religious verdicts, forbidding the Bosnian Muslims to collaborate with the *Ustasha* government which had encompassed their country under German and Italian accord. And here comes the Mufti of Jerusalem, the prestigious spiritual authority with the reputation of his city, representing both the Nazis in Berlin and the Muslim Brothers in Egypt, and telling them: "No, no, no, forget about that. That verdict is not valid anymore." And in 1943, when he visited all those four cities, he convinced the local religious leadership to come out in support of the Muslim recruits, thus mobilizing some twenty one thousand people to serve in the Waffen-SS Division No 13, notoriously known as the *Hanjar* Division, which in Turkish and Arabic means simply "dagger", as a symbol of the war itself.

As the Arabs could not care less about Jewish extermination in Europe, and in fact their Chief Palestinian Mufti, Haj Amin, was collaborating with the Nazis, leading the two parties to share the idea of the "final solution", the infamous British White Paper had been issued by British Prime Minister, Neville Chamberlain, the co-author of the Munich Agreement, a few months before the outbreak of the war, and stipulated that 75,000 immigration certificates would be authorized by the mandatory power to incoming Jewish refugees, in spite of the exile from the land since 1937 of the Palestinian leader who already was seeking collaboration with Nazi Germany and was aided by the Nazis in the disturbances of 1936-9. According to Walid Khalidi, one of the senior scholars of Middle Eastern affairs, when that quota was exhausted, further Jewish immigration would be contingent upon Arab agreement, "which clearly would not be forthcoming"[57], because since the beginning of the Zionist settlement in Palestine, the Arabs had been dead set against Jewish immigration. It was supposedly the memorandum written by Musa Alami and George Antonius, two of the prominent Palestinian leaders, in the absence of Haj Amin, and signed by all Arab senior officials and submitted to the British High Commissioner in Palestine in 1936, which complained about British unjust policies in Palestine, that started to tilt that policy towards the issuance of the White Paper. Musa Alami joined the Palestinian delegation in 1939 to the London Round Table which directly triggered the publication of the Paper.

The White Paper, which came on the heels of the Arab Revolt of 1936-9, during which Nuri Pasha of Iraq mediated a truce between Haj Amin and the British, which held together only until the Peel Report was published in 1937, recommending the partition of Palestine between Jews and Arabs, and the second phase of the Revolt exploded in more violence and vitriol due to the report's recommendation which was totally rejected by Palestinian nationalists, supported by other Arabs and Muslims. The outburst of renewed violence caused the banning that year of the Arab Higher Committee, and Haj Amin its head fled to Lebanon, where the ruling

---

[57] Walid Khalidi, *Journal of Palestinian Studies* Vol. XXXV, No1, Autumn 2005, pp. 60-79.

French tolerated his continued fight against the British in Palestine. Only when the War broke out, he and his colleagues who were in exile with him, were asked to leave. They all sought refuge in Iraq and associated with a coterie of military and political leaders who supported the Palestinian cause. The British sent emissaries to Haj Amin so as to cater favor with the Arabs and to convince him to endorse the White Paper. Nuri Sa'id Pasha, the Prime Minister of Iraq, was instrumental in convincing Haj Amin and his colleagues (Musa Alami and Jamal Husseini) and he also agreed to put Iraqi forces at the disposal of the British in their war against the Axis, if a deal was worked out with Haj Amin. But apparently due to Churchill's opposition, the deal fell through. As a result, Haj Amin became soon involved with the Iraqi pro-Nazi Rashid Ali (Kilani) and his co-conspirators' coup, backed by the Muslim Brothers in Egypt. So, a front of anti-British and pro Nazi actors was formed in April 1941, which put in direct jeopardy the British domination of the Middle East. When the British sent troops and reentered Iraq in May to quell the revolt, Haj Amin (and Jamal) fled to Iran, thence to Turkey and then to the Axis countries and Nazi Germany, which he served until the end of the war.

But the crushing of the Rashid Ali coup only escalated Arab animosity towards Britain on account of its Palestinian policy, despite the White Paper and the London Round Table which were basically a positive response to Arab demands. So, the British, and their loyal ally Nuri Sa'id, wished, in the absence of exiled Haj Amin, and after his short-lived conspiracy with Rashid Ali, to see in the secular, liberal and highly intellectual and respected Musa Alami, the substitute leader of the Palestinians with whom they could do business, but the Alami-Nuri Pasha collaboration created Palestinian resistance, that was rooted in the pre-1936 Rebellion. The politically active Palestinians had been then divided into two camps: the Councillers who backed Haj Amin and sat in his Council, and his opponents led by Raghib Nashashibi, the patriarch of the century old rival family to the Husseinis in Jerusalem. During the Arab Rebellion, particularly in the second phase that generated the Peel Commission and its Report, scores of the Nashashibis were assassinated, and that created widespread hatred and retaliation between those two clans. The assassinations, guided by the Mufti from his exile in Lebanon, as part of his struggle against the British and the Jews, were calculated to eliminate his compatriot Palestinians who were suspected of collaborating with either of his perceived enemies, of passing information to them or of mediating the sale of lands to the Jews, which the Mufti had prohibited in a *fatwa* (religious verdict). Assassination had been established in Arab and Muslim lore as a persuasive comment against opponents on disputed policies since the times of the first Caliphs, most of whom had been murdered by dissidents.[58]

Of course, the opposition put the blame for those murders directly on Haj Amin, but his status as the most popular leader of the Palestinians, in spite, or perhaps because of his exile, was not diminished, precisely as the British were struggling to shore up their reputation among the Arabs and to tarnish the image of their bitter Nazi enemies. The disastrous and recalcitrant attitudes of the Mufti as the head of the Palestinian national movement, also brought frustration upon catastrophe on the Palestinians who, backed by other Arabs and Muslim Brothers, also rejected the November 1947 UN Partition Plan for Palestine, confident as they were that it was in their power to prevent any Jewish state from surviving under their relentless onslaught. But after their designs were frustrated during that war, most Palestinians found themselves under either Egyptian rule in the Gaza Strip, or under Jordanian rule in the West Bank, and their burning nationalistic fervor found itself subsumed under the respective nationalisms of their Arab occupiers. The same development unfolded among the Palestinian minority which

---

[58] Ibid. p. 70-1.

remained in Israel, and the many Palestinians who became refugees in other Arab states, mainly in Syria, Lebanon and the Gulf Area.

The disastrous leadership of Haj Amin, like its motivations which were distilled in his vicious hatred of the Jews and Zionists, that emanated from both his religious Islamic background and his nationalist fervor, was not discredited by his successors in the Palestinian movement. On the contrary, Yasser Arafat, who became the iconic leader of the Palestinians after him, had also a personal affiliation with the Muslim Brothers in Egypt, in addition to his embracing the revolutionary and violent nationalist path of his renowned predecessor and spiritual mentor in whose hateful and genocidal path against the Jews he walked in his terroristic career. Israeli Arabs, who reminisce the struggle for independence of their people since the days of Haj Amin and Arafat, when their chances to attain their goals seemed close at hand, have no reason today to relinquish what is for them a glorious and proud past, and sink in the gloom of today's politics which carry no promise for them anymore than for the Palestinians at large.

In any case, after the dust of the 1948-9 War settled, the Palestinians made an attempt to revive their nationalism under Ahmed Shukeiri and even to install a provisional Palestinian government in Gaza, before those efforts were scuttled by other Arab parties which were not particularly interested to see a new militant nationalism emerge in their midst and pose threats to them. It was not until 1960 that another scion of the Husseini family, a Palestinian refugee who studied engineering in Cairo, Yasser Arafat, who was disgusted by the inter-Arab manipulation of the Palestinians, established the *Fat'h* Organization, which is an acronym for the Movement for the Liberation of Palestine (in reverse order, because in the right order it would amount to *hatf*, unpleasantly meaning "sudden death"). *Fat'h* also has a historical-religious meaning of its own, signifying taking over and occupying lands in the holy wars (Jihad) that Islam waged against the world since its inception. Arafat later united his movement with other Palestinian splinter groups under the umbrella of the PLO (Palestine liberation Organization), that was supposedly to be overseen democratically by a PNC (Palestinian National Council), in which all components of Palestinian nationalism were represented. A constitution, dubbed the National Palestinian Charter, was adopted by the Council in 1964 and amended in 1968.

The 1967 Six-day War brought in another major development as both the West Bank and Gaza came under Israeli rule, and the latter found itself in control of about a third of the Palestinian people (1.5 million out of five). Arafat and his PLO now created a new focus for Palestinian nationalism, which was "liberation" from the "occupying Israelis". That effort was vociferously backed by the Israeli Arabs and enhanced by the fact of its acceptance and recognition by most of the world. While previously there was little resonance to the Palestinian clamor for "liberation" of their entire territory of Palestine from the "Zionist occupation", namely the elimination of Israel, the post-war claim or liberating their "occupied territory" gradually filtered into the nations which had previously supported Israel, and turned the PLO, from a shunned and criticized terrorist organization into a respectable movement of national liberation, of which the Arabs of Israel were usually proud, albeit without fanfare. The spread of PLO recognition by the world became the major achievement of Palestinian nationalism. Over the years, following two disastrous *intifadah*'s, (uprisings), the first during 1987-92, the second (Al-Aqsa, celebrating the place where it erupted) during 2000-2004, the Oslo Accords were negotiated and signed in September 1993, which were supposed to put an end to Israeli-Palestinian clashes. The Accords were signed by the PLO leadership, which won in consequence its gradual rule of the West Bank and Gaza, under the PA (Palestinian Authority), pending the attainment of full statehood, which would have fulfilled the wishes and aspirations of the Palestinians, and brought to rest the relentless claim of the Israeli Arabs that if that wish is achieved, their resentment against Israel would recede and they would feel more at ease living in Israel and taking up its citizenship once the clash of interests between the country and their people is resolved.

Beyond the territorial clashes with Israel, Palestinians, like other Arabs and Muslims, have been caught up in the periodically surging trend of radical Islam, which has always resulted in the tension, and often competition, between secular nationalism and the requirements of political Islam. This is nothing new if one takes into consideration the antecedents of Palestinian nationalism where Islam had played a prominent role and its dominant figure was simultaneously a political leader and an Islamic cleric, similar to Bishops Abel Muzurewa and Desmond Tutu in Africa and Makarios in Cyprus. In the 1920s, the Palestinian national movement was indeed led by the Great Mufti of Jerusalem, Haj Amin al-Husseini, who played up in religious terms his opposition to both the British and the Zionists. In the 1930s, Izz a-Din al-Qassam, another Syrian cleric who settled in Haifa, undertook extensive religious and political activities in northern Palestine that soon lent prominence also to his leadership. He then founded a militant group, *al-kaff al-aswad* (the Black Hand) as an instrument of armed struggle against the British and the Jews in contended Palestine. He called openly for Jihad against both, until the British killed him in battle in Ya'bed (northern Samaria) in 1935.During the Palestinian Revolt of 1936-9, the Muslim Brotherhood based in Egypt established a number of lodges in Palestine that later grew into a full-fledged network. The Muslim Brethren in Egypt and Palestine developed a two-pronged line of activism, not unlike its al-Qassam antecedent: struggle against both the British occupation and the perceived Zionist menace. The 1948-9 war of the Arabs against fledgling Israel split the Palestinian Arab population into five different slices. A majority fled east and either moved across the Jordan River to Transjordan or settled in the Jordan-dominated West Bank. A large group concentrated in the Egypt-dominated Gaza Strip. A minority, about 150,000 Palestinians, remained within the state of Israel and became known as the Arabs of Israel. Others moved to neighboring Arab countries, where most were confined to refugee camps, or traveled to Western countries and labor-hungry Arab countries, like the Gulf Emirates, to seek education, jobs and good fortune. But they all shared and cherished the historical tradition and narrative of their roots, exploits and leadership which confirmed in stone the genesis of their struggle against Zionism and the British for an independent Palestine.

0It is noteworthy, however, that Muslim radicals have not monopolized Islamic thinking and sloganeering either in the Palestinian national movement in general or within its offspring within the Arab Israeli population. Mainstream Palestinian nationalism too, like most local forms of Arab nationalism, has made use of Islamic symbols and vocabulary to characterize enemies, to imply modes of action again them, and to define the nature of the Palestinian community and its struggle, thus linking key religious and secular concepts.[59] Terms like Jihad, *shahid, fidayeen,* and the emphasis on the centrality of Jerusalem, all attest to the Islamic discourse that was ingrained in Palestinian nationalism at that early stage. Add to that the symbolism of the usage of Islamic terms in Arafat's *nom de guerre* (Abu Ammar), the very meaning of *Fat'h* as explained above, and the names of his PLA brigades:al-Aqsa, Hittin, Ein Jalut, Qadisiyya (all names of great Islamic battles), and you have a wide sampling of the depth and the extent of the Islamic hold over Palestinian nationalism.

In the 1980s, the Islamic bloc emerged as a powerful constituency in the West Bank and Gaza, boosted by three Islamic colleges in Jerusalem, Hebron and Gaza and by professional associations of

---

[59] See Sylvia Haim, *Arab Nationalism,* UC Press, Berkeley, 1962; N. Johnson, *Islam and Politics of Meaning in Palestinian Nationalism,* Kegan Paul, London, 1982; and Bernard Lewis, "The Return of Islam", *Commentary,* (Winter, 1976).

doctors, engineers, lawyers, students and others, which soon evinced their loyalty to the Islamic umbrella. But it was not until the *intifadah* in late 1987 that the Muslim radicals united their ranks under the Hamas banner and began to pose a serious challenge to the established leadership of the PLO. Since that time, Hamas has competed with Fatah for the souls and the political allegiance of the Palestinian masses. The signal was sent, loud and clear, that as against the national aspirations of the Palestinians and their ethnic-national-cultural claims, personified in and by the PLO, and led by Arafat, they posited the viable Muslim alternative, which engraved its Muslim mark on Palestinian identity, and was led by another popular and charismatic Gazan figure -- Ahmed Yassin, the presumed author of the Hamas Charter. Hamas sought to conquer Palestinian nationalism and counter the PLO Covenant, by promulgating its own Charter during the initial stages of the *Intifada* (February 1988). To comprehend the width and depth of the ideological rift between the two brands of Palestinian nationalism, let us briefly summarize their Charters which are contained in their platforms which constitute their respective identity cards, while keeping in mind that parallel tendencies developed among the Israeli Arabs, who have also divided between secular nationalists and Islamic zealots. So, when these different tendencies voice or announce their fealty to one party or another, they thereby also confirm their loyalty to the respective platforms as the hardcore of their ideology.

The PLO Charter not only spells out the boundaries defining the Palestinians as a people and a nation, including Israeli Arabs, with their inherent culture, ethos, ethnic affiliation and historical specificity, but also relative to other Arabs and Muslims. Above all, the Palestinians are called upon to crystallize their dreams and aspirations by means of a continuous armed struggle against a specific enemy – Zionism. Thus, the whole concept of a nascent Palestinian nationalism was made to hinge upon a dialectical interaction with its sworn enemy. This battle to the finish, as reflected in the Charter, does not allow for compromise or negotiation. The goal is to destroy Israel and replace it with a Palestinian state, thus fulfilling the Palestinian dream and also the realization of the Israeli nightmare. The Palestinian Covenant, indeed, traces, step by step, the contours of Palestinian nationalism, which remain intact in theory, though the Palestinians had pledged during the Oslo process to amend the clauses that run counter to the recognition of Israel. However, since the Palestinians were never asked by Israeli negotiators to recognize Israel as a Jewish state, or to accept Zionism as the national liberation movement of the Jewish people, Israel's recognition of Palestinian national rights and of the PLO as their national representative, remain one-sided. Israeli Arabs, who were never asked to renounce that platform, nor have they ever volunteered to do so, remain implicitly committed to the same principles, delusionary as they might be. Temporarily, the practicalities of the Oslo Process, though deficient in satisfying Palestinian ambitions, have for a time shelved the "armed struggle" as a tool of policy, and conversely generated a fruitful collaboration between Palestinians and Israelis on security matters, and turned temporarily to domestic development and state building, mainly under the guidance of Prime Minister Salam Fayyad, a pragmatic economist, who was been able to harness world economic support for construction and development, instead of watching the West Bank destroyed once and again by war and terror. This has helped change the image of the Palestinian leadership in the West, from terrorists to statesmen and partners for negotiations, much to the relief of Israeli Arabs who saw their dream of a nearby Palestinian state accomplished. However, when the negotiations between Israel and the PLO soured and the Oslo process came to an impasse, the Palestinians turned to threatening that they would discontinue their security cooperation with Israel and to accuse it of "occupation". Nonetheless, well concerned about the survivability of their PA without Israel's protective presence, they have been pursuing their collaboration in security, intelligence and economic affairs with Israel, though they continue to pay hateful lip service to their nationalism. We may summarize the nationalist message of the PLO thus:

a. Palestine is the homeland of the Palestinians, but at the same time Palestine is part of the greater Arab homeland, and the Palestinians are part of the larger Arab nation. This means that while the Palestinians express their attachment to the land of Palestine (*wataniyya*), and state their particularistic identity, they are also aware of their belonging to a larger ethnic whole (*qawmiyya*), in terms of ethno-cultural descent, historical heritage and linguistic affiliation. The Palestinian Charter also states that the Palestinian identity is an innate, persistent characteristic that does not wane away, and it is transferred from father to son. In other words, the fact that the Palestinians have been dispossessed and dispersed as a result of the disasters that befell them, does not detract from their nationhood or their national character. Moreover, Palestinianhood is defined not only by the land ("those who lived in the land until 1947"), but also by ethnic descent ("anyone born to a Palestinian father after that, within Palestine and outside of it"). Outside this ethnic definition, only Jews who were in Palestine "prior to the Zionist invasion,"[60] would be considered Palestinians, presumably a tolerated minority. So, apart from this exception, Palestinian nationalism equates nationhood-peoplehood with Arab ethnic descent. These are terms that the Israeli Arabs embrace enthusiastically.

b. The outer circles of Palestinian nationalism are its Arab and Muslim identities. Palestinian nationalism not only declares

---

[60] Arab literature marks the beginning of the Zionist invasion as the year of the Balfour Declaration in 1917.

itself to be part and parcel of Arab nationalism in general, but also alerts the Arabs that they all face the same enemies: Imperialism and Zionism, and therefore they should all be mobilized to push out the foreign threat. The Palestinians, however, being at the forefront of that battle, which is part of their identity, undertake to be the vanguard of all Arabs in that undertaking. Islamic identity is invoked in the context of Palestine as the Holy Land, hence the urgency to restore it to Islamic hands in order to safeguard freedom of worship there and the control of Muslim (and Christian) holy places, since a Christian minority exists among the Palestinians. Palestinians also regard themselves as part of the Third World ("the forces of good, progress and peace") that they also vowed to mobilize to their cause in the unified battle against Imperialism and Zionism. Peculiar to Palestinian nationalism, however, beyond the outer definitions of the threatening enemies who have to be monitored and thwarted, is the *sine qua non* assumption that the survival of Palestine and the Palestinians hinges upon the utter destruction of the Zionist entity, in all its manifestations: political, military, cultural, economic and social. This means that, unlike other nationalisms which aspire to independence, and to throw the yoke of their occupier (not to eliminate him), here we see the very *raison d'etre* of Palestinian nationalism inherent in the destruction of Zionism. This explains the stringent anti-Zionist objections voiced by Israeli Arabs when they refuse to join Israeli Zionist political parties and strongly repel the idea of the Jewish national state which denies theirs.

Prima facie, nationalism and Islam amount to a contradiction in terms: one is secular, the other religious; one is founded on particularism, the other claims universalism; one asserts this-worldly aspirations, the other promises the hereafter. Thus, while the PLO document encompassing their National Charter had been deliberated, debated, argued, amended and repeatedly voted upon before it was adopted by the PNC, the Hamas Charter was written by some of its leaders, and only then promulgated to the public. Consequently, while the PLO Charter has been considered a man-made political document, albeit of constitutional import, which also provides for the instrument of its own amendment (Art. 33), the Hamas document creates the impression of reflecting universal, immutable and eternal truths that are not liable to change. The PLO Charter uses political language, though sometimes bombastic and flowery, but the Hamas Charter is wholly anchored in Islamic parlance. Not only are Islamic symbols and vocabulary often invoked, but most articles are backed by quotations from the Qur'an and *Hadith*, the two sources of Islamic law that are acknowledged by Muslim radicals. The juxtaposition of the Charter's clauses with these holy texts inextricably lends to the former the sanctity of the latter.

Most interesting and relevant, is the PLO avoidance of direct attacks on Jews as such and purporting to struggle against Zionism only; but Hamas unabashedly also launches anti-Semitic broadsides against the Jews, often citing such notorious texts as the *Protocols of the Elders of Zion*. For the Hamas, Jihad is justified not only against Zionists who have "usurped Palestine," but also against the worldwide evil of Jews that threatens to undermine all societies, including the Islamic, in order to take them over and dominate them. Moreover, while also acknowledging the Palestinian particularistic aspirations to liberate Palestine (that is, after all, the top of the Palestinian agenda), Hamas regard this task as a holy and religious mission, incumbent upon all Muslims of the world. Thus, while the PLO Covenant appeals to the Arab world for support, the Hamas appeal is directed to the Islamic world at large. The very fact that Hamas declares its affiliation to the supranational movement of the Muslim Brothers, and its dedication to the reconstitution of the long defunct Islamic Caliphate (since the fall of the Ottoman Empire in 1923), indeed makes their program universal. The PLO platform had committed itself totally to a political and military *modus operandi* in order to attain nationhood, and that required the definition of the contours of Palestinian nationalism as hinging on the undoing of the Zionist enemy. The Hamas Charter also outlines a socio-cultural and religio-moral code of conduct and action, calculated to raise Islamic consciousness and to conquer Islamic societies from within before they turn to the elimination of their enemies.

For Hamas, since the entire land of Palestine is *waqf* (a Muslim holy endowment), accorded by Allah to all generations to come of Muslims, no one is allowed to negotiate it away. Hence, all the international talks, negotiations and peace conferences are deemed a "loss of time", and any intercession by foreign powers in the Arab-Israeli dispute as "imperialism's collusion with Zionism. While the PLO has envisaged institutions and civil processes to implement its platform, Hamas, leaning entirely on *Shari'a* Law, states its purpose to establish an Islamic state in the entire expanse of Palestine, with presumably state institutions as designed by the Holy Law of Islam. Palestinian nationalism, from this point of view, is also incorporated into the *Shari'a* as part of the universal Islamic *Umma*.

The division among Israeli Arabs reflects the same bifurcation that exists among the Palestinians in general, between nationalists and religious, therefore it is worth addressing the contours of that divide. Palestinian nationalists of the secular trend, who perceived the real danger of Islamic takeover, although they continued, until recently, to dismiss it officially as insignificant, also realized that modern and secular nationalism, based on the rejection of Israel and of Zionism was not enough to thwart the all -out internal attack of the religious trend against their very roots and vision. As against the flowery promises of the PLO to establish a Palestinian state through negotiations and cooperation with Israel, which the PLO leadership failed to deliver over the years, the Hamas posited an alternative way of all-out Jihad and struggle, and an appealing ambition to get it all by war, sweat, blood and tears. Somehow, frustration from negotiation with the Israelis which delivered no benefit for the Palestinians, created an ambience of resistance and sacrifice which seemed much more promising and feasible than the vain pledges of the PLO. This was exemplified for the rank and file Palestinians by the PA corruption, world travel and luxurious living of its leadership, versus the humility and modesty of the Hamas' Sheikh Ahmed Yassin and his cohorts, who cared about the people's problems and tried to solve them, instead of just squandering public money in an extravagant lifestyle the people could ill-afford. It was this state of mind which brought victory to the Hamas in the first democratic elections of the PA in 2006 where both rivals participated. The voters were disgusted with the PLO conduct and failures, perhaps more than they were enthused by the Hamas alternative. It is this state of mind and affairs which enabled the Hamas one year later to take over rule in Gaza, as a separate regime from the PA in the West Bank.

A national ethos, which took shape only within recent memory, was created by nationalists who confronted the Hamas onslaught over the past few years and wished to lend some depth to Palestinian identity and history. Indeed, the Palestinians today rewrite their history so as to incorporate in their ancestral background the Cana'anites and the Jebusites[61]. They profusely use the succession

---

[61] In addition to this prevailing theme in recent Palestinian publications, even such respected scholars as Sari Nuseibeh hark back to this myth as if it were a fact of history. See his jointly authored book with Mark Heller, *No Trumpets, No Drums*, Hill and Wang, New York, 1993, p. 32.

of calamities that befell them in 1948, 1967, 1970 and 1982[62] to pull their ranks closer; they cultivate, like the Jews of Israel, an almost mystical connection to the land; they promote their particularistic history and culture; they are today brandishing national symbols (e.g., flag, headgear, anthem, slogans, elected institutions, stamps, literature and poetry, passports, police and other security apparatuses), in preparation for assuming the paraphernalia of full-fledged independence, which will bring with it sovereignty, currency, armed forces, and all the other attributes of national existence that they are yearning for. A particular effort has been deployed, while demonstrating against the Jewish state laws together with Israeli Arabs, by stripping the Jews from any claim to the land and especially Jerusalem, and by rewriting history, insisting that Jewish history was a fraud and that the alleged Jewish attachment to the land was fake. Finally, they elevated the figure of Yasser Arafat, their national symbol for over a generation, almost to the level of a cult of personality, much to the exclusion of other major personalities in the Palestinian pantheon of heroes.[63]

Most significantly, these elements appear in Palestinian writings and thinking, not only as the self-defining traits of Palestinian nationalism, but also as the requisites setting them apart from, and

---

[62] The 1948 War, which generated Israel's independence and the problem of Palestinian refugees, is often termed *al-Nakbah* (the Disaster), and so is the defeat of all Arabs by Israel in 1967, which ended in Israel's takeover of the West Bank and Gaza. In 1970 the PLO was forced out of Jordan following Black September, and in 1982 the PLO was forced by Israel out of Lebanon.

[63] Previously prominent names in the Palestinian national struggle, such as Abu Iyyad and Abu Jihad, or his latter day aides such as Abu Mazen and Abu 'Ala', or his opponents such as the Hamas leaders or Faruq Qaddumi, were seldom mentioned in the Palestinian hierarchy of heroes. Only more recent heroes who died dramatically, like Abu Ayyash (the Engineer), or did not otherwise pose an immediate threat to Arafat, such as ailing Ahmed Yassin (until his death), were mentioned. After Arafat, the Palestinian leadership split between the PLO and the Hamas, and the unifying figureof Arafat has receded into the historical background.

often pitting them against, the enemy – Israel, Zionism, the Jews – because they are the ones who are perceived as posing a challenge and a menace to the Palestinians, and it is to them that the Palestinians feel constrained to respond. For example, the Cana'anite claim is clearly geared to legitimize the Palestinian title to the land that has been snatched from them, as they see it, by the Zionist Jews who built Israel, and who themselves base their claim on their line of descent from the biblical Israelites who had conquered the land from the Cana'anites. Thus, if the Cana'anites are neatly established as the forebears of Palestinian Arabs, then the claimed Jewish experience in the ancient Holy Land, which was based on aggression and conquest in the first place, becomes a fleeting episode in history, and the Palestinians come full circle by justly (a "just peace" is one of their slogans) restoring possession of the land to its original legal owners. But then, the Cana'anites were neither Arab, nor certainly Muslims. However, like President Sadat of Egypt who could strike the balance between his Pharaonism and his Arabism and Islam,[64] or Saddam Hussein of Iraq who claimed the ancient heritage of Mesopotamia's Hammurabi as his own, but did not also desist from his Iraqi, Arab and Muslim identities, so have Palestinian nationalists learned to juggle their identities with dexterity. It is also significant that the Cana'anite antecedent is particularly popular among Palestinian Christians who, aware of the massive doses of Islam currently injected into Palestinian (and general Arab for that matter) nationalism, would hark back to a non-Islamic past in which they can find solace against the pressures of revivalist Islam around them. At any rate, Palestinian nationalists, Arafat foremost among them, have discovered that old is beautiful. And so, much like the Prophet of Islam in his time, who lent depth to the history of Islam by claiming an Abrahamic root to it, the Palestinians today assert,

---

[64] See R. Israeli, " Sadat Between Arabism and AFricanism", *Middle East Review,* 2, Spring 1979, pp. 39-48. See also from the same author, *Man of Defiance: a Political Biography of Anwar Sadat,*, WEidenfeld and Nicolson, London 1985.

as part of their nationalism, that their ancestry was in fact Canaan-
ite, and that Jesus Christ was also Palestinian. This is music to
Israeli-Arab ears, though they do not dare yet to state it publicly lest
they provoke the Jewish majority among which they live, but some
of them are willing to avow those feelings discreetly in friends' ears.

Both Hamas and the PLO tacitly agree, however, to their joint,
though not necessarily coordinated, campaign to disinherit the Jews
of their patrimony. The religious Muslims insist that the entire land
of Palestine is *waqf* (as part of the earliest *fat'h* conquests by Muslims, which lend to it a permanence, sanctioned by Allah as a Muslim inheritance for all generations to come. Therefore, they accuse
the Jews as liars and usurpers who have manufactured a false history
in order to take over Muslim holy lands, a wording that is not far
from what we read in the Israeli Arabs' Vision Document. The PLO
people hurl more or less the same accusations against Israel and
refuse to share the common holy sites with Israel on the grounds
that the ancient inhabitants of the land were Palestinians, hence
their adamant refusal to recognize Israel as a Jewish state. Moreover,
in order to justify the annihilation of Israel, their peace negotiations
with Israel notwithstanding, they have launched a campaign of
iconizing and martyrizing infamous PLO terrorists who had mass-
murdered in the last decades thousands of Israeli civilians in restaurants, hotels, buses and other public places. "Moderate" Abu Mazen
himself or his representatives, have been attending ceremonies to
call public squares, public events or public installations, like sports
fields, after the names of the fallen *shahid*s ("martyrs"), and inviting
Palestinian youth to follow their model. Everyone understands that
when children are educated to believe that blowing up entire Jewish
families celebrating holidays or traveling in public transportation,
is an ideal to be emulated, then the murderers are worshipped as
heroes. And when the PA devotes a substantial portion of its budgets which it obtains from outside donations to pay pensions to the
families of those dead "heroes" or to others who were caught and

incarcerated in Israeli jails, then hardly any hope can survive for any future accommodation between the two peoples internationally or integration of Israeli Arabs domestically. All the more so, when this message is amplified in children's textbooks, in the PA-sponsored media, in public addresses of the leaders and in sermons in mosques.

The PLO leadership, in their desperate attempt to retain the dwindling loyalty of the masses, has set on a course of de-legitimizing its partner to the Oslo Accords, and in this national effort it hardly risks any criticism by its Hamas rivals at home, or by the Israeli Arabs who watch them very closely. For, as Marcus and Crook have shown[65], one of the primary objectives of the PA (and certainly of the Hamas) is to delegitimize Israel in order to facilitate its subversion, then destruction and takeover. This takes place daily, in a campaign of indoctrination where blunt incitement predominates rather than positively bequeathing civilizational values to their people in their media and educational networks. That campaign encompasses denial of the right of existence of a Jewish state, many libels, hate messages and false accusations that Israel massacres innocent Palestinians, especially children, and blood libels long unheard of in Europe where they were born a millennium ago but today can be harshly punished. These libels are so massive, pervasive, repetitive and recurrent that there is no point to argue or refute them systematically. To achieve these goals, through violent anti-Semitic campaigns, the PA has mobilized its academics, who more often than not regard themselves committed to the service of their emerging state rather than to academic inquiry and truth. For example, textbooks in the PA can cite a non-existent "Talmudic passage", without caring the least about intellectual honesty or about the credibility of their future scholars, whom they educate to

---

[65] Itamar Marcus and Barbara Crook,"Anti-Semitism among Palestinian Authority Academics", in *Post-Holocaust and anti-Semitism,* No 69, 1 June, 2008, published by the Jerusalem Center of Public Affairs, 2008.

lie and to overlook academic standards of honest research.

Examples abound. For one, the history of the Middle East has been totally revised and re-written, with a view to erasing all records of Jewish presence in Palestine/the Land of Israel, archaeological sites and world-recognized authoritative histories notwithstanding. The Authority probably believes that by delegitimizing Israel under academic trappings, it can achieve a respectable and irrefutable denial of the historical link between the Jews and Palestine. So, they first create the infra-structure of the evil Jews who pitilessly "massacre Palestinians" and "drink their blood " for breakfast, and then follow that up with the creation of fictional narratives to prove that Judaism is racism. These traits are presented as the unchangeable character of the Jews by the mobilized academics for the "educational" programs of the Palestinian Authority, both in textbooks and in the media. In 1998, PA "historians" held a conference where historical revisionism was devised, not as an individual endeavor by historians who would have legitimately a dissenting point of view to present, based on archives or other evidence that they discovered, but under the PA directives, geared to strengthen Palestinian nationalism by eliminating their competitors. In fact, Dr Yussuf al-Zamili, Head of the History Department of Khan Younis Government College of Education, presented to the conference the approach of the educational system of the PA, whose goal would not be to teach the historical truth but rather to convey a political history aimed at denying Israel's right to exist in the land of Palestine, so as to cement Palestinian national feeling of prevalence in all Palestine.

When it became too much for even manufacturers of history to strip the Jews completely from their history, due to the compelling evidence to the contrary that has been engraved on the ground for millennia, Palestinian academics simply adopted the strategy of borrowing the ancient identity of Hebrews as their own, claiming that those ancient tribes were both Arab and Muslims (more than two millennia before there was Islam), thus refuting today's Jewish claim to the land. One of those "historians" who was handpicked by Arafat as his adviser and chief librarian, Jirar al-Qidwa, has been the champion of this "replacement theology", which he assiduously diffuses via the PA TV broadcasts. He unabashedly converted biblical Jews into Arabs, two millennia before Arabs from Arabia invaded Palestine and subjugated it. He wrote:

> Regarding the Israelites, they were Arab tribes and among the purest... And believe me, by Allah's name, that my blood has more of the Israelites' blood and of the blood of ancient Hebrews than has the blood of Netanyahu and Sharon.[66]

To strengthen this point, the Jerusalem Daily, *al-Quds*, carried for weeks on end in July and August, 1996, three years after Oslo, a daily page of chronicles on the history of the "Palestinian-Cana'anite" people. In that column, academics from the West Bank explained how Israeli academic findingss bolster the Palestinian claims to age-old Cana'anite roots in the land. Delegitimation of the Jews and their link to Israel also found expression on the Islamic level. Though Islam came to the world long after Judaism and Christianity, it claims a fresh renewal under its aegis of the ancient divine notions that Jews and Christians had betrayed, until Allah sent to humanity the Seal of the Prophets and the senior among them, Muhammed, who in one stroke turned the two monotheistic predecessors into forgery and distortion. In presenting Moses and Jesus as Muslim Prophets, he passed the accusation of forgery to their followers. So, Jirar al-Qidwa, the scholar-mercenary of the PA, stated:

---

[66] PA TV, June 5, 1997 (incidentally, or perhaps not, also the 30th anniversary of the 1967 Six-Day War, which unwittingly triggered the revival of Palestinian nationalism. Cited by Marcus and Cook, op.cit. p 2.

Judaism is not a religion in the full sense of the word, and is not a nation at all…Where does this religion come from? The source of Judaism is Mosaic Law… which is the continuation of Islam of our Master Abraham… Several researchers [who remain unnamed] have found in the Bible, when translated correctly [namely by Muslims] texts [where are they?] that prove that it is the continuation of Islam [nevermind that Judaism had preceded Islam by two millennia][67].

New heights of denial were reached by a Palestinian university lecturer who, during a recent PA TV program on religion, taught that Moses, a Muslim, brought "the Muslim Children of Israel out of Egypt" and referred to the subsequent Israeli conquest of the Land of Israel as "the first Palestinian liberation of Palestine". However, he corrected the Biblical narrative by claiming that the conquest was led not by Joshua, but by Talut (King Saul), who was also credited for having slain Goliath. This is not only a manufactured version of the Bible which has no legs to stand on, but it even runs counter to the Qur'anic tale (Sura 5) of the Children of Israel and their land. This lecturer, Dr Omar Jarara, who teaches at the *Najah* University in Nablus, is but the latest link in the long chain of Palestinian usurpers and forgerers of sources, who for the sake of serving the Palestinian cause and boosting Palestinian nationalism, can go to great lengths to toe the political line dictated by the PA. His outrageous "innovations" go even further. He said in that interview on National TV:

We must make clear to the world that David in the Hebrew Bible has no connection to Dawid (*Dawud)* of the Qur'an, that King Solomon in the Bible is not

---

[67] PA TV, November 3, 1998, Cited by Marcus and Crook, op. cit. pp. 4-5.

connected to the Qur'anic Suleiman, and neither are King Saul and Joshua Bin-nun. We have a great leader Talut, who defeated the nation of the giants and killed Goliath. That was a great Muslim victory. The Muslim Children of Israel went out of Egypt under the leadership of Moses, and unfortunately, many researchers deny the Exodus of those oppressed people who were liberated by a great leader, like Moses the Muslim, the Believer and great Muslim, who was succeeded by Saul, the leader of these Muslims in liberating Palestine. This was the first Palestinian liberation by armed struggle to liberate Palestine from the nation of giants led by Goliath. This is our logic and this is our culture[68].

To top it all, and incredibly in any civilized society, during the gloomy peak-days of the Coronavirus crisis (March-April, 2020), while Israel was busy training Palestinian medical teams to test their patients for infection and treat the infected; and while Israel was also bent on providing some of its much needed equipment for the protection of Palestinian medical teams and treatment of their infected patients, the Palestinian authorities in both Gaza and the West Bank came out with the most abominable libels, lies, accusations and threats against Israel, which only showed their obsession with theories of conspiracy, and ungratefulness for the aid they received. Yahya Sinwar, the Hamas leader in Gaza, an ex-prisoner in Israeli jails, threatened on his TV channels that if Israel, who permits hundreds of trucks loaded with food and other necessities daily into the Gaza Strip, should deprive that Hamas territory from food or equipment to treat the virus, he would order his forces to confiscate them by force from Israel, on which he took the occasion

---

[68] PA TV (Fat'h) Feb 15, 2012.

to heap all sorts of curses and insults as is his wont[69]. The Palestinian Authority in the West Bank was more elaborate than that, though no less venomous and no less ungrateful for the aid it was receiving. That innate conspiracy inclination, also filtered across the border into some Israeli Arabs, who while at first were ashamed to show signs of infection, and were later convinced by their leaders and doctors, that they should yield to the general directives of Israeli authorities and submit to treatment, certainly absorbed some of those libels and calumnies, which did not mitigate their usual suspicions from Israel. It is hard to comprehend why sick people would resent medical help, but in that culture of shame, where to submit to the conspiracy of the enemy who caused the pandemic might reflect a weakness, this is only one illustration of the mental incompatibilities between the Jewish majority and the Arab/Muslim minority.

Indeed, in the reports monitored by the Palestinian Media Watch (PMW),[70]authored by Nan Jacques Zilberdik and Itamar Marcus, under the title of "Israel prefers profits to saving Israeli lives from Coronavirus" - says PA Government spokesman, "moderate" PA authorities were cited in a long list of outrageous statements which constituted such instances of vicious incitement against Israel and Jews, that the Israeli media, accustomed to those libels and lies did not even bother to mention them, which did not prevent Israeli Arabs, who feed directly from the Palestinian media, to swallow them avidly, without a word of comment or criticism on those abominable libels against Israel who treated them for that deadly scourge and handed generous aid to their Palestinian kin across the border. Israeli public opinion was not insensitive to that act of insensitivity. Those outrageous lies and calumnies can be essentialized in these main claims, but their harrowing details are there cited

---

[69] Gaza TV, 8 April, 2020.
[70] PMW Bulletin, of 5 April, 2020

in full:

- Israelis spit at Palestinians and touch their ATMs to spread Coronavirus;
- Israeli prison guards seek to infect Palestinian prisoners with Coronavirus; and
- Israelis "carry out quality suicide bombing attacks from afar… without explosives or explosive belts… using the Coronavirus as… biological weapon" – op-ed in official PA daily.

Today's divided house among the Palestinians impels us to tackle in the aggregate the two seemingly contradictory concepts of secular nationalism of the *Fat'h* model which dominates the PLO, and the Islamic nationalism of the Hamas type. The general trend toward Islam, that has emerged from the "Arab Spring", only complicates the issue further and precludes any definite iron-clad conclusions from emerging yet. For today, a competition has been raging, covert or overt, between the two worldviews, aimed at converting public opinion to their respective causes and forcing a decision between applying the sacral-dogmatic-scriptural approach of the Hamas in contemporary life or, on the contrary, making the temporal-pragmatic-legal way of the PA to prevail. The nationalist aspect would normally base its appeal on the secular and particularistic notion, and is presumably also followed by most Israeli Arabs, though the religious trends are not absent there either. The latter would claim a more universalistic approach derived from some divine authority. Hence the dichotomy between the secular-nationalistic political culture, which would tend to adopt rational, if often mythical or manufactured, measures, some based on compromise and negotiation to achieve its goals, versus the religious-dogmatic imperatives of self-righteousness and single-mindedness, which usually often lead to fanatical and unbending conduct. Hence the near impossibility to bridge over the two philosophies, as we have seen in the frustrating attempts to create a *rapprochement* between the PLO and the Hamas over the rule of Palestine during the Oslo years, and down to the open rift, no longer just political rivalry, between Ramallah and Gaza. In many Islamic entities, like in Iran, Afghanistan, the Sudan, Pakistan, the Gaza Strip and others, the Islamic movements take over from incumbent "secular" regimes, as the latter are not considered "Islamic enough." Yet, due to the general mood of Islamization, which implies filling the vacuum left by failing "secular" regimes, and the struggle among the Palestinians over the souls of the same constituency, the PLO has accepted, as we have shown, much of the Islamic vocabulary, rhetoric and symbolism.

Israel's position regarding a settlement with the Palestinians is determined by a democratically elected government, which would negotiate, sign and enforce any agreement. It is impossible, however, to identify the "Palestinian position" because no single entity represents the Palestinian people; it is a divided house, with two competing ideologies, two kinds of nationalism and two rival authorities and political entities. Therefore, Palestinian delegations negotiating with Israel reflect the views of only one part of the Palestinian people and Israel has no assurance that any agreement would be enforceable on those representing other factions. The Palestine Liberation Organization (PLO) runs the Palestinian Authority (PA), which is supposed to govern the Palestinian-controlled areas of the West Bank along with the Gaza Strip. Following the *coup* in 2007, however, Gaza has been ruled by Hamas. The PLO has signed agreements with Israel and expressed a willingness to reach a settlement that would create a Palestinian state beside Israel. Hamas, however, is guided by Islam and opposes any negotiations with Israel and has called for its destruction. That bifurcation is also detectable within Israeli Arabs, with the secular among them siding with the PA and its Fat'h leadership, while the Islamic Movement is condemning the Oslo process and vowing to pursue the negative and aggressive path of Hamas. In an effort to unify the Palestinian leadership and create a single governing authority, third parties have attempted to mediate a reconciliation of the two factions, but so far (April 2020) they have been unsuccessful. Hamas remains opposed to negotiations with Israel and also dismisses the prime ministers chosen by the PA, resulting in the Palestinian Legislative Council where the Hamas had won the majority in 2007, being boycotted by the PLO and the PA, and the latter's government being boycotted by the Hamas. These and other disagreements over the distribution of power have prevented the two sides from agreeing on elections and the re-unification of the PA's rule in the territories. Significantly, since there were no elections held in both Palestinian camps since 2007, both rival leaderships and governments have been devoid of legitimacy. Can one imagine a President, a Prime Minister or a Parliament in the West or in Israel continuing to hold office a decade or more after their legal term of office had been invalidated? Only the Arabs in Israel, who have participated in three successive national election campaigns (1919-2020) which were contended precisely on the grounds of the legitimacy of government, understand the unconstitutionality of this situation.

Israel views the luck of reconciliation of the two parties as an indication that the Palestinians are no longer interested in negotiating a peace agreement. In 1993, Israel recognized the PLO and signed a series of agreements with the aim of achieving an end to the conflict with the Palestinians. Hamas, however, rejected these agreements and has sponsored terrorist attacks against Israel. Unless Hamas changes its policy and recognizes Israel, ceases terror and accepts the previously signed agreements, Israel and the international community have said that the group cannot be a party to negotiations. The leaders of Hamas have consistently insisted that they will not meet these conditions; therefore, Israel has made clear that it would not work with a Palestinian government that includes Hamas. As long as Israel did not recognize the PLO as the "sole representative of the Palestinians," and did not hand to it the rule of the West Bank and Gaza before any elections were held, the question of the legitimacy of the Palestinian government she would have to deal with was left open to whatever the Palestinian people would elect. The Oslo Accords, signed between Israel and the leadership of the PLO in 1993, however, shifted the debate between the two rival Palestinian groups from abstract ideology to practical politics. Though both groups called for the end of Israeli "occupation", a tenet that was shared by Israeli Arabs too, – the signature of those agreements indicated that the PLO was prepared to eschew violence, and to negotiate with the Israelis in order to achieve their goal, while Hamas remained committed to a holy war to drive them out of what it considered Islamic territory, that is, Palestine. The divide between the compromising position of the PLO and uncompromising views of Hamas with regard to peace talks with Israel has then aggravated the already tense rivalry between them, which also parallelly reflected on the divided opinion among the Israeli Arabs.

The PLO has agreed to negotiate on the basis of a two-state solution that would lead to the creation of a Palestinian state beside Israel, a proposition also supported by most of the Arabs of Israel. Hamas, however, backed by the diehard zealots of Ra'id Salah's Islamic Movement of Israel, maintained that the entire Land of Palestine must be cleansed from the viciousness and impurity of the "occupiers," and that only a single state under Islamic rule allows for the possibility that other faiths can coexist within it. When Islam does not prevail, they claimed in their platform, that means that bigotry, hatred, controversy, corruption, oppression, war and bloodshed prevail, as is evidenced by the existence of Israel itself. Hence, Hamas insisted that Muslims were obligated, following the model of the Prophet, to fight and kill Jews wherever they can be found, or at least ban them from Islamic land if they refuse to submit to its beneficial hegemony. Given this belief, how could Hamas, or its supporters among Israeli Arabs accept reconciliation with the Zionist entity? However, in view of the above-said about PLO nationalism and its disenchantment with negotiations with Israel, which have failed to meet the Palestinian ambitions, the Palestinian factions find themselves closer to each other than they were before. For, the PLO's express negation of a Jewish state in the Land of Israel, and their opposition to Israeli settlers and to the unification of Jerusalem, much more to President Trump's "deal of the Century" which envisages annexation of parts of the West Bank to Israel permanently, in fact create a new common denominator between the two bitterly rival factions. Paradoxically, then, outside peace attempts with Israel produce contention and rivalry at home among the Palestinians, while warmongering and discord with Israel are likely to unite them again. These are the horns of the dilemma faced by Israeli Arabs too.

The bottom line is that the Hamas-PLO split is not only organizational for now, but also ideological, political, personal and practical. The two groups have literally been killing each other, as well as arresting each other's members and doing everything possible to gain the upper hand. Hamas totally dominates Gaza and seeks a foothold in the West Bank in the hope of seizing control there as well. The PLO is doing everything it can, often with Israeli help, to suppress Hamas and to reassert control over Gaza. Their ferocity to one another, and the exclusion of each other, have not allowed so far any reconciliation between the parties to be concluded, despite the ongoing efforts to achieve it, and it seems that in the long run personal divisions have also aggravated the rivalry, which due to its territorial and religious characteristics, has been growing into an unbridgeable enmity. Neither the PA nor Hamas have proved to the other party that their formula of salvation has been more successful than the other's, thus at least giving to the latter the benefit of the doubt, since their path was not tried while the PLO's has proved a resounding failure. In addition, the aura of blood and sweat, in contrast to the soft image of the PLO, which is accused of submitting to the Americans and the Israelis despite its failure to get any closer to Palestinian statehood, has attracted some Palestinians, including part of the Israeli Arabs, to seek another path to a solution to their national problem. While the PA realizes its weaknesses, which emanate from its compromising approach compared to the aggressive and daring image of the Hamas, it cannot afford to embrace the Hamas too warmly for fear of losing Western and Israeli support to which it owes its survival. But Hamas, which is funded by Iran and other Muslim quarters, has little to lose from its brazen belligerence, and much to gain from its victimization in the Western world, and these are arguments that find resonance with Israeli Arabs. The turmoil in the Arab world since 2011 certainly pumps propitious winds into the sails of Hamas, inasmuch as it showed that U.S. allies or proteges, like Mubarak or Ben Ali, and Abdallah Saleh, were let down, while it was the independent revolutionary spirits of Qaddafi and Assad, Hizbullah and Hamas, who went on fighting, even against all odds. They reasoned that better to die fighting with honor than live under humiliation.

Following Arafat's death in 2004 and the lack of decisiveness of Abu Mazen's leadership, Hamas continued to irritate the PA, especially as it showed its capacity to manage the affairs of the Gaza Strip despite all the adversities, and to emerge from its first war with Israel (2008-9) with an increased sympathy from the Muslim world, notably Turkey, and all Leftists and "humanitarians" in the Western world who have been lamenting the "siege on the unfortunate Palestinians in Gaza". However, it is noteworthy that most of the Western world boycotts Hamas as a terrorist organization, though some popular sympathy has been evinced for its aura of "heroic resistance". For a while, Hamas even thought of pressing their bombardments and shelling against Israel to force her to retaliate, thereby wrecking the entire idea of Oslo and forcing reunification of the entire Palestinian people under its intrepid leadership; but as the civilian cost of this folly kept mounting on both sides of the border, the Hamas leadership had to yield temporarily to its responsibilities and agree to a long term cease-fire (*hudna)*, which calms the situation without yielding one iota strategically, ideologically or in *Shari'a* terms, in its endeavor for supremacy in the Palestinian camp. At times, the *shari'a*-sanctioned *hudna* on the model of the Prophet's Treaty of Hudaibiyya, was felt as too restrictive and excessively binding for the Hamas, though it was also breakable as the Prophet had done in his time, so they downgraded it into a less binding and looser term of *tahdi'a* which meant an informal understanding to calm things down, without any commitment to perpetuate it. Arafat had tried in his lifetime, to overtake Hamas on the right, by resuming the rhetoric of Jihad, brandishing Islamic vocabulary ("a million martyrs to reconquer Jerusalem") and hailing the Hamas heroes, like Ahmed Yassin, as his own. The Islamic radicals of Hamas, in turn, claimed in Arafat's time, and continue to claim today, that the PA represented only half of the Palestinian people in the West Bank, the other half being under their ideological grip, in addition to that part of the Palestinians people under their rule in Gaza. Radical Muslims sometimes speak the same language as the nationalists, using the same words with different meanings. Take, for example, this passage from the Hamas Charter:

> Hamas is a humane movement, bent on human rights, and is committed to the tolerance inherent in Islam, as regards attitudes to other religions. It is only hostile to those hostile to it or stand in its way in order to disturb its moves or to frustrate its efforts…Under the shadow of Islam, it is possible for the three religions: Islam, Christianity and Judaism, to coexist in safety and security. Safety and security can only prevail under the shadow of Islam… The members of other religions must desist from struggling against Islam over sovereignty in this region. For if they were to gain the upper hand, then

fighting, torture, and uprooting would follow (Art.31 of the Charter).

The words of humanity and tolerance are there, but what do they mean? Are freedom and tolerance valid when attached to the provision of "under the shadow of Islam?". Similarly, Palestinian PLO leaders have been publicly committed to promoting democracy, freedom, civil rights and the like, but as soon as their leaders are criticized the security forces move in and arrest the critics. Fearing that he will lose power in any election, Abbas has simply refused to schedule new elections since the Hamas won them in 2006, and therefore he has no legal popular mandate to govern the PA. Nevertheless, he continues to be recognized by the international community as a legitimate leader. The Palestinians have been preparing a constitution in expectation of achieving independence. This does not necessarily mean, however, that a future Palestinian state will be a democracy. Any political entity can have a "constitution," like the one embraced by Iraqi strongman Saddam Hussein, couched in lofty terms and encapsulating the most humane and generous terms, but the question is whether it is applied in practice. For example, do independent courts exist to protect and defend it? Will it provide for the civil rights and freedoms that Americans, Israelis or Israeli Arabs take for granted? Similarly, elections do not ensure democracy. In Iran, for example, people elected the Islamic regime over the authoritarian one provided by the Shah and his underlings. But who can be sure that the majority of the people there do not regret their choice now and would now rather reverse course it if they could? In practically all Islamic countries, the choice will always be between some sort of authoritarianism and Islam. This has also happened in Egypt, Morocco, Tunisia during the last year of the Arab Spring, and will likely also play out in Libya, Syria, the Yemen, and perhaps Palestine where Islamic political parties have dominated the public square. The last Palestinian election in 2006 saw the Islamic party, namely Hamas, win the vote. That election was a direct result of President George W. Bush's push for democratic reforms in the PA, but what emerged was an autocratic regime that has continued to deny its people fundamental freedoms, such as freedom of speech, freedom of the press and freedom of assembly, and practically scuttled the Oslo peace process. Israeli Arabs would only reluctantly admit that they are better governed than any Palestinians across the border; but like any colonized people who cannot wait to shrug off the rule of their colonizers, only to miss and become nostalgic about the far better rule by their colonizing occupiers, the Israeli Arabs, like other Palestinians, cannot wait to see the end of Israeli rule which they view as a colonialist power. But they also realize due to their better acquaintance with Israeli politics than other Palestinians, that this illusion and wishful thinking is not about to be fulfilled.

The peace process was crucial during its two decades of empty and vain on and off negotiations because it permitted at least an intimate contact between the parties, which enabled them to know each other, and to continue to cooperate in security matters on the ground in spite of the incitement and libels that the PA feels constrained to hurl at Israel, for it has become the victim of its own propaganda. It cannot suddenly reverse its accusations and calumniations of Israel while it had for decades consistently demonized its rival as the epitome of evil. Israeli Arabs know from their experience that their government is not so bad, the best proof being that they refuse to envisage any transfer to a Palestinian state if and when there is one. At any rate, during the protracted negotiations between Israel and the PA, sometimes direct and other times via American mediation, it became clear which obstacles the parties have overcome, but also they became aware of the gap between what they regard as negotiable in a give-and-take horse-trading, and what they might deem as non-negotiable under any circumstances. Negotiable issues usually regard assets and other measurable quantities, the renunciation of which would mean material, real estate or financial loss. When a party to the negotiations sensed that the sustained loss could be compensated by other assets or, that by giving up some, one gets some other, one may have been inclined to negotiate and come to some compromise, because the disagreement is quantifiable, measurable and therefore compromisable. When, on the other hand, the parties advanced religious- or value-related arguments or claims, the debate went one notch up. The value attached by one party to one element or another, like a holy place, a vital interest of *sine qua non* character, or a matter of national prestige and standing, is immeasurable and only subjectively evaluated. It might be hugely significant for one party but totally insignificant to the other, or of equal value to both parties, or simply because it is so important for one, as to make the other covet it too. The contested value may be moral, cultural, or religious, and as such it becomes utterly unnegotiable, and this is the moment we enter the domain of qualitative debate. For example, while it is possible to negotiate a territorial swap between Israelis and Palestinians, none of the parties is prepared to relinquish Temple Mount/Haram al-Sharif in Jerusalem totally to the other, at the price of excluding itself from it. The bottom line consequence being, that the more the Israeli Arabs are detached from value-related arguments the more likely would they be to soften their positions; conversely, the more Islamically and nationalistically inclined would they become, as seems to be their inclination at present, the more aggressive and uncompromising on the settlement of Palestinian affairs.

In any process of conflict management, and more so of conflict resolution, the quantitative issues would tend to be resolved and agreed upon first, while the more qualitative ones would tend to be relegated to the end of the process. To reach the elusive "agreements" of Oslo I and II, for example, Israel had to pay in quantitative terms: partial withdrawals from territories and partial independence to the Palestinians, euphemistically termed by the

Israelis:"redeployment," "self-rule," "autonomy" and "state-building." Israel, having spent many of her trump cards on this quantitative stage of settlement, has very few arrows left in her quiver for the much more qualitative debates that will follow regarding Jerusalem, Palestinian statehood, borders, settlements, refugees, and any number of intractable issues. In other words, Israel has already disbursed many of its concessions before the negotiations even started, thus making any further retreats increasingly difficult. The built-in contradiction between the Palestinian resolution to get to their key qualitative issues, such as the return of Palestinian refugees to Israeli territory, or exclusive control of Temple Mount, and the equally rigid determination of the Israelis to foil those attempts, has stonewalled the process ever since. Thus, while the PA leadership can survive only as long as it can deliver to its public any sort of Israeli concessions, it will become a lame duck when Israel draws the line and refuses to retreat any further. That is not only the reason for the impasse in the negotiations, but if an effort is made to force the issues on which both sides cannot yield, the explosion and final breakdown of the process will prove inevitable, and will vindicate those who had held no hopes for it *a-priori*, both within the Hamas and their Israeli Arab followers. The PLO demand to freeze Israeli settlement as a prerequisite to renew the negotiations, for example, is only a pretext to avoid them. For in all previous negotiations since Oslo, the talks and discussions were never ceased due to Israeli settlements, and when in 2000 Prime Minister Barak offered a 97% withdrawal from the West Bank in return for the Palestinian recognition of the finality of the conflict, his plea was rejected out of hand in Camp David, proving that for the Palestinians land, territories and settlements were less important than bringing the conflict to its final point. That leaves room for Israelis to assume that the Palestinians are hiding some of their ultimate aims, like replacing Israel, not living side by side with it. The Palestinian and Israeli Arab vicious condemnation of the idea of the Jewish state and the

Law of the Nation State amply corroborate this assumption.

In the wake of the failure of the PA to deliver a state, Hamas will become a more attractive alternative. The PLO's assumed will to negotiate and compromise did not end Israel's control over Palestinian lives. Hamas can then make the case that it is time to adopt a policy driven by the infallible and history-tested tenets of Islam, which preclude any negotiation or compromise over the *waqf* land that had been accorded by Allah to all generations to come of Muslims. The Islamic radicals on both sides of the Israeli boundaries already call for a return to the violent struggle to liberate Palestine in which it is more worthy to die as martyrs in *Jihad* resisting the Infidel "occupiers", than submit to the humiliation of accepting the usurpation of Muslim lands by the despicable enemies of Allah and Islam. The next phase of Palestinian nationalism, therefore, remains uncertain. If negotiations with Israel resume, maybe under the impetus of Trump's "deal", and result in the creation of a truncated and demilitarized Palestinian state, the more secular nationalists, on both sides of the Israeli border may claim to continue to dominate Palestinian society. If negotiations fail to resume however, the radical Muslim trend may reshape Palestinian society in its image, as they have already begun to do in Gaza. Given their view that their mandate is divinely inspired, the radical Muslim nationalists are certain to be more consistent, determined and relentless in the attainment of their goal, as they have been in Afghanistan, Libya, Syria, Yemen and anywhere else where Islam has taken over from other failed secular nationalists.

Summary

Viable Alternatives

The Arabs in Israel seemingly aspire to the simple formula of attaining democracy and equality within Israel, something that should be reachable as a matter of course in any free society, but when examined against the background of the complicated and often ambivalent attitudes of majority and minority and their interrelationships, it turns out to be hiding more than it is revealing, and when the Arab aspirations are dissected to their minute details, they transpire as impossible to fulfill. For example, for Jews to be called "the People of Israel" is a natural appellation which signifies that Jews are a nation, and therefore deserving of self-determination and statehood. For the Arabs, there is no Jewry, only Judaism as a faith, therefore every time they mention Jews in any context, it is in conjunction with Muslims and Christians as one of the three monotheistic creeds. This is of crucial importance because according to this interpretation, t Jews are relegated to live as a religious group in various countries of the world, just like Muslims and Christians who dwell in many places, justifying the PLO Charter which in its 20th clause denies Jewish nationhood, and PLO doctrine assigns them only their religious grouping as Jewish, side by side with Muslims and Christians who will constitute the nationals of the "democratic Palestine" that they envisage, though the designation of that future country as Arab and Muslim is part of the context.

In that worldview, all the formulas of "two state solutions", or "two states for two nations" are empty of meaning, because ultimately the Jews are meant to melt as a minority into another Arab state of Palestine, where with the return of the Arab refugees to their places of 1948, and when their demands to de-Judaize and de-Zionize it are fulfilled, as the Israeli Arabs desire, their demographic impact will turn the country into an Arab one. When the Israeli Arabs are told that their pipedreams will never be implemented, they counterattack that this is racism and incitement against them. We are here facing not only different and contradictory views and aspirations which cannot be overbridged because they are qualitatively unnegotiable, not quantitatively given to compromise half way. The clear consequence then is that the Arabs, who for the moment are on the losing side which does not seem to ever accept the other as the established majority in the land, had better be advised to change course as a result of changing the diskette, learning how other nations, in other times and places, have faced this kind of reality and made the best out of their situation instead of just whining and complaining in eternity. The Jews themselves had internalized that lesson for two millennia of dispersion and persecution, before they gathered strength and launched the marvelous and successful experience of modern Israel.

What remains for the Arabs of Israel to pursue is either to join the endless (and failing) struggle of the Palestinians to seize possession of part of what they claim to be their lands from Israel and Jordan, or to settle as a minority for their lot in Israel and to integrate in it, relinquishing the dream to undermine it and turn it into a binational state, or attempt a restart of a new life in the vast Arab world where they can contribute from the tradition of democracy, higher education and science and technology that they have absorbed during the three generation of their upbringing in Israel. All of those options can be hard and painful, but in the final analysis, after years of difficulties and many tribulations and drawbacks, a settlement will be found. Since antiquity, many people have moved and restarted their lives, out of their own volition or compelled by wars to move on[71]. The exciting experience of the Americas which began only half a millennium ago, is itself the result of the movement of peoples around the world. Many examples of one-sided movement, or exchange of populations have taken place following the world wars, and more good than misfortune resulted from them ultimately, despite the natural human recoil from watching people uprooted, carrying bundles on their heads and babies on their backs, or venturing with flimsy boats on stormy waters to try to come to a safe shore. Let us look at some lived experiences in the past:

One precedent that should be particularly attractive as a model to Arabs is Turkey which is both Muslim, a former ruler of the Arab space, and a close ally of much of the Arab and Islamic worlds nowadays. The triumphant new Turkish Republic headed by Ataturk abolished the Ottoman Empire in 1922 and signed a formal peace agreement with Greece at Lausanne in 1923. On the Greek side, the bitter pill of defeat and withdrawal from Turkish territory was difficult to swallow due to the quick and surprising (though short term) successes it had experienced since the Balkan wars, which had enabled that small country to double its territory and to encompass a Greek population of almost 5 million, but also to raise the rate of non-Greek minorities, essentially Muslims (Turks and Albanians) in its controlled territory, to 20% by the end of W W I. This untenable situation, similar in scope to the Arab minority in Israel today, amidst the tensions that had built up by then between

---

[71] R. Israeli, *Who is Right and Who is Left: The Fate of Weak Polities Among Mighty Empires,* Strategic Books, TX, 2018.

Christians and Muslims, pushed the Greek government to the necessity to deport thousands of its Muslims to Anatolia and at the same time begin to absorb in its midst most Greeks of western Anatolia where it had been crushingly defeated. The population exchange was executed fairly quickly, attaining the goal of ethnic-national homogeneity. Thus, while in 1906, nearly 20 percent of the population of present-day Turkey was non-Muslim, by 1927 only 2.6 percent has remained. This exchange, which was commissioned by the League of Nations, would not have been acceptable internationally today, as ethnic cleansing stemming out of population transfers and exchanges of population are considered abhorrent and contradicting human rights and the rights of individuals to make their choice, instead of letting governments decide for them. That is the reason why the actual but involuntary exchange of population that took place between Israel and the Arab world in 1948-50 when 750,000 Palestinians turned into refugees in Arab countries and were replaced in Israel by an equal number of Jewish refugees from Arab lands, has never received an international stamp of approval. But because of the unanimous decision by the Greek and Turkish governments that minority protection guarantees would not suffice to ameliorate ethno-religious tensions in their respective territories after the First World War, population exchange was then promoted as the only viable option. Had that logic obtained in the Arab-Israeli dispute, maybe the resulting wars, displacement and conflicts between the parties could have been greatly reduced if the Palestinian refugee issue had been solved.

Another salutary effect of this exchange of populations stemmed from the exclusion of every kind of foreign intervention and of the possibility of provocation coming from the outside, that had been rampant during the Capitulation system that European powers had imposed on the dwindling Ottoman power at the end of the 19th Century. This could be achieved most effectively with an agreed exchange of population, while the best guarantees for the security and development of the minorities remaining in place after the exchange, were those provided by the laws of both countries and by the supposedly liberal policy of Turkey and Greece with regard to all communities whose members have willingly assumed their duty as Turkish or Greek citizens. In the case of the Middle East dispute, no comparable settlement could be envisaged, because no liberal government had ever emerged in the Arabs countries to guarantee the rights of the Jewish minorities, while the liberal democracy of Israel could never succeed in ensuring the total loyalty of its 20% Arab minority, which remains closer to the enmity of its Arab kin towards its country- Israel than a positive bridge for peace and rec-onciliation between the two.

Other positive effects of the population exchange which made it acceptable and practicable to the norms of the time, though they would certainly (and perhaps wrongly) have been rejected today, were:

1. The population exchange between Turks and Greeks was seen as the best humane remedy in a situation that demanded a quick and efficient resolution to the growing tensions between those two intertwined populations. In other words, much like Schechterman after W W II, who may have embraced this exchange as a precedent and model to settle the dislocations of German minorities in Europe, the Norwegian diplomat Nansen, who was the main architect of the Turkish-Greek exchange, believed that what was on the negotiating table at Lausanne was not only ethno-religious nationalism, but a practical problem that had to be resolved. He believed that

rather than leaving majority and minority locked in perpetual friction and conflict in permanence and for eternity, it was vastly more humane, economic, rapid and practicable in the long run to effect the painful surgery immediately rather than let the wounds fester indefinitely that would turn any solution vaster, more difficult and unfeasible in the future. That is exactly what was not done with the Palestinian refugee problem, which has grown in four generations from 750,000 to 4,5 million and become practically insoluble, while Arab leaders are encouraging the Palestinians to dream about their "right of return" and preparing and rehearsing them violently to achieve that goal, and Israel blatantly refusing any notion of allowing repatriation of those refugees who would endanger its very existence.

2. The Lausanne agreement promised that the possessions of the refugees would be protected, and it allowed migrants to carry "portable" belongings freely with themselves. It was required that possessions not carried across the Aegean Sea be recorded in lists; these lists were to be submitted to both governments for reimbursement. After a commission was established to deal with the particular issue of belongings (mobile and immobile) of the populations, this commission would decide the total sum to pay persons for their immovable belongings (houses, cars, land, etc.). It was also promised that in their new settlement, the refugees would be provided with new possessions equivalent to the ones they had left behind. Greece and Turkey would calculate the total value of every refugee's belongings, and the country with a surplus would pay the difference to the other country. All possessions left in Greece belonged to the Greek state and all the possessions left in Turkey belonged to the Turkish state. Because of the difference in nature and numbers of the populations, the possessions left behind by the

Greek elite of the economic classes in Anatolia was greater than the possessions of the Muslim farmers in Greece.

3. When the Commission of the League of Nations arrived in Greece, the Greek government had already settled provisionally 72,581 farming families, namely about a quarter million souls, almost entirely in Macedonia, where the houses abandoned by the exchanged Moslems, and the fertility of the land made their establishment practicable and auspicious. Conversely, in Turkey, the property abandoned by the Greeks was often looted by loose arriving immigrants before the influx of immigrants of the population exchange. As a result, it was quite difficult to settle refugees in Anatolia since many of these homes had been occupied by people displaced by war before the government could seize them.

4. In Turkey, the departure of the independent and strong Greek economic elites, left the dominant state elites unchallenged. This was the moral advantage in the rather sad fact that during the war years Turkey lost around 90 percent of the pre-war commercial and bureaucratic class. The emerging business groups that supported the Free Republican Party in Turkey in the 1930s could not prolong the democratic rule of a single-party without an opposition, because transition to multiparty politics, which depended on the creation of stronger economic groups in the mid-1940s, had been stifled due to the exodus of the Greek middle and upper economic classes. In Greece, by contrast, the arrival of the refugees broke the dominance of the monarchy and old politicians and favored the Republicans, though increasing grievances of the refugees caused some of the immigrants to shift their allegiance to the Communist Party and contributed to its increasing strength, while the government, with the support of the King, responded to the Communists by establishing an authoritarian regime in 1936. In these ways, the population exchange

indirectly facilitated changes in the political regimes of Greece and Turkey during the interwar period.

5. In effect, the dynamics generated by the exchange of population ultimately caused the abolition of the monarchy in Turkey and the rise of the Republic. For while Sultan Mehmet VI accepted the humiliating Treaty of Sevres which placed most Anatolia under Allied and Greek control, the Turkish nationalists in Ankara rose against it and prepared to resist it and to block its implementation. Thus, in 1922, after they had secured most national borders, the Ankara government became the dominant authority in Turkey and in effect replaced the rule of the Sultan, forcing the Allies to convene the Lausanne Conference to replace the failing validity of the Treaty of Sèvres. And when invitations to participate in the conference were extended to both the Ankara-based government and the Istanbul-based Ottoman government, and they were followed by the abolition of the Sultanate by the Ankara-based government on 1 November 1922 and the subsequent departure of Sultan Mehmet VI from Turkey, the Ankara-based government was left as the sole governing entity in Anatolia. The Ankara-based government, led by Mustafa Kemal Atatürk, moved swiftly to implement its nationalist programme, which did not allow the presence of significant non-Turkish minorities in Western Anatolia, and negotiated and signed the "Convention Concerning the Exchange of Greek and Turkish Populations" on 30 January 1923. In fact, by the time the agreement was to take effect, i.e. 1 May 1923, most of the pre-war Greek population of Aegean Turkey had already fled. Thus the exchange involved the remaining Greeks of central Anatolia, for out of the 1,200,000 total Greeks, only 189,916 were still behind in Turkey that time.

6. In Greece, where the exchange of population caused most dislocations due to the number of refugees which was much

higher than in Turkey in both relative and numerical terms, they termed that torment as "the Asia Minor Catastrophe", preceding the Palestinians by a quarter century, who would also call their exodus in 1948 a catastrophe (*Nakbah*). Significant refugee displacement and population movements had already occurred following the Balkan Wars, World War I, and the Turkish War of Independence, causing almost all Greek Orthodox Christians to be expelled or formally denaturalized from Turkish territory. On the other hand, the Muslim population in Greece not having been affected by the Greek-Turkish conflict remained almost intact. Thus 354,647 Muslims moved to Turkey after the Lausanne agreement. Those Muslims were predominantly Turkish Muslims, as well as members of other communities such as Greek Muslims, Muslim Roma, and Albanians. Much of the remaining Greek population of Anatolia has been subject to pogroms and discrimination that brought ultimately to its exodus too.

This process can get even faster in open and democratic societies, like in Israel, where the minority can vent its grievances publicly and the majority can gauge the level and intensity of the menace to its hegemony. The process can then gather more momentum when the grievances of the minority are met and then in the name of the democratic rules of the game, more demands are advanced with more insistence. The host society then splits between those who continuously yield to the demands of the minority, in the name of democracy, humanism, fairness, farsightedness, civil rights, pragmatism and under the self-guilt they feel toward the "oppressed" minority; and those who would rather toughen their attitudes, reinforce their means of coercion and demand fulfillment of national duties and ritual identification with the state as prerequisites for equal rights, and they advocate law and order and a stricter control of the unruly minority. Conversely, in pre-democratic and non-democratic societies things are much simpler and much less affected by torments and dilemmas. Minorities flee away from danger and seek refuge among their kin: like German Jews in Palestine in the 1930s, Rohinga Muslims in Bangladesh or Syrian Muslims in Jordan and Turkey in the 2010s. In those cases, either the refugees run away for their lives under the continued threat of war and destruction, or are encouraged by the ruling tyrants to pack up and go. Those migrations under duress are sometimes dubbed "population exchange", "transfer of populations", "refugee movement", "exodus" and what have you. The Balkan wars and World War One are one example where Armenians were removed or exterminated, Greeks and Turks exchanged populations and Bulgars roamed the Balkan Peninsula, one minority arousing another in a chain reaction that could not be halted.

The lessons to have been learned from all these morbid experiences was that when national problems are not tackled as such but are dismissed as "communal" (like in Cyprus where the Greeks and Turks are still battling for their separate national existence); or "refugee" issue (such as the Palestinians who have been rotting in refugee camps for four generations now), or an "exchange of population" (like the Greek-Turkish dispute), the wounds are bound to remain festering until a permanent national resolution is produced. Take for example the massive population transfer of Jewish refugees from Europe to Palestine between the two world wars. Granted that there was a Zionist ideal to settle Jews in Palestine as an expression and encouragement of renewed Jewish nationalism, so as to implement the Jewish National Home envisaged by the Balfour Declaration, there were also some European thinkers and leaders who regarded the movement of European Jews into the Middle East as necessary from their own point of view in order to solve the "Jewish problem". Incidentally, at that time, plans were also rife to dispatch the surplus populations of over-populated countries in Europe to new agricultural settlements in less populated countries under the sponsorship of the League of Nations. It is true that in the wake of serious pogroms against the Jews of Europe, Zionists talked of finding temporary havens for Jewish refugees, which meant that Jews could also take shelter anywhere their safety was assured, for example the Uganda Plan to settle European Jews in East Africa, but ultimately Zionism remained committed to Zion, i.e. to the concept of a Jewish homeland in Palestine/ the Land of Israel.

At the end of W W I only 55,000 Jews were settled in Palestine, after some 30,000 more had been deported by the Ottomans or ran to safety from them during the war, and not all of them were Zionists. Only following the Balfour Declaration of 1917 and in the wake of the Paris Peace Conference, did the Zionists begin to press systematically for a Jewish homeland in Palestine under the British Mandate. That voice was heard as a result of the League of Nations' formal recognition of the historical connection of the exiled and wandering Jewish people to Palestine, and its instruction to the British to facilitate the establishment of a Jewish national home, whatever that meant, in order to put an end to the Jewish exile. Indeed, despite the harsh conditions of life in Palestine in the 1920s, some 37,000 Jews flocked into the country during the years 1919-1923, many of them fleeing civil war, pogroms, revolution and the upheavals of Eastern Europe. But close to half of the newcomers emigrated from Palestine back to Europe as soon as unrest seemed to diminish there and disturbances began mounting in Palestine in 1921. From that time on, Jewish immigration to Palestine became subject to political considerations of the ruling power. In response to violent Arab demonstrations in 1921, the British limited Jewish immigration to the "absorptive capacity" of the land. The Zionist Organization was in charge of selecting the people to enter under the quotas set by the British, in view of the fact that the demands for free immigration by far outnumbered the imposed restrictive quotas. Despite these limitations, however, Palestine continued to be a refuge for the European Jews in the 1920s and thereafter. In the 1920s the large Jewish population of Poland came under attack on both nationalistic and economic grounds. They would perhaps have gone to America to follow up on the vast Jewish immigration wave from Eastern Europe at the turn of the century, except that by then the gates of the New World were all but closed. To escape persecution and harassment, over 23,000 Polish Jews went to the Holy Land, bringing the total Jewish population of Palestine, the *yishuv*, to some 154,000 by the end of the decade.

Those refugees were welcomed by the Jews with mixed feelings. For while the Zionists encouraged Jewish immigration to the land, they were less exhilarated with the "bourgeois" accretion to the socialist coloring that the pioneering spirit had given to the fledgling state- building. Thus, even though the country was practically the only half-open haven for Jewish refugees, the Zionists felt somewhat uneasy about the new waves, for they were apparently much more concerned about the quality and ideological coloring than the quantity of the newcomers. Other displaced Jews had been resettled in the Crimea and the Ukraine as a result of the dislocations caused by the Russian Revolution. During the decade of the 1920s some 100,000 Jews lived in the new agricultural settlements in the Soviet Union, some of them in the Ukraine and in the Crimean Peninsula, under the project known as the American Jewish Joint Agricultural Corporation which was financed by US Jews and carried out in close cooperation with the new Soviet State. Thereafter, massive movements of Jewish refugees originated in Nazi Germany, and during the years 1933-38 some 150,000 German Jews fled the Nazi terror. Most of these refugees went to France and other European countries. The Jewish exodus increased drastically after September 1935, when the Nuremberg Laws stripped the Jews from their German citizenship and from political and economic rights. Of the 100,000 German Jewish refugees who went overseas during this period, 80,000 ended up in Palestine, in what is known as the 5th *Aliya* which injected an invaluable momentum, energy, innovation and culture which later made modern Israel. But all these figures paled in comparison with the millions who roamed the roads of Europe when Hitler invaded Poland in September 1939, and panic-stricken people began fleeing from the cities, suffering the ruthless bombings of the German *Luftwafe*. Many went south into Hungary and Romania, others to France, still others to Palestine and Iran, and from there back to France and England. Some 300,000 Polish Jews, i.e. 10% of Polish Jewry, fled from Western Poland as it came under Nazi rule, eastward to the territory occupied by the Soviets, before the borders of partitioned Poland were sealed.[72]

In view of the dire conditions of Jewish existence in Europe after 1933, on the one hand, and the growing opposition in America to change the immigration laws that would have allowed the mass transfer of Jewish refugees from the gathering storm in Europe, on the other, the Evian International Conference was convened in 1938 to try to tackle the issue, but it ended in a resounding failure. It was convened at the initiative of United States President Franklin D. Roosevelt who perhaps hoped to obtain commitments from some of the invited nations to accept more refugees, although he took pains to avoid stating that objective expressly. It was true that Roosevelt desired to deflect attention and criticism from American policy that severely limited the quota of Jewish refugees admitted to the United States, but since the conference was attended by representatives from 32 countries, and 24 voluntary organizations as observers, there was an expectation that some of those representatives would announce their readiness to absorb some refugees, but it was not to be. Golda Meir, the attendee from British Mandate Palestine, was not permitted to speak or to participate in the proceedings except as an observer. Some 200 international journalists gathered at Évian to observe and report on the meeting. Germany

---

[72] See Chapter 9 of R. Israeli, *Palestinians Between Israel and Jordan*, {Praeger, NY, 1991).

responded to the news of the conference by saying essentially that if the other nations would agree to take the Jews, it would help them leave, so many of them would have been saved, had the nations not been so obtuse to Jewish suffering. Two exceptions were the Dominican Republic and Costa Rica who were prepared to discuss the matter. Thus, not only did the conference end in failure, but it unwittingly helped Nazi propaganda by showing that Germany was "generously" ready to let Jews go, but there was no one to accept them.

In the Winter of 1939-40 the Soviets began a massive transfer of parts of the Polish population under their rule to the Russian hinterland, in order to cut them off from their native land and supposedly to decrease their hostility toward the Soviet state. Many Polish families were torn apart, and hundreds of thousands were exiled to remote settlements and camps in Siberia and Central Asia. Up to 30,000 Poles, including some Jews, were shipped every day eastward, in a 6,000 mile journey made under sub-human conditions. By 1941, the Polish government in exile claimed that close to two million Poles had been deported into the Soviet Union. More massive uprooting of people ensued when the Russians decided to invade Estonia, Latvia and Lithuania and to annex them to the USSR. In 1940-1 35,000 Latvians disappeared without a trace, and tens of thousands more followed the Poles into exile in the depths of the Soviet Union. The fate of East European Jews was the same or worse. Many of them were made refugees by the Soviets after they had been driven eastward during the Nazi invasion of 1939. Thus, about two million Jews, some of them refugees from Poland, some inhabitants of Soviet-ruled East Poland and others who had lived in the Baltic states, came under Soviet rule. Those who had fled from Nazi-occupied territory were particularly harassed and persecuted by the KGB for the "crime" of maintaining their ties with their relatives who remained in Nazi-ruled Western Europe. Therefore, Jews who had fled to the Soviet Union, were deported farther east; in all, the number of Polish Jews who migrated to Russia was estimated at 400,000. Other Jews, although far fewer, made their way westward into Nazi-held territories, ignorant of Nazi horrors, but fleeing from Communism, or in order to renew their ties with their families in Poland. Stories abound about Jewish families who crowded trains heading west, running away from the Soviets, or heading east, running away from the Nazis, who crossed each other on the railway, not knowing that both had no firm shelter to rush to in the chaos of the war. The confusion was indeed so complete, the shock of war and deprivation so deep, and the ignorance of the conditions on the ground so total that Jewish refugees in the trains heading in both directions were just running away without knowing where they would land.

In this major upheaval that afflicted Europe and the world, there were also many refugees from Soviet-occupied territory in Finland, where over 400,000 people were displaced from their land, amounting to 10% of the total Finnish population. To add insult to injury, the Russians incarcerated the Finns who remained in Soviet-occupied territory and sent them to their own camps above the Arctic Circle where many perished. Some of those refugees started returning home in 1941 when they took advantage of the German invasion of the Soviet Union to reclaim their lost territory. In 1944, those people were again refugees for the second time, when the Russians turned the tide of the war and reoccupied the Karelian Isthmus and the area around Lake Ladoga. After the war, the redistribution of ethnic groups affected some 18 million people in Europe and particularly led to the movement of German minorities numbering some 12 million in Czechoslovakia, Poland, Hungary, Romania and Yugoslavia. All of them were resettled in Germany. The Sudetenland of Czechoslovakia and the western territories of Poland, which had been inhabited by these Germans, were repopulated by Czechs, Slovaks, and Poles. Other population transfers took place between the Soviet Union and Poland and Czechoslovakia that involved agreements based on "territorial compromise". As a result, some 2 million people were relocated, thereby reuniting Ukrainian, White Russian, and Lithuanian minorities with the main bodies of their people in their native Soviet republics; and Poland became almost totally inhabited by Poles, which added to its homogeneity and stability. To this one can add the compulsive transfer of 154,000 Turks from European-Slavic-Christian Bulgaria to Asian-Turkish-Muslim Turkey. The greatest authority on European refugees, Joseph Schechterman, favored the transfer of ethnic groups as a solution to nationality problems that had proven to be insoluble in any other way, however unjustifiable some of the cases in his study may have been. He also emphasized that some of the hardship and suffering accompanying the transfer could be alleviated by agreement and organization, as they were accomplished at the Potsdam Conference.

Against the background of his extensive first-hand experience in Europe, Schechterman seems to have been lenient toward forcible removals of minority populations when they were motivated by the genuine necessity to eliminate a danger to the stability of the state or an inducement to domestic irredentist aspirations that were backed by neighboring countries from the outside. Expulsions, however, were found to be unjustifiable when they were motivated by a deep resentment against the role played by minorities during W W II (such as the Germans in the Sudeten lands). Even though this feeling of bitterness by the majority for being betrayed by their countrymen, was understandable to Schechterman, much more than the urge to punish the offenders, he saw insufficient justification for so drastic a measure as wholesale expulsion of entire minority groups. He regarded the notion of guilt, and its corollary –retribution- as a fundamentally individual category, and therefore inapplicable to collectives. He contended that guilt had to be established with regard to every individual involved, for even if the majority of a minority group were guilty of a specific offense, the group in its totality might not be legally or morally accountable for the offense committed by its members. This was the big advance in attitude towards displacement of people after W W II, compared with the wholesale dislocations after W W I when entire populations were uprooted by the Greeks and Turks, under the pretext of "mutual exchange" of populations by agreement, in order to settle their national accounts with their perceived enemies.

Thus, the underlying idea of a compulsory transfer of entire populations has nothing to do with guilt or penalty, or even with abstract justice; it is in essence a preventive measure, not a retaliatory one. If large sections of an ethnic minority within a state consistently negate their allegiance to that state, repeatedly create frictions, conflicts and challenges to its legitimacy, look for guidance from and display allegiance to their national state abroad, nourish irredentist tendencies and thus jeopardize the integrity of the state and its national security, and express fundamental values that are at variance with the majority and perpetuate them in their educational system; and if all attempts to reconcile this minority and integrate it into the framework of common statehood, with equal rights and duties, fail, then – and only then- might there be recourse to forced population transfer (or expulsion, or ethnic cleansing). Because then, it is not a matter of just racism, incitement or bias, but a pragmatic choice between eternal misery for both majority and minority, or a horrible but provisory travesty of justice for the minority, which will be healed in time and permit both sides to live free of conflict for ever after. Shechterman also argued that the existence of such a resentful minority within the affected state represents a permanent source of jeopardy, and only the elimination of this danger in permanence, i.e. the removal of the entire ethnic group, is likely to erase the menace. The Prophet Muhammad's mistreatment of the Jews in Medina may be seen in this light (or rather obscurity), as the only solution open to him bi view of the perceived challenge they posed to his rule; and so were the repeated expulsions of the Jews in medieval Europe (England, France and Spain). The Nazis went much further, because expulsion would not satisfy them, although in the beginning of their rule they allowed thousands of Jews to depart from Germany to Palestine with part of their properties; but, ultimately, they proceeded from ethnic cleansing to genocide when they adopted the "final solution".

On the other hand, suppression or deportation of even a great number of persons directly guilty of extreme nationalistic anti-state activities cannot necessarily serve the purpose, because it does not eliminate the root cause of the problem- namely the presence of an ethnic entity whose views and objectives have proved to be incompatible with the survival or the security of the state to which its members reluctantly belong. Thus, unless the territory on which such a minority lives is detached from the state in question, there seems to be no alternative but a wholesale transfer of the disloyal population to the state to which it professes allegiance. This is not a punitive measure but a prophylactic one, that is a matter of highest state expediency, not retribution. Schechterman expressed a deep respect for the indomitable spirit of a minority group that refuses to live under the state authority of another people and strives for unification with a neighboring state, for there is nothing inherently reprehensible, to his mind, in such irredentist tendencies. However, when they become a manifest danger that cannot be eliminated in any other reasonable way, the ethically neutral preventive measure of transfer (or ethnic cleansing) must be resorted to. In some instances of population transfer, the above principles of justification were not observed, such as the compulsory removal of the German minorities from Yugoslavia and Hungary. None of them was a minority facing a German state across the border and looking toward a union with it, and there was no irredentist danger and no tangible threat to the integrity of the state territory. However, these minorities were a source of friction and sometimes acted as a fifth column; nonetheless, since they did not represent any immediate menace to the safety of Hungary and Yugoslavia, or to the peace of their regimes, Schechterman thought that their compulsory transfer was too harsh a measure. For the removal of these groups, as well as of the Germans from Romania, lacked the decisive preventative aspect of any justifiable transfer scheme. Instead, these cases were seemed as examples of retaliation against the Germans and caused unnecessary hardship and suffering to their victims. The cases of the Germans in Poland and Czechoslovakia, on the other hand, had an iron-clad justification.

As we have observed, transfers of population in post W W II Europe, have been of three kinds:

1. A bilateral exchange of population (Polish-Soviet, Soviet Czechoslovak, Hungarian Czechoslovak);

2. A unilateral removal (Germans from Czechoslovakia, Poland, Romania Yugoslavia and Hungary;

3. The "voluntary" flocking of the hundreds of thousands of Jewish survivors of the Holocaust to Palestine and then Israel. The quotation marks around voluntary are due to the miserable situation in which the survivors were and when no other country was ready to accept them (Canada's Trudeau only recently, and belatedly (November 2018), apologized for turning back a 900 refugee ship of refugees from the *Sho'a*, many of whom were eventually murdered).The British mandatory power did not welcome them into Palestine either, and they had to infiltrate there illegally, while those who were seized in high sea were redirected by the British Navy into Cyprus where they were interned until the establishment of the State of Israel in 1948.

While the bilateral removals involved state treaties and provided for the right of choice by the population concerned, the unilateral relocations involving Germans were compulsory and arbitrarily initiated by the governments ruling the territories from which the refugees were evacuated. Nevertheless, the forced transfers of Germans from the Czech Sudeten, from Hungary and from the Polish recovered territories, were sanctioned by the Big Three in Potsdam. The settling of the Sudeten and of the recovered territories by Czechs and Poles, respectively, was voluntary. In general, compulsory transfer was regarded by jurists as inconsistent with the democratic concept of human rights, because the loss of lands, homes, properties and roots, for resettlement in other countries constituted an individual travesty of justice for many. Only the Jewish "voluntary" running away from the inferno of Europe failed to raise any moral or legal concerns anywhere, and when it did, it was considered "illegal" and the British did everything they could to scuttle the entire movement, for if they accepted the stream of Jewish refugees they would have had to face the fury of the Arabs who had collaborated with Hitler in the "final solution", and could not countenance the absorption in Palestine of the survivors of that tragedy. Had it not been for the sympathetic conduct of the French and the Italians in providing facilities for those gathering refugees from all over Europe to embark from their ports to Palestine, who knows how many of them could have been rescued?

As we saw above, ideas promoting the transfer of populations were rife in post W W I Europe, and some of their authors regarded the League of Nations as responsible for redressing the chaos caused by mixed populations, in order to bring about happiness through population redistribution and homogenization. In the period immediately following W W II, many statesmen, writers, and scholars concluded that ethnic shifting of minorities was the only way out of the territorial and minority maze in Europe. Others, however, emphatically rejected the idea on moral, practical or political grounds. Some thought that the principle of transfer runs counter to democratic values; others abhorred the human disruption it caused. Still others clung to the utopian ideas of "human brotherhood", "understanding", "harmony between peoples" and "universal love". The moralists said that the transfers subjugated individual rights to the rights of the collective, thus degrading people to mere atoms of the ethnic group to which they belonged. The democratic-minded feared that even the most humane transfer was inconsistent with the rights of individuals in established democracies. Some opponents of transfer did not hesitate to term it "criminal", even if it resolved the complex problem of the mixture of ethnic, religious and other minority groups, because it created hardships on those who had to undergo that painful process. Others feared that following the enormous personal hardships and injustice occasioned by transfer of populations, uni-national states would be created that, in turn would intensify and promote exclusive nationalism or even chauvinism. Multi-ethnic states, on the other hand, were thought to promote cooperation, collaboration, living together, sharing, understanding, and tolerance, and enrich the social, intellectual and psychological aspects of their makeup. With a hindsight of 160 years in America following the Civil War (1861-5) and 70 years after the turmoil of World War Two, one can say that today's permanent clashes between whites and blacks in the US, and the second thoughts that are voiced about the multi-culturalism in Europe that had allowed millions of Muslim immigrants in, do not seem to uphold those optimistic ideas about the desirability of mixing ethnic, religious, national and linguistic groups in one nation-state[73]. Nor does the permanent friction between the Jewish majority and Arab minority in Israel offer any more optimistic solution than an eventual population transfer or exchange.

In Asia too international transfers of population, as well as internal migrations, have been part of the scene. In 1931, for example, one seventh of Malaya's population were Indians, who had immigrated from Madras and spoken Tamil. Most of them had been

---

[73] See R. Israeli, *Retreating from the Mirage of Multi-CuLturalism?: The Cases of Holland, Britain and Israel*, Strategic Books, TX, 2018.

imported to satisfy local labor demands and had settled there with their families. Chinese who migrated south to the Malayan Peninsula today constitute about one third of the population there. In China Proper, there was need to remove in the 2,000s millions of people to allow the construction of the huge four dams in the upper Yangtse Valley. In these cases, however, a reverse process took place compared to European migrations: While in post-war Europe the idea was to resolve minority ethnic problems and to bring more homogeneity and stability to its states, Asia, just like contemporary Europe, has created more problems by disturbing long term local ethnic and religious uniformity through massive injections of alien migrants. Remember that in China, even the millennial-old domestic migration of northern Chinese to the south has perpetuated there the usage of the term *Hakka* (stranger, guest, alien culturally). Indeed, those countries have known more ethnic turbulence since their local demographic balance has been disturbed by the incoming populations. Some 15 million Chinese are estimated to have migrated to other Asian or Western countries by 1940. Sizeable Chinese minorities exist in practically all countries of southeast Asia, and the jealousies and competition they raise among the local and native populations have generated disturbances, massacres, bigotry and acts of discrimination. In the years 1941-44 eight minority nationalities were deported by the Soviets to Siberia and the other Soviet territories, including Central Asia, even though they had often lived in their national territories for centuries. All in all, at least 1, 5 million people were involved in those transfers, which were rationalized in terms of potential "treason" during wartime. Today, under a more liberal policy, voices are being raised by some of them, such as the Tatars of Crimea, to be allowed to return to their homelands, a demonstration of the fact that ethnic loyalty and allegiance to a certain land and certain people, sometimes are much stronger that the designs of the statesmen who had imposed the transfer.

The Jewish story of migrations, voluntary and forced, has been characterized by *perpetuum mobile.* The stereotype of the "wandering Jew" has been indeed incrusted in the Jewish and international mind, since Jews have been experiencing more history than geography, but have remained also imbued with a powerful sense of survival and durability against all odds, as they have been predisposed to migration and horizontal mobility as circumstances required. Many of these migrations were considered as mystical and religious experiences, such as the ancient exodus from Egyptian slavery into freedom in the Promised Land. Others, like the forced exiles from the Holy Land following the destruction of the two Jewish commonwealths and the Temples which symbolized them, were regarded by the Hebrew Prophets as divine chastisement for Jewish sinfulness and misconduct. In the course of those two exiles the Jews did not cease to dream about another desirable "transfer" that would gather them again in the land of their ancestors. In the Diaspora, they moved from one country to another, wandered between continents, abandoned host cultures and adopted others as circumstances required. In other words, migration became a second nature to the Jews, as a tool of survival, or as a sign that they would not implant themselves anywhere for good pending their repatriation to their Holy Land. They were indeed compelled to leave their country in the Land of Israel, or their dwellings in Europe and the lands of Islam, or they flocked out of their own volition to the New World or back to Palestine/Israel. Choice and necessity have both played roles in the Jews' propensity to migrate. They always wished to return to Israel when they could not, or were banned from it, but as soon as they were offered the chance to repatriate to their ancient land they often opted to go to other lands of opportunity. This has given rise to a typically Jewish paradox: a cult of rootedness, a permanent vow to return to the Land of Israel, a pledge to never forsake Jerusalem; and at the same time, an almost inexplicable attraction to the Diaspora. It also seems that the Diaspora has been almost a prerequisite for rootedness in the Land of Israel. The Israeli national anthem celebrates that paradox by containing the phrase: "We hope to be a free nation in our country", more than a century after the beginning of Jewish resettlement in Palestine and 70 years after modern Israel was established.

Jewish migrations became more stabilized and unidirectional since and due to the systematic Nazi genocidal massacre of the Jews of Europe, which eliminated most of European Jewry; and the counter process of the establishment of Israel in 1948 which channeled most Jewish migrations to the Jewish state, which at 70 could boast of being home to more than half of world Jewry (7 out of 13 million). Namely, Israel has become the shelter of more than the Jews murdered by Hitler and his gang, and the focus of Jewish existence in the world, while most of the other half is based in the US, which had grown until 1948 as the main and the most numerous, powerful and influential Jewish center, with its close to 6 million half assimilated Jews, who have had to recognize that that they have been removed from their dominance of the world Jewish scene. A certain stabilization of migrations was in effect after W W II, until the Arab Spring and the wars in the Muslim world, and then the Middle East, and especially the Afghani, Iraqi, Libyan, Yemenite and Syrian civil wars that broke out at the turn of the 21st Century, provoked a new wave of massive migrations from the Middle East and Africa to Western Europe, especially Germany.

Bibliography

Foundatioanl Documents

The Qur'an

Protocols of the Elders of Zion

Arab Vision Papers (in Israel)

Supreme Court Document 4112/99, *Adala* vs the City of Tel Aviv

Mussawa Report of November 2006, written by Yussuf Jabbarin

Modern Arab History and Contemporary Problems, Part II for Tenth Grade, No 613, (Ramallah/Gaza, Palestinian Authority)

Outstanding Examples of our Civilization for 11th Grade (Ramallah/Gaza, Palestinian Authority)

The New History of the Arabs and the World, (Ramallah/Gaza, the Palestinian Authority)

Islamic Education for 8th Grade(Ramallah/Gaza)

Convention Concerning the Exchange of Greek and Turkish Populations, 30 January 1923

Two-volume report of the Orr Commission to investigate the October 2000 Arab Rebellion in Israel, 2001

Written and Electronic Media

*Adala I*nternet Site

*Al-*Sirat Weekly

Commentary,

Fasal al-Maqal, Nazareth

Haaretz

IMRA January 27, 2008, extracted from an ISA Report

The Jerusalem Post

Journal of Palestinian Studies

Middle East Review

PMW Buletin

Post-Holocaust and anti-Semitism

al-Quds

http//www.mfa.gov.il/NR/rdonlyres/75FC2B98=A581-4C89-
88AC-7C3C1DiBC097/0/Terrorism2007report.pdf

www:al-minbar.cc/alkhutab/khutba.asp?mediaURL=5473, accessed
1 February 2002.

Books

Andric, Ivo, *The Bridge on the Drina*, Dereta, Belgrade, 2011.

Ariely, Dan, *The (Honest) Truth About Dishonesty*, Harper Collins,
NYC.

Bat Ye'or, *Islam and Dhimmitude: Where Civilizations Collide*, Fairleigh Dickinson University Press, Lancaster, 2002.

Berko, Anat, *The smarter Bomb: Women and Children as Suicide
Bombers* (Hebrew), Miskal, Tel-Aviv, 2010.

Bostom, Andy, *The Legacy of Islamic Anti-Semitism*, Prometheus
Books, NY, 2008.

Erlich, Hagai,, *Introduction to the History of the Middle East* (Hebrew),
Vol. 6, The Open University.

Gaylin, Willard, *Hatred, the Psychological Descent into Violence*, Public Affairs, New York, 2003.

Goldstein, Phyllis, *A Convenient Hatred: The History of Antisemitism*,
Facing History and Ourselves, Brookline, Mas, 2012.

Haim, Sylvia, *Arab Nationalism*, UC Press, Berkeley, 1962.

Harari, Yuval Noah, *Homo Deus: A Brief History of Tomorrow*, Vintage Books, London, 201.

Harel, Israel, Foes, not Friends", *Haaretz,*, 17 June, 2011, part II, p. 2.

Hertzberg, Arthur (ed), *The Zionist Idea,* Atheneum, NY, 1979, p. 16.

Israeli, Raphael, *Man of Defiance: a Political Biography of Anwar Sadat,*, Weidenfeld and Nicolson, London 1985.

Israeli, Raphael, *Palestinians Between Israel and Jordan*, Praeger, NY, 1991.

Israeli, Raphael, *Islamikaze: Manifestations of Islamic Martyrology,* Frank Kass, London, 2008.

Israeli, Raphael, *Islamic Radicalism and Political Violence: the Templars of Islam and Sheikh Ra'id Salah,* Vallentine Mitchell, London, 2008.

Israeli, Raphael, *Old Historians, New Historians, No Historians,* Wipf and Stock, Oregon, 2016 .

Israeli, Raphael, *The Oslo Idea: the Euphoria of Failure,* Transaction, New Jersey, 2012.

Israeli, Raphael, *From Arab Spring to Islamic Winter,* Transaction, New Jersey, 2013.

Israeli, Raphael, *Retreating from the Mirage of Multi-Culturalism?: the Cases of Holland, Britain and Israel,* Strategic Books, TX, 2018.

Israeli, Raphael, *Dying as a Shahid: Martyrdom in Islam,* Strategic Books, TX, 2018.

Israeli, Raphael, *Muslim Minorities in Modern States: The Challenge of Assimilation,* Transaction, N.J, 2009.

Israeli, Raphael, *Hatred, Lies and Violence IN the World of Islam,* Transaction, NJ, 2014.

Israeli, Raphael, *Paranoia, Inferiority Complex and Fanaticism: Muslim Attitudes Towards Jews,* Strategic Books, TX, 2018.

Israeli, Raphael, *Who is Right and Who is Left: The Fate of Weak Polities Among Mighty Empires,* Strategic Books, TX, 2018.

Israeli, Raphael, *The Intractable Dispute: Why the Muslims and Arabs Are at Loggerheads with Jews and Israel,* Strategic Books, TX, 2019.

Israeli, Raphael, *The Odd Couple: The Aberrant Relations Between Turkey and Israel,* Strategic Books, TX, 2019.

Israeli, Raphael and A. Benabou, *Savagery in the Heart of Europe: the Bosnia War (1992-5),* Strategic Books, Texas, 2013.

Israeli, Raphael, *Suicidal Democracy: Israel's Future in the Arab Environment,* Strategic Books, TX, 2019.

Israeli, Raphael, *The Hidden and the Obvious with Israeli Arabs (Hebrew),* Jerusalem, 2016.

Johnson, N. *Islam and Politics of Meaning in Palestinian Nationalism,* Kegan Paul, London, 1982.

Mahajneh, 'Alaa, "The Arab Language and the Native Status of Arabs in Israel" (Arabic) in the *Adala* Internet Site.

Murray, Douglas, *The Strange Death of Europe,* London, 2016.

Nuseibeh, Sari and Mark Heller, *No Trumpets, No Drums,* Hill and Wang, New York, 1993.

Schivelbusch, Wolfgang, *The Culture of Defeat,* Picador, New York, 2001.

Shueftan, Dan, *The Palestinians in Israel,* (Hebrew), Zmora-Bitan, Tel-Aviv, 2011.

Articles

Israeli, Raphael, " Sadat Between Arabism and Africanism", *Middle East Review,* 2, Spring 1979, pp. 39-48.

Israeli, Raphael, "Islamikaze and their Significance", in *Terrorism and Political Violence,* Fall 1997, pp. 96-121.

Khalidi, Walid, *Journal of Palestinian Studies,* Vol. XXXV, No 1, Autumn 2005, pp. 60-79.

Lewis, Bernard, "The Return of Islam", *Commentary,* (Winter, 1976).

Marcus, Itamar, and Barbara Crook,"Anti-Semitism among Palestinian Authority Academics", in *Post-Holocaust and anti-Semitism,* No 69, 1 June, 2008, published by the Jerusalem Center of Public Affairs, 2008.

Zilberdik, Nan Jacques and Itamar Marcus, PMW Bulletin, of 5
April, 2020.

Analytical Index
Names, Places, Terms and Events